EXTRAORDINARY PRAISE FOR *BRAVING IT*

FINALIST FOR THE BANFF MOUNTAIN BOOK COMPETITION

"*Braving It* is a detailed portrayal of terrain so harsh it would give any seasoned outdoorsman pause, complete with grizzlies, brushes with hypothermia, and a growing bond that is honest, hard-earned, and touching."

—*MEN'S JOURNAL*

"*Braving It*, the book, is a metaphor for the wilderness—the call of the wild—that James Campbell evokes in this masterfully told story. Every time I set the book down, I pondered the lessons learned, and couldn't wait for my next sojourn into its pages. When it ended, I longed for the adventure to continue and pined for the beauty of Alaska. So I picked it up and read it again, savoring every page."

—ERIC BLEHM, AUTHOR OF *THE LAST SEASON*, *FEARLESS*, AND *LEGEND*

"Campbell, through his descriptions and thoughtful reflection, brings to life the Arctic's great beauty, expanse and values as a wilderness and testing ground—a 'final frontier' for a certain kind of seeker. . . . *Braving It* is a smart, insightful book that should be read by fathers and daughters everywhere—and by anyone who looks to wild country as 'part of the geography of hope.' "

—*ALASKA DISPATCH NEWS*

"Any of us who've watched daughters grow up to be strong and capable in the backcountry will delight in this book—it's a wonderful new world in many ways!"

—BILL MCKIBBEN, AUTHOR OF *THE END OF NATURE* AND *WANDERING HOME*

"James Campbell describes . . . trips to Alaska, where father and daughter faced off with grizzlies, battled clouds of mosquitos, capsized in a freezing river—and pushed the bond between them to its limits."

—*NATIONAL GEOGRAPHIC*

"As a father of daughters and lover of adventure, I found *Braving It* to be spot on—riveting, profound, open-eyed, and deeply touching. Campbell's struggle to understand and measure up to the stark and stunning Alaskan wilderness and, more importantly, to his teenage daughter—to find his place in the lives of both—becomes our struggle, too. A must-read for every striving parent and every teen striving to understand his or her parents."

—DEAN KING, AUTHOR OF *SKELETONS ON THE ZAHARA* AND *THE FEUD*

"Campbell's prose captures both the difficulties and pleasures on offer in the extreme wild. . . . Parents who enjoy Campbell's adventures vicariously might find themselves contemplating their own family outing."

—*RICHMOND TIMES-DISPATCH*

"*Braving It* is a beautiful and original book, an antidote to the screenification of modern life. As a father enters the country of middle age, and a daughter edges toward adulthood, they share an epic Alaskan adventure. Among the dangers they encounter is an unexpected one: fleeting time. Countering this is the gift the father gives the daughter and the writer gives the reader: The gift of the elemental now, of moments of wind, fire, water, snow, beauty. And of equally primal moments of human love and connection."

—DAVID GESSNER, AUTHOR OF *ALL THE WILD THAT REMAINS: EDWARD ABBEY, WALLACE STEGNER, AND THE AMERICAN WEST*

"A touching and riveting true story of hope and adventure."

—*ALASKA BEYOND*

"[Campbell's] daughter, Aidan, [is] worthy of a book-length tribute. . . . *Braving It* [is] as much about parenting as it is about adventure, though in Campbell's book the two concepts are often inseparable."

—*ISTHMUS*

"With humor and honesty, Campbell brings readers along for the adventure, which is full of swarms of hungry mosquitoes, the fear of grizzly bears, and the push-pull relationship between a teenage girl and her father. . . . Campbell expertly blends facts on the flora, fauna, and general life in the Alaskan bush with his reflections on being middle-aged, with many adventurous years behind him, as opposed to his daughter, whose quest for adventure has only just begun. Informative, humorous, and full of a love of nature."

—*KIRKUS REVIEWS*

"A delightful and sometimes harrowing tale of the Alaskan bush."

—*SHELF AWARENESS*

BRAVING IT

*A Father, a Daughter,
and an Unforgettable Journey
into the Alaskan Wild*

>>>>>>>>>>>>>>>>>>>>

JAMES CAMPBELL

B\D\W\Y
BROADWAY BOOKS
NEW YORK

Library of Congress Cataloging-in-Publication Data
Campbell, James, 1961–
Braving it : a father, a daughter, and an unforgettable journey into the Alaskan
wild / James Campbell.
First edition. | New York : Crown Publishers, 2016.
Identifiers: LCCN 2015030811 | ISBN 9780307461247 (hardcover) |
ISBN 9780307461254 (trade paperback) | ISBN 9780307461261 (ebook)
Subjects: LCSH: Campbell, James, 1961—Travel—Alaska. | Campbell,
Aidan, 1998—Travel—Alaska. | Fathers and daughters—Alaska—Biography. |
Alaska—Description and travel. | Wilderness areas—Alaska. | Wilderness
survival—Alaska. | Coming of age—Alaska. | Backpacking—Alaska. | Canoes and
canoeing—Alaska. | Arctic National Wildlife Refuge (Alaska)—Description and
travel. | BISAC: BIOGRAPHY & AUTOBIOGRAPHY / Personal Memoirs. |
FAMILY & RELATIONSHIPS / Parenting / Fatherhood. | NATURE /
Ecosystems & Habitats / Polar Regions.
Classification: LCC F910.7.C36 A3 2016 | DDC 917.98/04—dc23 LC record
available at http://lccn.loc.gov/2015030811

ISBN 978-0-307-46125-4
Ebook ISBN 978-0-307-46126-1

PRINTED IN THE UNITED STATES OF AMERICA

Book design by Anna Thompson
Maps by Paul J. Pugliese
Cover design by Eric White
Cover photograph by Dave Musgrave

10 9 8 7 6 5 4 3 2 1

First Paperback Edition

FOR MY FATHER, WHO SHOWED ME THE WAY.

AND FOR MY DAUGHTER AIDAN.

AND YET THERE IS ONLY ONE GREAT THING
THE ONLY THING,
TO LIVE TO SEE THE GREAT DAY THAT DAWNS
AND THE LIGHT THAT FILLS THE WORLD.

—ANCIENT INUIT SONG

THERE ARE ONLY TWO LASTING BEQUESTS
WE CAN HOPE TO GIVE OUR CHILDREN.
ONE OF THESE IS ROOTS; THE OTHER, WINGS.

—HODDING CARTER,
WHERE MAIN STREET MEETS THE RIVER

CONTENTS

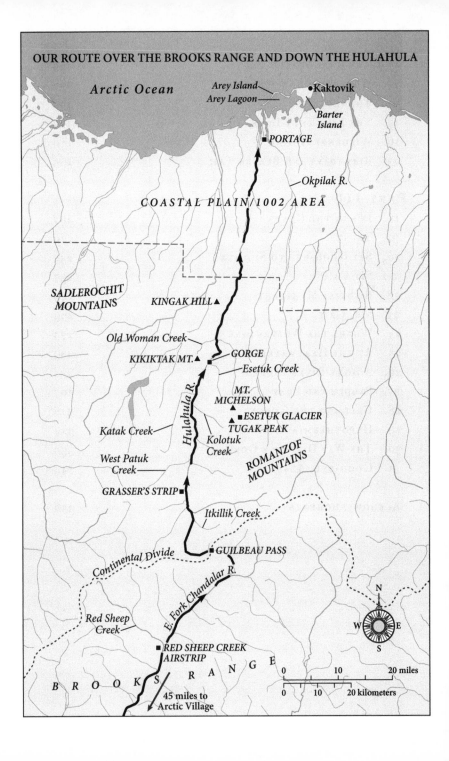

OUR ROUTE OVER THE BROOKS RANGE AND DOWN THE HULAHULA

Arctic Ocean

Arey Island
Arey Lagoon
•Kaktovik
Barter Island

■PORTAGE

Okpilak R.

COASTAL PLAIN/1002 AREA

SADLEROCHIT MOUNTAINS

KINGAK HILL ▲

Old Woman Creek
KIKIKTAK MT. ▲ ■ GORGE
Esetuk Creek

MT. MICHELSON
▲ ■ESETUK GLACIER
▲ TUGAK PEAK

Katak Creek

Hulahula R.

Kolotuk Creek

ROMANZOF MOUNTAINS

West Patuk Creek

GRASSER'S STRIP ■

Itkillik Creek

GUILBEAU PASS ■
Continental Divide

E. Fork Chandalar R.

Red Sheep Creek

N
W   E
S

■ RED SHEEP CREEK AIRSTRIP

B R O O K S   R A N G E

0   10   20 miles
0   10   20 kilometers

45 miles to Arctic Village

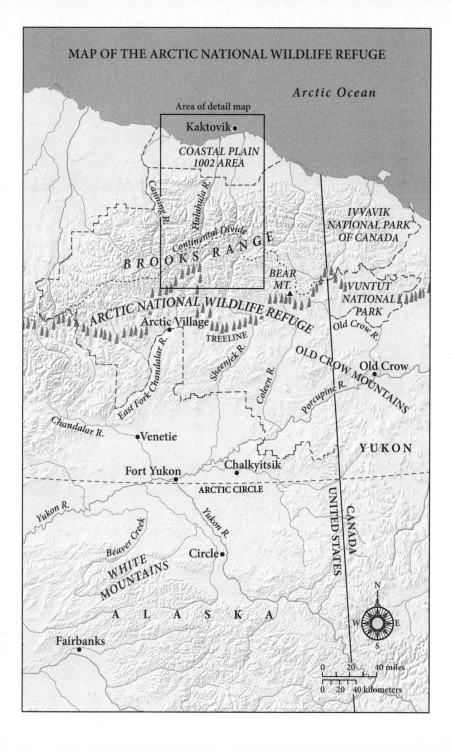

MAP OF THE ARCTIC NATIONAL WILDLIFE REFUGE

Arctic Ocean

Area of detail map

Kaktovik •

*COASTAL PLAIN
1002 AREA*

IVVAVIK
NATIONAL PARK
OF CANADA

Canning R.

Hulahula R.

Continental Divide

B R O O K S   R A N G E

*BEAR
MT.* ▲

VUNTUT
NATIONAL
PARK

ARCTIC NATIONAL WILDLIFE REFUGE

Old Crow R.

Arctic Village •

TREELINE

OLD CROW MOUNTAINS

Old Crow •

Sheenjek R.

East Fork Chandalar R.

Coleen R.

Porcupine R.

Chandalar R.

• Venetie

YUKON

Fort Yukon •

Chalkyitsik •

ARCTIC CIRCLE

Yukon R.

Yukon R.

CANADA
UNITED STATES

Beaver Creek

Circle •

WHITE
MOUNTAINS

N
W   E
S

A L A S K A

• Fairbanks

0   20   40 miles

0   20   40 kilometers

PROLOGUE

M Y DAUGHTER AIDAN HADN'T YET entered kindergarten when I made a series of trips to the Alaskan Arctic while researching and writing my first book. She loved my stories, and as she listened, she said that when she was a "big girl" she hoped to join me in Alaska. I told her that, yes, one day we would go together. She accepted this answer until her freshman year in high school, when she began to remind me of my promise on what seemed like a weekly basis.

The more I thought about it, the more it seemed like the right time to take her on an Alaskan adventure, or perhaps a series of adventures. In traditional Eskimo cultures, although gender roles were well defined, adolescent girls would sometimes accompany their fathers on extensive hunting and trapping trips while boys stayed behind in the village. The idea was that it was important for boys and girls to switch roles in order to acquire the others' life skills. Boys would learn to sew, tan, weave, and cook, and girls would learn how to hunt, survive in the wilderness, and make tools and weapons. I believed that, at fifteen, Aidan was ready for a similar experience. She would be old enough to appreciate it and responsible enough to carry her own weight. Perhaps, too, her encounter with wilderness would evoke the same feelings of wonder it had in me.

From John Muir and Aldo Leopold (fellow Wisconsinites) to Rachel Carson, Annie Dillard, and Wendell Berry, literature teems with musings on the power of nature. Leopold memorably called it "meat from God." Edward Abbey called wilderness a "necessity of the human spirit." Henry David Thoreau's saying "In Wildness is the preservation of the World" makes the bold claim not that we must save wildness but that wildness has the potential to save us.

In preparation for our adventure I asked Aidan to read Wallace Stegner's "Wilderness Letter." In it Stegner writes about wild country as "a part of the geography of hope." I'd always loved that line—"the geography of hope." But in rereading the letter before passing it on to Aidan, I was drawn to another phrase: "the birth of awe." Yes, I thought, in Alaska, Aidan might truly feel awe. Short of that, I wanted her to learn concrete life lessons in common sense, self-sufficiency, confidence, and competence.

By February 2013, after deciding to do a self-guided, three-week paddling trip somewhere in Arctic Alaska, we were auditioning rivers, running them in our imaginations. There was the Firth, a mighty river of steep canyons that straddles the border between northeastern Alaska and Canada; the Hulahula, a scenic, hundred-mile-long stretch of water that tumbles from the Romanzof Mountains of the Brooks Range to the Arctic Ocean; the Canning, which parallels the Hulahula and runs along the western border of the 19.5-million-acre Arctic National Wildlife Refuge;

the Sheenjek, which in 1956 motivated environmentalists Olaus and Mardy Murie to develop the idea of a wilderness preserve in the Arctic; and, finally, the Porcupine, a six-hundred-mile historic trade route that winds through dense boreal forest en route from Dawson City in Canada's Yukon Territory to the Gwich'in Athabaskan community of Old Crow, also in the Yukon Territory, and then southwest into Alaska.

All are wild and beautiful rivers with the ability to inspire and terrify. That is the thing about awe: beauty and fear are inseparable. The Inupiat, of Alaska's harsh Arctic coast, have a word to express the duality: *uniari,* "nervous awe." The Tununirmiut of Baffin Bay call it *ilira,* and distinguish between it and the raw fear—*kappia*—that one might feel if he or she were thrown from a canoe into an icy Arctic river.

In April we pored over maps and began to assemble our gear. Then, in May, I got a call. Heimo and Edna Korth, my cousin and his wife, about whom I'd written *The Final Frontiersman,* had just left the bush for the village of Fort Yukon, on the Yukon River, where they traditionally spend the summer months. For the rest of the year the Korths live 120 miles to the north, deep in the foothills of the Brooks Range, where they raised three daughters. Heimo and Edna are some of the last hunter-trapper-gatherers living in the Arctic National Wildlife Refuge.

Heimo wanted to know if I'd be willing to come up in July and August to help him build a new cabin on the Coleen River. Earlier that month, during spring breakup, as the river ice thawed and melted, the Coleen River had rerouted itself, spilling into a side channel; the Korths' current cabin, which sat along the banks of that channel, was in jeopardy of being washed away. Heimo explained that he had already done some of the preliminary work. He'd picked out the new site upriver, cleared some of the trees, and sketched the outline of the cabin with an axe and a shovel. His only caveat was that we'd have a lot of work and we'd have to do it fast to get most of the cabin built before the cold came.

I was tempted by the invitation. I'd always wanted to build a cabin in the woods, nursing dreams of heading to Canada or Alaska and living off the land, but as a young man I instead went to an eastern city for college. It was a good place, but hardly an appropriate training ground for a mountain man. After college I got sidetracked, following the beaten professional path to Chicago and New York, and eventually left the path for the mountains of Colorado. Then, a decade and a half later, a deep homing instinct led me to return to rural Wisconsin.

In each place I lived I found joy. In Colorado I went to graduate school, which I paid for by working construction and landscaping, and sometimes helping out an old rancher whose sons had left for the city. In return the rancher gave me some first-edition Zane Grey novels from his book collection. But I had never followed the needle pull of the compass north as Heimo had.

I mulled Heimo's offer over for a few days before approaching my wife, Elizabeth, with an idea: what if Aidan and I were to go up together to help him? Elizabeth had never been a supporter of our Alaskan river trip idea and viewed this new plan with equal skepticism. Aidan was not new to the wilderness, but she still had lots to learn, and Elizabeth thought we should start out with something less risky—the Boundary Waters, for instance. The Boundary Waters is a 1.3-million-acre wilderness, with twelve hundred miles of canoe routes, that straddles the border between Minnesota and Ontario. It's remote country—by Lower 48 standards—but it is not Alaska.

Elizabeth's biggest worry: bears. Like many other Lower 48ers, my wife believes that nearly every Alaskan thicket hides an angry, frothing-at-the-mouth grizzly. She's no city gal, either. She's done her time in the woods. But the thought of her oldest daughter wandering around in bear country scared her. She'd read that a grizzly kills in a gruesome fashion, delivering a deadly blow to the head with a force akin to a twelve-pound splitting maul swung by an NFL linebacker, before seizing the back of its prey's neck and severing its spine. Grizzlies have a bite force of over 8 million pascals, a metric unit of pressure, powerful enough to crush a bowling ball. Elizabeth wondered why I would want to risk taking Aidan to Alaska, especially when she could learn the kinds of life skills I was talking about right here at home.

By that, Elizabeth meant that we have land where we keep bees and tend a garden, pick cherries, apples, mulberries, and plums for jam. There is no shortage of work. We were getting chickens, so there was a chicken coop and run to build, wood to cut and split, and perhaps one day maple trees to tap and sheep's milk cheese to make. Nevertheless, I could tell that Elizabeth was wavering. When she made me promise that wherever Aidan went I would be beside her with a shotgun, loaded with lead slugs, I knew that she had decided to let Aidan join me. Now I had to hope that Heimo and Edna would, too.

Heimo didn't know Aidan—his second cousin once removed—from Adam, and when I called to broach the possibility of her coming, he proved leery of taking on a teenage girl. He was full of questions that boiled down to just one: could she hack it?

I made a modest pitch. I am one of my daughter's biggest fans, and occasionally one of her toughest critics, but I didn't want to raise expectations. I told Heimo she might prove herself useful. After thinking it over for a couple weeks, he called back: he and Edna were willing to give Aidan a chance.

I still had to sell Aidan—and perhaps myself—on the experience. We'd be swapping a river trip for a three-and-a-half-week stint of cabin building. Would there be opportunity for Stegner's "birth of awe"?

I was straight with her about the experience; I didn't sugarcoat it. It would be hard, sweaty, and dirty work. We would get blistered, scratched, and scraped limbing trees and lugging them out of the woods. There would be bugs—clouds of them. We would be wearing the same pair of work clothes day in and day out, and after a while the animal smell of our own bodies would offend us. We would encounter Nature with a capital N, including the possibility of running across a grizzly, *Ursus arctos horribilis,* or a cow moose protecting her calf.

For tools, we would be using axes, drawknives, pickaxes, and saws. If one of us got cut badly, we'd have to make an emergency call by satellite phone and hope that someone could come and airlift us out. Because the nearest hospital is two hundred and fifty miles away, in Fairbanks, we would be a minimum of twelve to twenty-four hours from medical help. The remoteness of where we would be, and what that meant in case of emergency, could not be overemphasized. In 2012, two scientists from the University of Alaska, Fairbanks' Geophysical Institute identified the Coleen River as the most isolated spot in mainland Alaska. The Arctic National Wildlife Refuge is roughly the size of South Carolina or the country of Austria, and combined with the adjacent Ivvavik and Vuntut National Parks in Canada, it is part of one of the largest protected ecosystems in the world.

Aidan had lots of questions, many more than when we were planning the river trip. She is a curious, inquiring girl, a committed student of the Socratic method: ask and you will be enlightened. When she's nervous or uncomfortable, the questions multiply. Heimo's invitation somehow made Alaska real for her, and her questions came in a torrent, like a spring cloudburst. How dangerous would it be? Would we have a first aid kit? What would we eat? What would we do about the bugs, the bears? Would a grizzly maul you? Kill you? How would we protect ourselves? Where would we get our drinking water? What if we got giardia? Would she be able to use the satellite phone to call home? Would there be a generator to charge her Kindle? Though she knew some of the answers, she asked the questions anyway. But then one day, after nearly two weeks of her hounding me, the barrage ended. She had reached a saturation point. A week later she announced with little ceremony, "Dad, I want to go." She sounded so confident that I began to worry.

Aidan, you see, is firstborn and eager to please. As a little girl she'd ask me, "Daddy, do you wish that I had been a boy? Is that why you gave me a boy's name?" Perhaps she heard the teasing from my buddies. It's a Gaelic name—Aidan—meaning "little fire," and is used mostly for males. My friends insisted that I wanted a son so bad I gave her a boy's name. By the time Aidan was two, I knew that was a lot of bunk. She was my sidekick. She was a tomboy, but still a girl who loved dolls, tea parties, and feather boas.

In answer to her question about whether or not I wished I'd had a son, I chose to be honest with her. I told her that I'd dreamed of having a boy, but not long after she came into the world, I knew I could never love a son more than I loved her.

Despite my reassurances, in school she made sure she could throw a football as well as the boys, field the highest punts, and run the fastest and longest. With a BB gun, and later a .22 rifle, she was determined to be a deadeye. When I brought home ducks, geese, or pheasants I'd shot, she'd get right in there and watch up close while I cleaned them. I'd offer her a brief biology lesson as she held the still-warm heart in her hands.

When she was seven I gave her the nickname Cap. Two years earlier, I'd started reading books to her in bed before school—everything from Kate DiCamillo and Mark Twain to J. R. R. Tolkien and Laura Ingalls Wilder. Her favorite of Wilder's books was *The Long Winter,* set in South Dakota during the brutal winter of 1880–81. When the train stops delivering food to the Ingallses' town, Pa Ingalls and the townspeople worry that they will starve until two young men, Cap Garland and Almanzo Wilder, make a dangerous trip across the prairie to bargain with a farmer for a supply of wheat. They return with enough to last the town through the winter. I told Aidan that she was my Cap Garland. At the time, I didn't realize the dynamic I was setting up: Aidan trying to fill the character's brave and determined shoes. But she never showed any signs of crumbling under the weight of her nickname. Actually, I think she was proud. She felt that I saw her as she wanted to be seen.

As a teenager, she's no different than she was in grade school. She still puts 100 percent into everything she does, so much so that occasionally she can be blindly driven, believing there's a straight line between commitment and success. Being goal-oriented and ambitious doesn't equip one to deal with the reality that sometimes, despite one's efforts, things don't work out as planned. I felt that a wilderness experience would teach Aidan about adaptability. In rural Alaska, Murphy's law is a near constant, a state of uncertainty that many kids these days are ill-equipped to handle. Between organized sports and school, their lives are planned, and managed, to a T. Someone always seems to be hovering, ready to dispense advice, problem-solving instructions, and directions. Decisions are made for them by principals, teachers, coaches, instructors, and us, their parents. Being in the woods, by contrast, is all about improvising.

My greatest hope for Aidan was that her encounter with a new world, most especially a wild one, would be one of the defining moments of her life—that the Alaskan Arctic would knee her out of her comfort zone and, simultaneously, throw her for a joyful loop. In reality, I had no idea what obstacles we would face, nor did I know how Aidan would react to them. Would we be taking on too much? Was I being unrealistic, irresponsible even, in thinking that I could take my teenage daughter to the remote wilds of the Alaskan Arctic?

PART I

>>>>>>>>>>>>>>>>>>

CHAPTER 1

INTO THE WILD

T HE JULY SKY WAS BLUE and brittle and the air over the craggy peaks of the White Mountains looked as if it could shatter. Below, mist wafted out of the thick woods along Beaver Creek. The water was high and cloudy with runoff.

I looked back at my daughter Aidan, cramped in her jump seat, her head resting on her backpack in a Dramamine-induced sleep. I was grateful that on this, her first flight in a bush plane, the weather was fairly calm. I saw the gold cross that was once my grandmother's hanging from her neck. My mother gave it to her just days before we left for Alaska. "To keep you safe," she said.

Thirty minutes later, I spotted the Yukon River, wide and wandering, with the sun on its back. A few hopeful Gwich'in fishermen had set out their fish wheels. Once the baskets would have been full of Chinook, or king salmon, as they're known in Alaska, but the great salmon runs on the Yukon seemed to be things of the past. In Fairbanks, we had heard that 2013 was one of the worst runs in modern history due to disease, a deteriorating gene pool, and "bycatch" by the Bering Sea pollock fleet, whose nets also picked up tens of thousands of salmon.

Not long after, I saw the town of Fort Yukon, a hodgepodge of tin-roofed cabins and dirt roads that dead-ended not far out of town. If not for the glistening school and the shiny, new health clinic, Fort Yukon would have looked like a frontier outpost hacked out of the woods a century ago.

A few minutes later we landed to pick up some supplies for Heimo. Daniel Hayden, our bush pilot, taxied our Helio Courier over to where another pilot was gassing up his plane. I woke Aidan, and Daniel popped open the doors. By the time I struggled out of the cockpit I knew that the other pilot was Kirk Sweetsir, an old friend. Kirk ran Yukon Air Service as a one-man, two-plane operation. Ten years previously, I'd flown with him a number of times and had once described him as a "pilot-philosopher." Having grown up in the river community of Ruby, Alaska, he had ended up in England, attending Cambridge University. But England couldn't hold him after his undergraduate years: too many lines, boundaries, hedgerows, and too much tight-lipped propriety—especially for an Alaskan.

Aidan wandered over to Kirk's Conex and read the sign: "YUKON AIR WELCOMES YOU TO: FORT YUKON (GWITCHYAAZEE), POPULATION 637, LOWEST TEMP: −75, HIGHEST TEMP: + 105, LO-CATED 8 MILES NORTH OF THE ARCTIC CIRCLE." By the time I took a few photos of her, Kirk had finished gassing up his plane. He walked over, shook my hand, and turned to Aidan.

"So the old man's taking you up to Heimo's. Gonna be hot and buggy." He looked at Daniel, who was trying to fit a window through the plane's door and laughed. "What are you trying to stuff in there? Is that for Heimo? I thought he was still using seal gut for windows."

Daniel laughed loudest of all. In Alaska, among the dwindling population of backwoods trappers, Heimo has a reputation for keeping things spare and simple. He still tucks his smallish cabins in the woods, making sure they're not visible from the air or the river. But as he gets older, he wants a few modern comforts: a big, south-facing window, for instance.

"Nope," I replied to Kirk. "No seal gut or walrus hide. Heimo's going twenty-first century. Actually, the plan is to have a few windows."

"Hmm," Kirk mumbled. "Heimo's getting civilized in his old age."

Daniel announced that it was time to go, and I shook Kirk's hand and make tentative plans to see him and his wife and their two boys on our return trip.

At an airspeed of one hundred miles per hour, Daniel followed the switchbacking lower Sheenjek due north and then headed northeast to the Coleen River corridor, all the while talking about the 1990s *National Geographic* documentary *Braving Alaska,* in which his family, the Haydens, and Heimo's family had been featured.

"It was great back then," Daniel said, "because we rarely left the bush. Not even in summer. So it was fun to have visitors. But that way of life is over. The world is not a physical place anymore. It's about technology." As Daniel talked, I pictured the footage of the entire Hayden clan, Daniel sporting a wide, happy grin as a long-haired child of the wilderness, and I wondered about the trade-off—laptops and iPhones for Conibear traps and skinning knives. Even Susan, Daniel's younger sister, who ran her own trap-line with a team of dogs, had swapped life in the bush for town.

"I still go out to the homestead, usually for a month or so to trap marten," Daniel said. "That's enough for me to reconnect. But I don't run dogs. I use a snow machine. Kibble is expensive, and you can wipe out a whole river feeding dogs on fish." Then Daniel pointed north to a line of high, treeless hills separating two broad valleys. "Our territory runs up against Heimo's right there."

Though their cabins are separated by eighty miles, for a long time the Haydens were Heimo's closest neighbors. They rarely saw each other, but Heimo considered Daniel's parents, Richard and Shannon, both friends and kindred spirits. Heimo had grown up in Wisconsin, Richard in Minnesota. Both had married native women, and both families had decided to make a go of it in a place most people have had the good sense to leave to the caribou, bears, and botflies. January temperatures often bottom out at 50 below, and with the plagues of mosquitoes, blackflies and hornets, the summers can be worse than the winters. Through perseverance, guts, and a bounty of good luck, mixed with heartbreaking misfor-tune, the two families carved out their lives in the kind of seclusion few people have experienced.

In 1882, a U. S. Census Bureau geographer classified the fron-tier as a place containing fewer than two people per square mile. That definition, I knew, was utterly inadequate here. The Korths and the Haydens were the only settlers for more than five hundred square miles. The nearest road, the Steese Highway, was nearly 250 miles away, on the south side of the White Mountains.

Daniel brought the plane down low over the river. The Coleen was the color of the Caribbean, a transparent turquoise. Aidan tapped me on the shoulder and pointed out her window at a small school of Arctic grayling holding in the current.

Minutes later, Daniel spotted Heimo and Edna near the river and made two passes to study the makeshift gravel bar runway. "Looks good," he said. "They've filled in the holes and dragged off the driftwood. The river's gone down, too, since the last rain. I was worried we might not even have six hundred feet." With the heavy load we were carrying, Daniel would likely need that much room to land the plane.

As he pulled back on the yoke, Aidan tapped me on the shoulder again. Gravel bar landings are risky, and Aidan wanted me to hold her hand. I squeezed it three times—*I—love—you*—and felt the urgent need to imprint on my brain the feeling of my daughter's hand as the tundra tires touched and the tail tire lowered and dragged. But Daniel put the plane down as if on a bed of feathers and we taxied back to the south end of the bar. Out the window I saw Heimo, dressed in hip boots, an old flannel shirt, a bandana, and his leather holster with the .44 Magnum. Ten years had passed since I saw him last, but apart from a week-old beard gone completely gray, he looked the same. Edna did, too, although I could see that she moved somewhat stiffly and that her black hair was also streaked with gray.

"Hey, Cuz," Heimo said as I exited the plane.

"Howdy, Old Codger," I replied, shaking his hand.

Heimo turned to Aidan as she stepped out of the plane. "We're going to work you hard." He laughed, extending his hand.

Aidan shook it. "My dad says you're a big joker."

"Oh." Heimo laughed again. "I ain't jokin'. We got lots of work to do."

Aidan gave me a look—not for the last time—that said, *What have I gotten myself into?*

She walked over to Edna, whom I studied for some sort of reaction, but her face remained impassive. I heard Aidan say, "I loved my slippers." During one of my trips north, when Aidan was four, Edna had made Aidan a pair of Eskimo slippers, using moose and caribou hide, short-haired strips of sealskin, small pieces of lynx (which many trappers pronounce "link"), and wolf fur. On the tops of the shoes, she'd added a white background of beadwork accented by beaded red, yellow, and blue flowers. They were works of art, and Aidan wore them day and night for years.

Edna smiled tentatively. When I'd first proposed bringing Aidan out, it was she, even more than Heimo, who had resisted the idea. While I was writing my book about the Korths, my relationship with Edna had sometimes become testy. Edna is from the small Yupik Eskimo village of Savoonga on St. Lawrence Island in the Bering Sea. I asked too many questions that, from her cultural perspective, were prying and intrusive. Heimo told me, too, one day as we basked in the spring sun along the riverbank, "Edna resents that I spend all my time with you now. She says she misses me."

Perhaps Edna agreed to let us both come out because she knew that Heimo needed our help and because she knew that she would not be with us. She had injured her back in a car accident while on a food run in town, and the work of cabin building was simply too hard for her. She was heading back with Daniel to Fort Yukon, where she would tend Heimo's salmon nets and her garden.

The sky was still free from clouds, and from where we stood, I could see massive Bear Mountain to the north, and what the Korths call Mummuck Mountain, meaning "breast" in Yupik, to the northwest, and the Porcupine and Strangle Woman Mountains—the Old Crow Range—to the east and southeast, just across the border in Canada. The sight was, I felt certain, what Wallace Stegner had meant when he wrote about being moved by a "timeless and uncontrolled part of earth," a world not reduced to the human dimension. I knew, too, that nothing in Aidan's experience, not the Northwoods of Wisconsin or the Upper Peninsula of Michigan, not even Idaho's Sawtooths, had prepared her for wilderness stretching in every direction. I remembered when I saw this place for the first time, more than a decade ago. I had felt both frightened and liberated; now I wondered if Aidan felt it, too.

Edna walked over to the plane. Before she climbed in, Heimo wrapped his arms around her. "I love you, Mom," he said. Instead of calling Edna Honey or Sweetheart, he'd always called her Mom.

We waved good-bye as Daniel taxied to the north end of the gravel bar. We heard him rev the Helio's engine, and when the plane rumbled past in a swirl of wind, spitting gravel and scattered sticks, we all waved again. As it disappeared downriver, Heimo spun in a circle with his arms outstretched, an Alaskan Zorba the Greek.

"Damn," he said, "I feel so lucky to live out here."

An hour later, after transporting our gear to the campsite, and setting up our tent, we walked with our fishing rods north along the river through willows and head-high cottonwoods, purple Siberian asters and yellow Arctic daisies, clinging to the sand, and tufts of white cotton grass. A flock of hooded mergansers croaked as they whipped by. Soon the caribou would be coming.

"I gotta show you this grayling hole," Heimo told us excitedly. "You'll love it. There'll be a breeze, too, so there ain't gonna be any skeeters."

We reached the gravel bar, and while I tried to tie on a small dry fly without the aid of my reading glasses, which I'd left back at camp, Aidan threw out a spinner. Seconds later her line was taut and bouncing.

"Look at that," Heimo said. "First cast."

Aidan was beaming. Our last few fishing outings had been family affairs in which I'd spent much of the time untangling lines, grumbling, and getting irritable. By the time I was ready to cast, Aidan had already brought in two fifteen-inch Arctic grayling. She held one up for me to see and grabbed its dorsal fin, which fanned out like that of a miniature sailfish. She laid it down and thumped it over the head with a rock, and the fish shuddered.

Heimo was lying among the smooth and silvery stones, too blissed out even to bother wetting his line. If Aidan could learn anything from him, it would be to live in the here and now, in what my Idaho writer-friend, John Rember, called the "thin moment of the present."

"Should I catch more?" Aidan asked hopefully.

"Keep fishing, if you want," Heimo said, propping himself up on his elbows. "We ain't in no hurry. It's six o'clock and the sun don't set till August."

CHAPTER 2

BUGS, BEARS, AND THE BATHROOM PROCEDURE

I WOKE IN THE MIDDLE OF the night to the sound of sandhill cranes, their coarse, whiskey-tinged voices traveling up and down the river, and for a moment I forgot where I was. I could have been back home, in Lodi, Wisconsin, where the cranes congregate in the local marsh.

I crawled out of the tent to watch for them but was quickly driven back in by the swarming mosquitoes, which rose out of the bushes like smoke. Although the Arctic is a desert—it gets less rain than Arizona—in summer it becomes a playground for over forty species of mosquitoes. Because of the two-thousand-foot-thick permafrost, the ground absorbs little water. Puddles, ponds, and ephemeral pools dot the landscape, perfect breeding places for trillions of mosquitoes.

I zipped myself into my sleeping bag and lay back and listened to the cranes' racket. They sounded happy, raucous, as if they were on an all-night bender. Above me, between the rain fly and the tent, I counted not sheep but dozens of mosquitoes and a handful of horseflies, attracted by the scent of human flesh. In Fairbanks, we were warned that, due to a wet spring and a late-season snow, this was the worst bug year in the Interior in decades. According to an article in the *Alaska Dispatch News,* titled "Bloodletting Worsens During Alaska's Legendary Mosquito Infestation," the mosquito population would be reaching its peak in July.

Morning came too soon. Hearing the crackle of a fire, I exited the tent. "Better move fast. Bugs are terrible bad," Heimo warned. After living in Fort Yukon among Alaskan Natives for two to three months of every year for the last thirty-plus years, Heimo had adopted their speech patterns, speaking in truncated sentences, dropping his definite and indefinite articles. He would say, "You get wood; I make fire." The only thing that distinguished him from the Native Gwich'in in Fort Yukon was his very noticeable Fox River valley, Wisconsin, inflection. Once a Cheesehead, always a Cheesehead.

"Gonna make pancakes," Heimo said. "Aidan like them?"

"Yeah," I said. "But she's still sound asleep."

"Is she a sleeper?" Heimo asked.

"Depends."

Like most teenagers, Aidan could crank off ten to twelve hours on weekends and over summer vacation and still wake up tired. But during the school year she was sleep-deprived, also like many kids her age. She would stay up till midnight studying and then, because she knew my school year ritual was to wake at 4:30 a.m., I would see a note in the kitchen by the coffeemaker asking me to wake her at 5:00.

I pulled a camp chair close to the fire to escape the mosquitoes. Heimo pointed to the sky overhead. "Osprey. Up there in the wind. They're cruisin'." I craned my head. The two ospreys looked like lost kites.

When Heimo said that we were going to need more wood, I pulled on my mosquito head net and left the fire. Mosquitoes poured out of the blueberry bushes. The old ones that had wintered over—snow skeeters, Alaskans call them—were slow and sluggish, but they still craved blood. The new crop was small, hungry, and quick.

I noticed a trail, followed it away from the campsite and the buggy underbrush, and gathered an armful of wood. Not until I walked back did it occur to me that the trail was wide and too well packed to have been blazed by Heimo in the few days before Aidan and I arrived. Then I saw large desiccated piles of scat, and attached to the bark of a spruce tree, I noticed light brown guard hairs. A scratching post? Then it dawned on me: it was a bear trail. Heimo had set up camp next to a bear trail. I thought of Doug Peacock's advice about picking a campsite in bear country. Choose a spot, he writes, that is not "on or near a bear trail, a potential feeding site, or a place where bears bed or travel to or from beds." My next thought was that Elizabeth, my wife, was going to kill me.

Although Alaska's huge coastal brown bears make the Arctic's barren land grizzlies look like pine martens, a hungry five-hundred-pound bear is nothing to trifle with. Genetically identical to the nine-hundred-pound coastal browns, the barren ground grizzly's habits couldn't be more different. Brown bears sleep a lot and frequent small areas, where game—especially fish—is plentiful. In contrast, hungry barren ground grizzlies prowl huge territories in search of food, especially in late summer as they enter a metabolic stage called hyperphagia, when, in preparation for hibernation, they will be trying to take in as many as 20,000 calories per day. At 82,000 calories, one average-size human being would satisfy a bear's caloric needs for half a week, saving it the trouble of digging up large areas of tundra in search of ground squirrels and roots.

I dropped the wood near the fire.

"What in the hell, Heimo; is that what I think it is—a bear trail?"

"Yup," he said, laughing so hard he could barely talk. "You noticed."

"We can't mention it to Aidan," I told him, "until she gets comfortable out here."

"Ah, hell," Heimo said. "We don't have to worry about bears. They hate the bugs, too, and most of 'em are in the mountains."

"Most of 'em are in the mountains," I muttered to myself.

For the next five minutes I glanced back and forth down the bear trail as if a grizzly was going to appear any moment. When the pancakes were done, I poked my head into the tent. "Breakfast is ready, Aidan."

She could hardly open her eyes. "It got cold last night, and I didn't sleep well. Daddy, can I sleep a little longer? I promise I'll get up early tomorrow."

I hesitated for a moment. This adventure was, in part, supposed to be a lesson in self-sufficiency and grit, and I didn't want to get started on the wrong foot. But, when Aidan called me Daddy, which she rarely did anymore, it was hard to say no to her.

"Sure," I said. "I'll eat your pancakes and make two more for you in an hour."

I knew Heimo was watching and listening, and I turned toward him somewhat sheepishly. Before coming up, I'd filled him in on what I hoped to accomplish by bringing Aidan to Alaska.

"Maybe it's the Dramamine she took yesterday," I said.

"Yeah," he said. "We got a lot to do, but let her sleep. I remember how my girls were when they were teenagers. I could have yelled *'fire!'* and they never even would have rolled over."

I'd always liked this about Heimo. He lived a hard, demanding life in a place that cut a person little slack, and could be opinionated and unsparing, but he also could be surprisingly tenderhearted.

At 7:45 Aidan unzipped the rain fly, crawled away from the tent, poured water from her water bottle into her hand, and splashed her face.

"Ahh," she said. "I bet I look a lot better than I did an hour ago, huh?"

"Prettiest girl for a hundred miles," I said.

She scowled. When she turned fifteen, it was as if someone had flipped her sensitive switch. She rarely let a perceived insult pass, especially if it involved her appearance." I take it you haven't seen yourself this morning, Dad," she countered.

"Ouch," Heimo said, looking at me. "She's right; you don't look too good." Then he poked the cast-iron skillet in Aidan's direction. "Got a crispy blueberry pancake for you. The girls loved 'em this way."

Aidan pulled a camp chair over to the fire. Heimo held up his hand as if to say, *Shhh.* Seconds later he said, "That's a Bohemian waxwing. Nice song, isn't it? Pretty far north for 'em, though."

By the time Aidan finished her second pancake, Heimo was no longer interested in birdsong. He was ready to build a cabin. But first things first: Heimo announced that he needed to introduce us to the dishwashing and bathroom protocols.

Washing dishes was a fairly straightforward job. We had one metal tub and one large pot, which we'd fill at the river and carry back to camp. The tub we'd use for soaking and washing, and the pot for rinsing. We'd leave the dishes out overnight to air dry.

The bathroom procedure was more complicated. First Heimo showed us the screen tent, the only place other than our sleeping tent where we could escape the bugs. "When those blueberries start percolating," he said, "believe me, you're gonna want to know where the 'honey bucket' is." Inside, surrounded by walls of mosquito netting, was a five-gallon bucket, our makeshift toilet. Next, Heimo led us forty feet into the woods, where he had dug a shallow hole. He'd put up a small piece of orange tape on a nearby tree as a marker.

"You bring the honey bucket here and dump it. What comes from the earth returns to the earth. But the hole ain't that deep, so be careful of the back splash," he warned us. He continued. "Then you get on your hip waders and walk down to the river and wash the bucket out. All the other animals shit in the river. Ours won't hurt it. Just make sure you don't clean the bucket upriver of where I get my water."

The bathroom procedure was not quick, as I soon discovered. At the end of the day, when I was worn out from cabin building, the prospect of answering nature's call seemed a daunting one. I learned to hold it till the next morning, waiting until waiting was no longer physically possible.

On the way back from the honey bucket hole, Aidan pulled my shirt and whispered something that I couldn't hear.

"Speak up," I said.

"Shhh. I don't want Heimo to hear."

We let Heimo walk ahead and then she said, "Dad, that bathroom tent is just thirty feet from the fire pit and twenty feet from Heimo's tent. There's not a bit of privacy. Mosquitoes or not, I'd rather use the woods."

"Heimo raised girls out here," I told her. "He knows when to turn his head."

"He better," she said. She kicked at the ground with the front of her boot. "And what about—" She hesitated and then blurted it out. "What about my period, Dad? What if I get it while we're here?"

"It's no big deal, Aidan," I told her. "Heimo raised girls. He knows all about that stuff."

Back at the campsite, it was as if Heimo had been eavesdropping on our conversation. And he was direct, no beating around the blueberry bush.

"Aidan," he said, "if you get your period, just wrap your stuff in toilet paper and we'll burn it in the fire. But let your dad know when you get it, so we can be extra careful about bears."

"Bears?" Aidan asked, alarmed.

"Yup," Heimo answered. "Bears smell the blood, which for them means food. It was the only time I was worried about the girls walking in the woods. When they had their periods, I made them stick around the cabin." A recent report from Yellowstone National Park had called the link between bear attacks and menstruation a myth, but who was I to question Heimo?

"Let's get going," he said. "We got five weeks of work to do and only three to do it in."

He grabbed the chain saw and made for the woods with git-'er-done gonzo. Aidan stood cement-footed.

"C'mon," I said. "Let's get going." I could tell she was obsessing over grizzlies and menstrual cycles.

"I don't like it, Dad. I don't like it at all," she said. "No privacy. Bears hunting me down."

"Give yourself some time," I told her as gently as I could. "You haven't even been here for two days."

To her credit, Aidan picked up a basket—packed with gloves, bug spray, bear bells, pepper spray, water bottles, mosquito head nets, a chisel, a hammer, and her Kindle—and followed Heimo's trail into the woods. I grabbed two axes and a shotgun and followed close behind her.

In a clearing a quarter of a mile from the campsite, Heimo waited for us near a large pile of logs. "These are yours," he said to Aidan. "They need to be peeled before we can use them on the cabin."

It was a shit job and Heimo knew it, but his eyes were fastened on Aidan. He was sizing her up. Would she be a whiner, or would she make herself useful?

I surveyed the logs. Although they'd been limbed and bucked to size, the bark was thick and knotted. *No way in hell,* I thought. *No way Aidan's going to be able to peel all of these.*

Aidan was no newcomer to peeling poles, but she'd never taken on a job like this before. Back home, in spring, we'd built a compost bin using black locust poles, and cut and peeled more poles for a chicken coop. Black locust doesn't rot and will last almost forever. But peeling live, fresh-cut trees, especially in spring, when the sap is running, is like sliding a knife through warm butter—except where there's a knot, the bark comes off in long, moist sheets. Stripping bark from sun-dried spruce logs was going to be an entirely different matter.

Heimo explained to Aidan that he wanted the bark off, the logs naked and honey-colored, so that the inside of the cabin didn't look like a dungeon. He took the small axe and went to work on the knots, after which he exchanged the axe for the drawknife, wedged the log with a small wood chock, and dug the drawknife's blade into the bark and pulled. He worked furiously, perhaps showing off a bit. He was sweaty and out of breath when he finished the demonstration.

Aidan ran her hand along the peeled portion of the pole and asked Heimo for the drawknife. She positioned herself over the top of the log and pulled, but the knife dug in too deep.

"Change your angle," Heimo said.

"Like this?" she asked, jerking at the handles of the knife. She completed a few strokes and then stopped dead at a knot. She dropped the drawknife. "Ouch," she said, shaking her hands.

"Yup," Heimo said. "If you don't whack off those knots first, you're gonna be in for a world of hurt."

Aidan tried again and got into a rhythm before she hit another knot. The drawknife jumped and almost hit her in the face.

"Ugh," she growled.

"Gotta be careful," Heimo said. "You'll bleed to death out here. Nearest hospital is a long way off. Hundreds of miles, and that's if you're lucky enough to get a plane."

Aidan tried again. She can be hardheaded, and while this can occasionally make her tough to deal with, I knew that for peeling poles it was a trait that would work to her advantage.

"Now you're steamboatin'!" Heimo said. "We got a lot of logs, so when you get tired, you can switch with your old man."

He explained that, after we've made some headway on the walls, we'd head downriver to where he was dismantling the old cabin. Although the managers at the refuge office in Fairbanks had given him permission to build a new cabin, they wanted him to cut as few trees as possible and use as many of the old logs and roof poles as he could.

"C'mon," he said to me, as Aidan continued to peel. "I want you to see the new cabin site."

He was excited again and eager to show me the place he'd picked out. He took off at a trot, but I walked backward, keeping my eye on Aidan.

Halfway down the path, he stopped and shouted, "Hurry up."

When I reached him, he said, "Couldn't be more perfect. It's in a clearing, but tucked in the trees, and close to the river, too."

"That means skeeters," I said.

"Yup," he agreed. "But we can light smudge fires. Besides, Edna and me will be thankful for the trees when it's fifty below and the wind's cuttin' through here."

Twenty more yards down the trail, Heimo stopped.

"Here it is. The cabin's gonna face south, and I'll use the window you brought right here." He pointed to what would be the front of the cabin. "Edna wants windows on each side, too. It'll be our home cabin, the one we'll grow old in, so I'm going to build it big—twenty feet by fourteen. Edna deserves it."

The cabins I remembered staying in when the girls were still living with Heimo and Edna were approximately thirteen by thirteen, six steps in either direction. They were comfortable and clean, and every square foot had a purpose.

Heimo continued to talk about where he was going to put the cache and the outhouse, and where he'd hang the meat racks. But I only heard every fourth word or so. I was looking back at the area where Aidan was peeling, watching her as best I could. I took my eye off her long enough to help Heimo notch two of the foundation logs. The process was a fairly simple one. We used a string and a pencil to measure and draw, or scribe, the notch. With the chain saw Heimo made a rough cut and then whacked out the chunk with the back of the axe. Then we shaped the notch with the small axe or a gouge chisel, tapping the end of the chisel with a hammer and watching as the sharp blade curled the wood. After we notched both ends of two logs, I walked back to Aidan's work area. My main concern was not bears but her cutting herself with the drawknife.

I called to her and she turned around. She was wearing thick gloves, pants, a long-sleeved shirt, a head net, and bear bells, and was already drenched in sweat.

"You okay?"

She ignored my question. "How long are we going to be out here, Dad?"

I scowled at her. "You're kidding, right? How long? Way too long to start asking."

She looked at me, laid down the drawknife, picked up her Kindle, and sat against the base of a tree.

"What are you doing?" I asked.

"Taking a break," she said.

"After forty-five minutes?"

When she didn't respond, I said, "Why don't you get back to work." I said it less as a question than a command.

"I'm tired and hungry," she replied.

"We came here to build a cabin, and you knew it."

"Fine," she said, getting up slowly. "I'll do the work, but I don't have to like it."

CHAPTER 3

PEELING POLES WITH
MARCUS MUMFORD

WHEN I RETURNED TO THE new cabin site, I saw that Heimo had finished notching the remaining two foundation logs, so we went to work on the wall logs. Cabin builders notch their logs differently. On all logs other than the foundation logs, Heimo lays his notches down, a vertical log fitting into a horizontal one tongue-and-groove style to prevent water from building up, freezing, and weakening the walls. Rather than making them square, he shapes the notches to fit the logs. Winter has a way of finding cracks and seams; the tighter the fit the better. Because big trees are hard to find in a land where it takes two hundred years for a black spruce to get fifteen feet tall, Heimo has to alternate his logs between thick end and thin end so that the cabin wall does not rise unevenly.

By the time the wall was two layers high, the clearing smelled of sweat, chain saw fumes, and bar oil, like a mechanic's shop, mixed with the lush scent of spruce pitch and wood chips and the sharp smell of mosquito dope (which deterred mosquitoes but seemed to summon the horseflies). The saw, with its air-cooled, two-stroke engine, was loud, too, but there was no way of getting around the odor of gas or the noise. Using handsaws, we would have to work until October, when the snow would likely be a foot deep.

Heimo shook wood shavings from his bandana and then picked up another log, which was badly bowed. When we lay it, bow up, on top of the other two logs, the middle stuck six inches into the air.

"I got a trick," Heimo said, and while I held the log steady, he made a vertical cut at the bend. As he sawed, the bow slowly fell. "Another inch," he said, "and she'll lay almost flat."

By the time he had cut a third of the way through the log the bow was almost gone. He inserted the front of his saw blade in the gap between logs and shaved off the small knots and ridges, alert, all the while, for the possibility of the saw kicking back in his face. When he tired, he handed me the saw and I finished the job.

"Okay, let's spike it," Heimo said. "We wanna get these logs as flush as we can. Use the butt of the axe on the spike. I ain't got a sledgehammer."

Heimo and I straddled the wall. Sitting close to where he had made the cut, we used our weight to press down the log. I spat on my hands, rubbed them together, and grabbed halfway down at the belly of the axe handle. Then I spat on my hands again.

"What's all the spittin' about?" Heimo said. I could hear the anxiousness in his voice as he readjusted his hold on the spike. "Watch out for my hands. I lose them and it's sayonara. I won't be good for nothin' out here."

Fortunately, I'd spent the winter splitting wood, and my aim was true. I struck the spike dead-on. It took eight more swings before the head of the spike lay flat against the log. My forearms ached.

"Think of how strong those old Wisconsin lumberjacks must have been," Heimo said. He stepped back and eyed the wall. "Looks good. Now it's time for more logs. We can see how Aidan is doing."

We were a quarter of the way down the trail when he stopped. "What's that?" he asked.

I heard it, too: *I will wait, I will wait for you.* "It's the chorus," I told him. "Mumford and Sons. Aidan's cranking her music to let the bears know she's there."

As we neared Aidan, Heimo danced a kind of Irish jig.

Perhaps sensing something, Aidan glanced back and smiled. "See, it's working," she said. "No bears." I wondered what had happened in the last two hours to change her mood. Then I saw a large log peeled clean of its bark. Progress.

"How 'bout some Led Zeppelin or Jimi Hendrix?" Heimo said.

"Who?" Aidan asked.

"Who? Who?" Heimo looked at me as if I was responsible for Aidan's question. "She don't know Led Zeppelin or Hendrix?"

"She knows Neil Young and the Stones," I said.

"Aidan," Heimo said, "on your next trip, I'm going to introduce you to some real music."

"Hunk Willam?" Aidan asked. "Bug Owen?"

Clearly pleased that Aidan remembered the story he had told us over breakfast about the Native Gwich'in of Fort Yukon and their affection for country music, especially Hank Williams and

Buck Owens, whose names they pronounce Hunk Willam and Bug Owen, Heimo wrapped his arm around her shoulder.

"She quicker than you with her comebacks," he said to me.

I replied that I'd been taking it easy on him, that soon I'd break out my wicked wit and skin him like a deer.

"Maybe when we're sitting around talking politics," I goaded him. "Who knows, maybe Sarah Palin will run for president in 2016. Didn't you take a picture with her in Fort Yukon? I'm going to circulate the rumor that she grabbed your butt and you told her that she had ten minutes to take her hand off."

"Go to hell," Heimo replied. "Edna wouldn't think that was funny."

Heimo and I had developed a rapport over the years and forgiven each other our differences. We simply agreed that when it came to things like politics, our riverbanks were not within hollering distance. We followed the Thomas Jefferson model. Jefferson is thought to have said, "I never considered a difference of opinion in politics, in religion, in philosophy, as cause for withdrawing from a friend."

The three of us were a curious bunch. Heimo is a sharp, self-educated (he barely graduated high school) conservative with secessionist tendencies. Alaska, especially the Alaskan bush, attracts iconoclasts, free spirits, and irreverent do-it-yourselfers who march to the beat of their own drums and mistrust most anything to do with what they call "the feds." Heimo's got the mistrust thing in spades, though he counts among his friends the federal bureaucrats, biologists, and wildlife ecologists of the Arctic National Wildlife Refuge office in Fairbanks and many employees of Alaska's various state agencies. Though he's never been south of the Mason-Dixon Line, he flies the Confederate flag over his cabin to protest governmental overreach. He grew up with a father who had been a union plumber and a dependable Democrat until the union ditched him at the time when he most needed its support, at which point his father vowed never to vote Democratic again.

I, on the other hand, have six years of college under my belt and the student loan repayment bills to prove it. In Alaska, a good college education doesn't have the currency it does in the Lower 48. Alaskans care about practical things, like whether or not you can butcher a moose, overhaul a truck engine, fly a plane, or identify animal tracks. I hunt and fish, have trapped a bit, own shotguns and rifles—though I am not a member of the NRA—and teach my daughters how to use them. But unlike Heimo, who has been living in the woods since he fled Appleton, Wisconsin, I have spent a portion of my life in Chicago and New York, and am still torn between my love for the "country" and my attraction to big, vibrant cities.

Aidan is still as green as spring. At fifteen, she is not especially interested in politics. What she really wants is a first-rate education and summers off to be a rafting guide out West. Regarding guns, which are a fixture in the Alaskan bush—Heimo and Edna rarely walk out the front door without a sidearm—she's less certain. Though she grew up with a BB gun and a .22, and has a single-shot .410 with a peashooter-size barrel, she doesn't like bigger guns. Their sound makes her jump and the kickback rattles her teeth. Nevertheless, somehow I've persuaded her that if she is going to be a responsible meat eater, she needs to learn to shoot, kill, and butcher. Back home, knowing where your meat comes from is an exercise in awareness. In the Arctic, it's the real thing.

Heimo was ready to carry back another log. We needed a big one to make sure the walls were balanced. He walked among the peeled ones, studying them, like a rancher picking out a prize steer.

"What do you think?" he asked, lifting the end of the log. "I like it because it doesn't taper too much." I seconded his selection and then we decided how we were going to carry it.

"Right shoulder," he said. "I'll give the ohook. You remember?"

"That's the word the whaling captain on St. Lawrence Island used, right?" I said.

During his first five years in Alaska, Heimo spent every spring on St. Lawrence Island. In 1976, after barely surviving his first winter in the bush, he went there to run a dry goods store for a friend. The Yupik people of Savoonga embraced him, and the village's hunters taught him hunting skills few white men had ever learned: how to hunt walrus, seal, and polar bear on the ice. Eventually they invited him to participate in their most sacred tradition—hunting the bowhead whale.

"You got it," Heimo congratulated me. "Once we sighted a whale, the captain would get into the *angyaq*. And then he'd yell 'Oooo-hooo—kk!' Like saying 'One, two, three!' We'd be running alongside the thirty-foot boat—they were still made of walrus skin then—pushing it like bobsledders across the ice. When the captain reached the *k* of *ohook*, we'd leap into the boat. First we'd paddle and then we'd raise the sail and follow a lead until the ocean opened up. I can still smell the stink of the whale and hear the sound of the blow—*Puhhh!* Man, that was exciting."

Aidan was peeling now to Florence and the Machine, and her bear bells jingled around her neck like wind chimes.

"She's gonna scare every bear within fifty miles of here." Heimo laughed. "You ready to hoist this puppy?"

On the *o* of *ohook*, we lifted the log off the ground to get a grip. Then, on the *k*, we hoisted it to our shoulders. I had the heavy end, and when the log hit my shoulder, I gasped. As I trudged down the trail, it dug into my neck, clavicle, and scapula. When we reached the cabin, we let it drop to the ground. Then we both sat down and slugged water from our bottles.

"Think you can spell Aidan?" he asked. "She was peeling hard, but we need those logs a little faster."

"Sure," I said. "Maybe she'll welcome the break."

When I reached her clearing, I saw that Aidan was fighting a knot. But she didn't notice me. She had dug down deep and discovered some primal gear, void of anything but pulling and peeling. If a grizzly ambled by it would have gone unnoticed. Only when I turned off her Kindle—the Lumineers this time—did she stop and look up. The sun was high in the sky, and there was not even the breath of a breeze. Her shirt was stained with sweat and the area smelled of freshly peeled spruce.

She invited me to admire her work. "This is a knotty one. But I'm getting better with the axe and drawknife."

"I can see that," I said.

"I can feel my muscles getting bigger," she said. "It's going to be great for cross-country skiing. Nobody will be able to double-pole better than me." She'd decided that peeling logs, pinned beneath the sun, was good strength training.

"Do I have to, Dad?" she asked when I told her Heimo wanted us to switch jobs.

"For a little while," I said. "Go learn how to notch and trim logs. When we get back home, we'll build our own cabin."

Reluctantly, she gathered her belongings among the wood shavings and chips and walked down the path toward Heimo. I picked up the drawknife and started in on a log. Ten minutes into the job my body was warmed up and I was lost in the rhythm of peeling. An hour in, however, whatever serenity or mind-body harmony I'd achieved was gone.

Peeling is hard, lonely labor under the best of circumstances, but with the sun at its zenith it was miserable work, too. I'd sweated through my shirt, and the horseflies, which can reputedly smell meat from over four miles away, had gotten wind of my scent. Thirty minutes later Heimo and Aidan came to rescue me. I stood and stretched out my back. My knees popped, and then I realized that my hands wouldn't move. My fingers felt fixed to the handles of the drawknife.

"Lunchtime," Heimo said.

"Good," I said without letting on just how glad I was for the break. "Seems I draw more flies than a caribou carcass."

Heimo asked Aidan and me to gather firewood on the way back to the campsite. Aidan slogged into the woods and picked up some smallish sticks.

"What you really need are these," I told her, ripping some brittle branches from under the canopy of a small black spruce. "They're great for starting a fire and they're usually dry, even in a hard rain." Aidan didn't reply. "Why so sullen?" I asked. I realized she was on the verge of crying.

"Are you okay?"

"I don't know," she said, cradling her armful of sticks. "Heimo got impatient with my questions and then he just ignored me. I don't know if he wants me here, Dad."

I dropped my branches and walked over to her. Over the years I'd realized that there were times when a father should not indulge his daughter and times when he should. Right then, I knew Aidan needed my support.

"You're a good worker and you're tough," I consoled her. "Don't let him get under your skin. He's just a little tense because he's got a lot to do before the weather turns. You'll prove your worth."

What I didn't say was that I had an idea about what had set Heimo off. Aidan could be a relentless question asker, especially when she was nervous and out of her element. She may have peppered Heimo so much that at some point he just grew tired of her questions.

Aidan set her jaw to stop the tears.

"Hang in there," I said clumsily. As we walked on I felt how inadequate my response had been. Elizabeth would have known intuitively how to comfort her.

Back at the campsite, Aidan started to build a fire.

"I'll help you," Heimo said, his irritation gone. "There's a strong wind."

"You got some nice, dry wood," he said, encouraging her. "You gotta always put the kindling upwind of your larger sticks. I like to bunch up the kindling first. Then I like to strip paper and crumple it up and put it underneath. When you light your match, use your body as a screen. Once the fire gets going, add some smaller pieces. Always remember: out here, you gotta know how to start a fire fast. It can be a matter of life or death."

When the fire caught, Heimo walked to the food cache and pulled off the tarp.

"How 'bout ramen noodles, PowerBars, and tangerines, the ones you brought from Fairbanks? That'll have to do for lunch until we shoot a goose or a beaver. Are you hungry, Aidan?"

Aidan brightened. "Yeah, that sounds good, especially the tangerines."

Halfway through lunch, Kirk Sweetsir flew over, and Heimo got him on the two-way radio.

"First time I've ever been able to see one of your cabin sites from the air, Heimo," Kirk said.

"Yeah, I know," Heimo answered. "I'll have to fix that."

If Heimo's cabin site was visible from the air, that meant people could find him—an idea he hated. It's not that he doesn't like people. In fact, he's good-natured, a result, perhaps, of living in such a severe place. But he likes people on his own terms. When he's in Fairbanks he's treated as something of a celebrity, but after a week of being recognized, he's climbing out of his skin and ready again for the solitude of the woods.

What he doesn't care about is inspiring copycats. He uses letters from wannabe survivalists as fire starter. If you push him, he'll admit that he wishes there were a few more trappers carrying on the frontier tradition, albeit at a fifty-mile or so distance. But he does not consider himself a proponent of a back-to-nature doctrine. Nor is he a wilderness purist. The key to living in the bush, he says, is to put the wilderness experience first and to bend civilization around that experience—to blend in a few small conveniences, not exclude them entirely. As for the American myth of the solitary hunter wandering the wild mountains, Heimo lived alone for six years, and the loneliness pushed him to the brink. During those first few winters, when the temperature bottomed out at 50 below for weeks and he had no one to talk to, no one to share his fears with, it took nearly all his will to carry out the simplest tasks. But he was young and full of life and large dreams. Now, he readily admits that if not for Edna and her companionship, he would not still be here. "A wolverine," he's told me on many occasions, "is a strict loner, but a man needs people."

Kirk was north of us, no longer overhead, but I could still hear him on the radio. "If you're still planning to die out here"—he chuckled—"make sure you designate a spot near the cabin where we can put you in the ground."

"Not here," Heimo replied. "Upriver. Just leave me for the wolves."

"Ten-four," Kirk said. "By the way, I spotted a herd of caribou. I thought they might be comin' this way. But they were headed for the Sheenjek."

By 1:00 p.m. Aidan had finished washing the dishes and I had given up on the hope of a power nap.

"Damn bugs," I said. "From the air this place looks like paradise, but on the ground it's a mosquito sanctuary."

Heimo chuckled. "You got that right. If I didn't have to get this cabin done, I'd never be out here now. I learned that decades ago." Seconds later he was gathering his tools, ready to make a beeline for the woods. Most of the time he kept his anxiousness about getting the cabin done in check, but he knew that summer was almost worn out. Soon the bears and the caribou would come down out of the mountains, the cottonwoods would be tinged with yellow, the willows would redden, hoarfrost would cover the tundra, sunfat blueberries would freeze on the bush, and ice would skiff the river's edge. Even as the sun sapped our strength and the mosquitoes challenged our sanity, he knew that we were losing light as the earth's northern axis turned away from the sun. Summer and its pedal-to-the-metal growth would pass in a panic.

"All right, let's get a move on," he said. "We got a lot to do, and I can feel it. Winter's comin'."

CHAPTER 4

FIRST THE RIVER GIVETH

THE GWICH'IN SAY THAT THE far north is where a man has room to dream. But I'd been lying with my eyes open since 4:30, jolted out of sleep by an anxiety dream—an image of Aidan being swept away by a rushing current.

By 5:00 a.m. I was listening to a squawking loon flying up and down the river, "Ack, ack, ack." At 6:00 a.m. I exited the tent and heard Heimo say, "When I hear that fire cracklin', I'll be out."

I got the fire going and filed and sharpened the saw's chain. Heimo soon emerged full of energy, already talking as he zipped up his tent's rain fly.

"Did you hear that red-throated loon? One thing people don't understand about this place when I tell 'em is that the Arctic is a lean country. So little food up here. There ain't many animals per square mile. It's not like Wisconsin. Last time I was down there, for my dad's funeral, I got up before sunrise every morning just so I could take a walk and listen to the birds sing."

Heimo took a step through the fire—his method for getting rid of the bugs—and I heard the crackle of incinerated mosquitoes as they fell from his pants into the flames. He unfolded his chair and something caught his eye. "Dragonflies," he said delightedly. "They're real mosquito hawks."

I hadn't said a word yet, and Heimo looked at me. "What's wrong with you?" He got a gleam in his eye and lapsed into a thick Wisconsin accent. "OOOOh, Christ," he began. "Ya musta been down to the Bucksnort Tavern last night poundin da beers wit da boys, eh? You in da doghouse with da wife?" Then he laughed. "You look like shit."

I put on my best Sheboygan, Wisconsin, voice. "Cripes, ya tink maybe I need a bratwurst and a Leinenkugel?"

Heimo seemed ready to continue our Cheesehead skit, but then he shook his head. "Nah. If I get in the habit of talking like that, Edna's gonna kill me. She hates it."

Hearing Aidan moving inside the tent, I set a pot of water on the metal grill. When it boiled I dumped two spoonfuls of cocoa and a bit of coffee from my charred tin percolator into a cup, poured in the water, stirred it, and let it cool.

The hot chocolate was my peace offering. The previous night, Aidan and I had fetched water at the spring, instead of the river, to avoid any chance of giardia, an intestinal infection caused by a waterborne parasite, the symptoms of which are extreme diarrhea, nausea, abdominal cramping, and fatigue. Though Heimo didn't think the precaution was necessary, I pointed out to him that if one of us got sick his plans for the cabin would be shot to hell. We'd brought along a filter, but we were thirsty so often that we would have had to filter round-the-clock to stay hydrated.

On the way back to the campsite, with our water bottles and a full five-gallon pail, I had lost my bearings. Caribou trails criss-crossed the woods and I led us down the wrong one. I was pissed at myself; I should have known better. I didn't have a compass, and going in I hadn't paid attention to the signs—a scarred spruce, a patch of blueberries, a small sinkhole. We couldn't see the mountains or hear the river; the woods were too thick. Aidan wanted to keep going. She thought she knew the way back to the campsite. I wanted to backtrack and return to the spring to reorient ourselves. We argued, she and I equally adamant about being right. It was a classic case of two stubborn people butting heads, each unwilling to give an inch. Ultimately, I played dirty. I said, "You do it your way, and I'll do it mine," knowing full well that she was too afraid of bears to leave me. Had she stomped off to find the campsite, I would have been obligated to follow her. Instead we walked back to the spring and got our bearings.

When we returned, Heimo was out of his chair, looking in our direction. "Where were you?" he asked. "I was starting to wonder."

"Dad got us lost," Aidan blurted out.

"You're shittin' me," Heimo said.

"Nope," she continued. "He took the wrong trail."

Later that evening, as I helped her haul water from the river for the dishes because she was afraid to go on her own, I said, "You know, that was low."

"Aw, come on, Dad," she replied. "I was just joking. Heimo didn't care. Don't you think you're being a little oversensitive?"

"Maybe," I said, "but that's not for you to decide. Now, go boil the water and do the dishes."

"You don't have to be so mean," Aidan said as she walked away. Twenty feet down the trail she turned. "Okay, I'll do them, but I'm not looking forward to being here, if this is how you're going to act. This isn't the way I imagined it."

"Me either," I said, raising my voice.

By the time we reached the tents, I'd already regretted the altercation. But I didn't apologize. It's one of the things my wife hates about me; I'm not quick to say I'm sorry. I've explained to her that I don't rush to make apologies. She says it's a lame excuse for not be willing to admit when I'm wrong. Maybe. With Aidan, right or wrong, I should have apologized. I've always been proud of my sense of direction, and my pride got in the way. I could have made a joke about men and directions. Then I could have taught her some very basic lessons in woodcraft, explaining what I did wrong—getting us lost because of my failure to observe—and what I did right—returning to our point of origin to reorient myself. After returning, we could have gone back to the spring and I could have shown her how to use a compass. Instead, I walked into the woods, ostensibly to collect firewood, and stewed over her words: "This isn't the way I imagined it."

That hit home. Aidan was here with me because I'd convinced her that the experience would be powerful. Deep down, however, I was afraid I wouldn't get it right. Could it be that one day she would look back upon this adventure with regret? Was I crazy for bringing her here, to what a good female friend, who raised a family on the Yukon River, called a "man's world and possibly the loneliest place on the planet for a teenage girl"?

Aidan had gone to bed early while Heimo and I stayed by the fire telling stories. By the time I went to bed I was prepared to say I was sorry, but she was already asleep.

This was all at the front of my mind as I carried the hot chocolate to the tent. Aidan was reading. I considered crawling in to say

I was sorry and to discuss what had happened the night before, but she looked comfortable and content. Let it be for now, I told myself. We'd have ample opportunity to sort things out.

"Your hot chocolate is ready, madam," I said.

Hoping to keep the mosquitoes out, Aidan opened the tent only wide enough to stick out her hand. As I walked back to the fire, I heard her slurp.

"It's perfect, Dad," she said. "Thank you."

Ten minutes later, she joined us. Heimo was tying on his bandana with one hand and grabbed the cast-iron skillet with the other. "Dammit," he said. "I got carpal tunnel so bad I can hardly lift the pan. I hate getting old."

Aidan was still sipping her cocoa, smiling at us. I envied her. Unlike us, she was a work in progress, not a work in regress. Yesterday, after putting in a day of peeling poles, she did an hour of jump roping and a plyometric cardio circuit she'd designed when she realized the gravel bar was more rock than sand and she wouldn't be able to run on it. Heimo and I sat in our camp chairs and, like two old men, complained about our worn-out joints.

I took the skillet from Heimo and poured in the pancake mix.

As he walked to the river to get water, I looked at Aidan. "Sorry about yesterday," I said. "I was stupid."

"Me, too," she replied. Then she cleared her throat. I thought she was getting ready to discuss what had happened, but instead she asked me how Heimo had changed in the decade since I'd last seen him.

I said I wasn't sure, that I hadn't spent enough time with him to know. This was a lie, a case of one proud middle-aged man protecting another. Despite his bounding gait, I knew that Heimo was feeling his age. Ten years ago he never would have admitted that he was tired or sore. Now, he had atrophy and impermanence on his mind.

In 2002, when I had been with him, he'd run a river in his canoe for the rush or climb a mountain for the view. Today, as he nears sixty, he has little inclination to push himself. These days he'd rather spend an afternoon picking cloudberries on the tundra with Edna or watching her fish—Edna loves to fish. When he hunts caribou, he rarely goes to the top of Mummuck Mountain to watch for them anymore. He waits for them to come to him. Carrying out 125 pounds of meat in his backpack once gave him a thrill. It made him feel like one of the early trappers of the Rocky Mountains. It brought out the Jim Bridger in him. Now he likes to shoot a caribou on the gravel bar so he can butcher it and float it down the river in his canoe.

What Heimo feared now more than anything else, I knew, was not being physically up to the challenge of living in the bush. The joke in Alaska is that a "sourdough" is someone who's "soured on the country and ain't got the dough to get out." But Heimo was here by his own choosing. When he first came north his parents had hoped Alaska was nothing more than a passing fancy. But Heimo understood what they had not; he'd found his place in the world.

That was the summer of 1975, when much of Alaska was still a geography of possibility, a de facto wilderness, held loosely in federal trust and open to anyone willing to bust his, or her, ass and line a boat up a river, build a cabin, set up a fish camp, butcher a moose, or trap enough fur to make a meager living. Today, the great irony of Alaska is that, because of the competing forces set in motion by the discovery of oil in 1968, and the decade-long land grab that ensued, it is a place divided by figurative fences. Despite the don't-fence-me-in spirit of individualism, every square foot of the state's 365 million acres has been surveyed and conveyed to one group or another. Alaska is a patchwork of federal, state, Native, and private landholdings.

Heimo built his first cabin on the Coleen River in 1978, when what is now the refuge was part of that great chunk of undesignated, if contested, federal territory. Its status soon changed. When President Jimmy Carter signed the Alaska National Interest Lands Conservation Act (ANILCA) into law, on December 2, 1980, 28 percent of the state, 104 million acres, was placed under federal protection, and the land that Heimo had homesteaded was formally declared part of the Arctic National Wildlife Refuge. Acknowledging that those living in the Alaskan bush "may be the last remnant of the subsistence culture alive today in North America," ANILCA explicitly allowed for the continuation of subsistence practices by Alaska's rural residents in some of the national interest lands, including the expanded Arctic National Wildlife Refuge. It granted renewable five-year "guest permits" to anyone who, like Heimo, had built his cabin in or before 1978. ANILCA further stipulated that permits could be transferred only to immediate family and were rendered null and void with the death of the "last immediate family member of the claimant residing in the cabin." Like many Alaskans, Heimo has a deep mistrust of anything that happens in Washington, D.C., but ANILCA's concession to homesteaders in the refuge worked out to his advantage. He was allowed to stay, while in some parts of Alaska, the government forcibly removed people from their cabins.

Aidan put down her hot chocolate, added wood to the fire, and poked the coals. Heimo, back from the river, took a long pull from his water bottle. He wiped his face with the back of his hand, a callused and leathery hand that had split hundreds of cords of wood, fleshed and stretched fur late into the night, scooped clotting blood out of the gut cavities of moose, survived frostbite, and held the small bodies of three daughters.

Aidan hadn't been around Heimo long enough to form an opinion of him. She had never encountered anyone remotely similar, and while she sympathized with him, it was hard for her not to be skeptical. Was he struggling to live out a way of life whose time had passed? Was woods savvy a kind of intelligence that had a place in the twenty-first century? If Aidan had asked Heimo what he was missing by living in the bush, his answer would have been quick and direct. "Not a damn thing," he would have said. Nevertheless, Heimo had become something of a relict.

As fewer and fewer people make their livings from, and off of, the land, our tolerance for people like Heimo diminishes. He considers himself a conservationist in the old mold—someone who practices conservation. He has no use for the environmental movement; it carries far too much political baggage for him. As a trapper who sells fur that is shipped all around the world, and a hunter who takes five caribou every year, he would have a tough time convincing many modern-day, environmentally minded Americans that he is anything but a killer. But unlike many of his detractors, he puts his values into practice every day of his life.

Heimo's Golden Rule is one that few but the most committed conservationists could ever live by. It's that nothing is ever wasted. Up here, you can use God's name in vain if the mosquitoes are chewing the shit out of you or if it's pouring and your rain fly is torn. But waste food and you are an irredeemable sinner. When you shoot a caribou, you use the entire animal. Caribou organs are a delicacy, their bones contain nutritious marrow, and their hides can be made into pants and blankets. Same goes for a moose.

You don't discard its tongue or cheeks, the meat on its face, the fat behind its eyes, or the brain. They are the equivalent of Sunday dinner, what you serve if a bush pilot–friend happens to drop in for supper or a long-lost cousin decides to pay you a visit.

Heimo sat down and poked at the fire. "I want to die out here, ya know, but to do that I need to be healthy."

"Huh?" Aidan asked. "That doesn't make any sense."

"Yup, that's fer sure," Heimo said. "I gotta stay fit. And now," he added, farting loudly, "I gotta use the screen tent." Heimo has the kind of gas that can clear a campsite, so Aidan and I gathered our belongings, quickly changed from our sleeping clothes to our pitchy, dirty, reeking-of-fish-guts work duds, and made a run for it.

IT WAS LUNCHTIME, and after a dose of ibuprofen to take the soreness out of my joints, I joined Heimo and Aidan at the fire. In the tops of the trees, white-winged crossbills were cracking spruce cones for the seeds. Clouds had moved in from the north, it had begun to drizzle, and Heimo had laid out his rain fly.

"Damn thing's torn," he said, pulling a needle and thread from the breast pocket of his Carhartt flannel work shirt. He told Aidan how Herman, an old Eskimo on St. Lawrence Island who had taught him how to hunt seal, walrus, and polar bear, never went anywhere without a needle and thread.

"Can be the difference between life and death out here," he cautioned her. "Especially in winter. It's saved me before. At fifty below, you tear your jacket or your pants, and you're screwed."

"I don't know if I'd want to be up here in winter," Aidan said. "No sun and forty below zero. That's not for me."

"You'd have to put some fat on. You know that," Heimo replied. "You get out on the trapline at minus forty, with a fifteen-mile-per-hour windchill, that's an air temperature of eighty-five below. Then you got no room for mistakes. It'll kill you quick."

"What up here can't kill you?" Aidan asked. The question hung there and she lowered her head, wishing she could take it back.

"Not much," Heimo answered. "Edna and me, we've paid the price."

Aidan knew the painful story. In the spring of 1984, the Korths—Heimo, Edna, two-year-old Coleen, and Millie, Edna's eleven-year-old daughter from a previous marriage—were living in a tent camp on the Coleen River, looking for a spot in which to build a new cabin so that they could expand their trapping territory. Heimo knew that if they were going to make enough money to stay in the bush, he needed to catch more fur. They were short on food and subsisting on the occasional goose, willow leaves, Indian potato, wild onion, and whatever grayling they could find in the feeder steams. It was just a week past breakup and the river was too choked with runoff for them to find fish in the main channel. Heimo remembered that they'd left a twenty-five-pound sack of cornmeal in a fifty-five-gallon drum at their cabin downriver. He knew, too, that there would be more ducks and geese there.

On the morning of June 3, Heimo loaded the canoe, positioned Millie in the middle, and set Coleen in Millie's lap. Edna took the bow, and Heimo sat in the stern to do the steering. They had no life jackets, but the section of river they'd be on had never been a problem.

Two miles down, Heimo saw a large white spruce, fallen during the spring flood, hanging low over the river. He paddled furiously but the current pulled at the canoe. They hit the tree's trunk and the canoe flipped over. The force of the collision threw everyone from the boat into the frigid water. When Heimo surfaced, he saw Edna hanging on to the gunwale. He saw something in the current and reached out. It was Millie. He grasped her jacket, pulled her toward him, and realized that she no longer had ahold of Coleen. The memory of what happened then is seared into his brain. He saw Coleen float by. But he knew that if he let go of Millie she would drown. He lunged for Coleen with one arm, but missed.

Instinct took over. Heimo dragged Millie to shallow water, swam back out into the river, and pulled Edna and the canoe to a gravel bar. Then he ran to the bank and raced downstream. "Coleen!" he screamed. He knew he would find her and rescue her and everything would be okay.

He ran a quarter of a mile downriver and then he ran back. Where was Coleen? When he reached Edna and Millie, he realized they were hypothermic and went into autopilot, gathering kindling and deadwood. He tried to light a fire but couldn't strike the waterproof match; his hands were shaking too hard. He tried again and again. When the match finally lit, the fire blazed and he dashed downriver again. He ran back and forth, screaming, "Coleen! Coleen!" At last he lost it. In his rage, he punched trees and heaved huge rocks into the river. Then he ran back to the fire. He knew he had to get Millie and Edna, who was crying hysterically—"Where's Coleen? I want my daughter"—back to the tent camp and under blankets.

At the camp, he covered Edna and Millie in caribou skins and tripped the Emergency Locator Transmitter (ELT). Then he went to the gravel bar and, kicking away the rocks, scratched SOS into the sand with his foot.

That evening, by the time the Civil Air Patrol out of Fort Yukon received the alert from the Rescue Coordination Center on Kodiak

Island, which had pinpointed the electronic signals emitted by the ELT, Heimo, Edna, and Millie were out on the gravel bar. Heimo had built another fire to keep them warm. When the plane arrived, the pilot followed the ELT signal to the woods. He circled time and again, concentrating on the signal. Heimo ran up and down the gravel bar, waving his arms wildly and shouting at the top of his lungs. "We're down here, you stupid son of a bitch. We're down here. God, please let him see us." Five minutes later he saw the pilot circle back in the direction of Fort Yukon. Until the pilot gave up his search, Heimo had believed that maybe—somehow— Coleen might still be alive. Now his last glimmer of hope faded. He had failed to save his daughter.

Later, a pilot for Arctic Circle Air and friend of the Korths heard that the RCC was still getting hits from the Coleen River. He took matters into his own hands, borrowed a company plane, and flew out to the river. He found Heimo, Edna, and Millie still on the gravel bar and air-dropped a message—"If it's an emergency and you need a helicopter, wave your arms." When Heimo waved, he tipped his wings to acknowledge that he understood and air-dropped another message—"I'm going to get help." He knew there was a helicopter based out of Arctic Village, where professors from the University of Alaska were doing archaeological work, so he radioed them.

Five hours after their friend discovered them on the gravel bar, Heimo, Edna, and Millie were in Arctic Village, where news of their tragedy quickly spread among the villagers. That night, as the sun began to fade, they flew to Fort Yukon. When they arrived there, a group of friends met them and took them in. They were exhausted. Edna and Millie fell asleep, but Heimo paced liked a caged animal. The following day, he, two Alaska state troopers, and a helicopter pilot flew up and down the river, but they never found a sign of Coleen.

Four days later a service was held in Coleen's honor at the Assembly of God church. Much of Fort Yukon was there. Heimo and Edna were numb. When the service ended and Heimo turned to thank everyone for coming, he stared into the crowd of friends and cried for the first time.

After the funeral, the villagers led Heimo, Edna, and Millie outside, where they had set up a traditional Gwich'in potlatch, with moose, salmon, fry bread, chicken, and potato salad. Heimo and Edna hadn't eaten in two days but they could only stare at the food. When the potlatch was over, the people of Fort Yukon presented the Korths with five hundred dollars in cash. People from as far away as Arctic Village had made small donations.

A week later, the Korths returned to the river. While Edna and Millie waited on a gravel bar where the plane had dropped them off, Heimo put on his hip boots and waded into the river, leaning into the current. Still muddy with spring runoff, it slapped cold at his thighs. Heimo crossed the river's main channel. In the shallows, he could see grayling holding where the current slowed. Then he saw the gravel bar that had been Coleen's playground. There among the knee-high willows and soft sand were Coleen's footprints, indentations from the pink boots she loved. Heimo knelt down and touched one of the prints. Then he walked back and forth and stamped them out, knowing that Edna would never be able to bear the sight.

At the far bank, he saw the canoe. His hand trembled as he reached for the bow rope. Before crossing the river again, he splashed water on his face and wiped his eyes. When he reached the gravel bar where Edna and Millie were waiting, Edna refused to get in the canoe. Heimo explained that the river was too high and the current too fast for her to keep on her feet or for him to carry Millie. When he finally coaxed her into the canoe, she sat in the middle, gripping Millie with one hand, clasping the canoe's rail with the other.

For the next three weeks, Edna, Millie, and Heimo worked for eighteen hours a day, taking advantage of the sun, to build their new cabin. It was hard, seemingly endless work, but it was the work that saved them.

HEIMO STOOD AND went to get wood. When he returned to the fire, he lay three large pieces under the metal grill grate. Sitting down, he said, "Yup, we've paid the price. Parents aren't supposed to outlive their children. That's not how it should be. After Coleen died, people wondered how we could come back out here. They thought we'd be haunted by the memories and tried to convince us to move to town."

Heimo stared at Aidan without speaking. Then he grabbed a stick and poked at the embers. "Their intentions were good, but what none of them understood was that we could never leave this place. Here, we're surrounded by her memories. Coleen is everywhere."

CHAPTER 5

DOWNRIVER

AFTER TEN DAYS OF WORK the cabin walls were waist high. Heimo was pleased with our progress and proposed we kick off early to attend to our personal hygiene. We were walking around with brown clouds of accumulated sweat, woodsmoke, and bug dope trailing us.

"Really?" Aidan asked, when Heimo interrupted her peeling. I could see the white sweat stains on the back of her shirt, and when she lifted her mosquito head net, the sweat from her forehead dripped down her face. "We get to punch out early," she said, standing slightly bent over, with her hands on her hips like an exhausted runner.

Heimo thought she was being sarcastic. "You're a bigger smartass than your dad."

"No," Aidan said. "I wasn't kidding."

"Ah, come on, I'm not working you that hard, am I?" he asked.

"Not for indentured servants," I said.

Aidan and I had been teasing Heimo that he was running a salt mine and depending on us for no-wage labor. Joking aside, the work was harder than Aidan had envisioned, the bugs ten times worse than she'd ever imagined. In Wisconsin the mosquitoes are bad, but Alaska's are plague-like. What's more, Aidan hated not being able to run and hated, too, not being able to call home and tell Elizabeth or a friend how much her arms and shoulders felt like they were going to fall off from all the peeling, how much she missed reclining in her bed and reading a book or walking down Madison's State Street in the long light of summer, how she detested hiding under a mosquito net in the hot sun, and how she sometimes felt trapped because I was often too tired at the end of a day to do anything but fish from a nearby gravel bar, and she was too scared to hike up- or downriver on her own.

We followed Heimo to the campsite. When we got back to the tents, Aidan gathered her towel, soap, shampoo, and brush. "I can't wait to wash up in the river," she said. "When I was peeling today, I smelled something awful. I couldn't figure out where it was coming from. And then I realized it was *me*. I smell like the monkey cage at the zoo." I started to contradict her, but I got a whiff and realized she was right; she did stink.

Minutes later, we were out on the gravel bar. Aidan was washing up at one end, while Heimo cleaned up at the other. I delayed my river bath to act as a sentry for Aidan, who was still worried about the possibility of a grizzly lumbering out of the willows. I sat on a piece of driftwood with my binoculars, glassing Mummuck Mountain for caribou, hoping that the herd Kirk had spotted from his plane might have swung this way. Downriver I heard Aidan plunge into the ice-cold Coleen. When I didn't hear her come back up, I lay down my binoculars and stood nervously, looking in her direction, fearing that she'd gotten caught in the current. As she surfaced, I breathed a sigh of relief and turned back toward Mummuck Mountain. She wanted her privacy and made me promise that I would face north while she bathed.

A few minutes later, I turned again and saw her wrapped in a towel and running my way with her clothes bundled up in her arms. She was out of breath when she reached me.

"What's wrong?" I asked.

"Nothing, nothing," she said, her voice straining. "F-f-freezing. I'm freezing."

Heimo and Aidan dried off in the sun and then I took my bath, which amounted to nothing more than a fifteen-second dunk in the river, a hurried lather, and another dunk. The water was so cold my head felt like it would crack open.

It was seven o'clock before we returned to the campsite. The wind had quieted and the bugs had gone on the offensive, so we ate hurriedly and got into our tents as soon as we could. By the time I crawled in, Aidan was lying on top of her sleeping bag, holding a small mirror up to her face. Her hair was brushed and pinned back in a ponytail. She handed me the mirror. I held it close and glanced at my reflection. There was a dead mosquito on my cheek and a streak of dried blood, and something—maybe snot—crusted on my chin whiskers.

"So," she said. "What do you think of yourself?"

"Solid B," I replied.

She laughed. "That's what I thought you'd say."

Then she grabbed the mirror and looked at herself. She was in the middle of one of North America's great wildernesses, and had just taken her first river bath in ten days, but she was still a teenager who needed reassurance.

"Seriously, Dad. Do I look pretty?"

"B plus, A minus," I answered.

"You'd make a horrible girl," she said, and reached in the corner of the tent and threw something at me—her stinky socks.

TWO DAYS LATER we headed downriver to fetch supplies from the old cabin. The early morning was sun-filled and breezy, but the wind had shifted out of the north and big, dark clouds scudded in off the Arctic with a suddenness that caught me by surprise. It was cold and getting colder.

We put on our life jackets and pushed the canoe into the water. "Let's go," Heimo said, his sense of urgency palpable. Aidan climbed into the middle of the square-back canoe and knelt while I sat in the bow and Heimo took the stern. He yanked at the starter rope on his five-horse Mercury kicker. The motor coughed, almost caught, and then cut out. "Damn thing's been acting up," he said. He pulled four more times before the motor finally rumbled to life. Thirty feet downriver, it sputtered and died. Heimo jerked at the starter rope four more times and then he gave up.

"Grab a paddle."

We floated along the riverbank for one hundred feet before paddling into the main channel. I felt the canoe settle into a set of small rapids twenty feet from the cutbank to our right. Aidan stared into the river's deep, green holes. "Look," I told her as the clouds parted and a reed of light shone on the distant Strangle Woman Mountains.

I was watching the light on the mountains when I felt the speed of the water increase. I noticed snarls of alder, willow, brush, and tree trunks dumped along the edge of the river, evidence of the kind of violence the Coleen is capable of. As we came around a bend I saw a sweeper, a large, uprooted white spruce tree, lying across our path, stretching halfway into the river.

"Sweeper!" I yelled. The only thing I could think was *Grab Aidan. If we spill, grab Aidan.*

"Paddle like hell," Heimo shouted. "Or we'll get sucked in."

I paddled as hard as I could and managed to turn the bow, but as I did I realized that Heimo had not swung the stern to safety. The back of the canoe would absorb the full impact of the crash. As the bow passed outside the reach of the sweeper I heard its branches scrape the side of the boat. I knew that if the back end hit we were still going to flip. I waited for the collision, but then I felt the canoe ease into slower water.

"Jesus Christ," Heimo said. "That was a close one."

Only when I heard the relief in his voice did I release my vise grip on my paddle. I rested it across the gunwales and leaned back in my seat.

"OOOOOahh." Aidan expelled the breath that she had been holding.

As the current slowed and we drifted, I could tell that the Coleen had changed. Heimo explained how during spring breakup, as the melting ice roared downriver, the Coleen rerouted itself and the main channel spilled into what was once the side channel, a quiet offshoot of the river that Heimo and Edna had admired over thirty years before when they built their first cabin here. The river had receded since spring, but I could still see the high-water marks along the bank.

The Coleen, like other Arctic rivers, is always shifting. One year there's an island, thick with willows and cottonwoods seeded by the wind, dividing the river. A year later it is gone, washed away by spring floods.

When we reached the cabin site we beached the canoe on a

little gravel bar. Heimo walked into the woods, concerned that the river had eaten up more of the yard than he thought. He worried that it would take the cabin itself before he'd had a chance to get everything out.

When Heimo was gone Aidan said, "Dad, I kept looking at the sweeper, thinking we weren't going to make it." Then she asked in a whisper, "Is that where Coleen died?"

"Farther downriver," I told her. "But not too far."

"I wondered," she added, "because Heimo seemed tense."

I'd noticed it, too, as soon as we sat in the canoe.

"It makes me want to cry," Aidan said. "Do you ever recover from something like that?"

"I hope I never have to find out," I replied.

I told her the story of Heimo and Shannon Hayden, the mother of our bush pilot, Daniel. Shannon had given Heimo a gift that he and Edna treasure. It had been almost twenty years since the death of Coleen, and Heimo was visiting the Haydens in Fairbanks. Richard and Shannon had made the move to town because of Shannon's failing health. While they were visiting, Shannon left the room and returned with a photograph. It was of Edna, young and beaming with the joy of motherhood, holding little Coleen in her arms. The image was so unexpected that Heimo didn't have time to clench his jaw and fight back the tears. The serrated edge of grief had smoothed over the years, but sometimes it still took him by surprise. Heimo looked away. When he turned back, wiping his eyes with the back of his hand, he saw that Shannon and Richard were crying, too.

Aidan knew something of death. She'd seen cancer kill her maternal grandmother. She knew, too, how the death of her grandmother still weighed on her own mother.

Heimo and Edna never had the chance to say good-bye to their daughter. They did not even have her body to grieve over. For months after Coleen's death, all Edna wanted to do was to lie in bed or sink into a grave. Sometimes Heimo would lie beside her and wrap his arms around her while she sobbed, "I want Coleen back." While Edna had curled up and cried, Heimo had been left with a mountain of guilt and an anger that rushed to the surface like a rain-filled river. He punched trees and hurled his axe at the ground. How could he, a man who had survived alone for six years, lose his daughter to the landscape he loved? How could the place that had saved and restored him also betray him?

But he had little time for grief or regret, however deep. There was much to do before winter came.

IT WAS COLD and Aidan and I were eager to move. We took the well-worn path to the cabin. On the way I stopped to show her the large cottonwood where Heimo's daughters, Rhonda and Krin, once carved totem pole–like faces into the thick bark. Both girls grew up on the river. Here, they had hunted, fished, and run their own traplines. When not roaming the woods, they had liked to draw and write stories. Both are now in their twenties, married, and living in Fairbanks. Rhonda has a young daughter, named Coleen for the sister she never knew.

Aidan was admiring the carvings, running her fingers over the ridges and shallow grooves, when Heimo yelled, "Hey, I'm up here and I need that list." Earlier that morning, Heimo and Aidan had put together a list of the supplies we needed.

Aidan entered the cabin yard and stopped. Up until she'd seen the girls' carvings and the neat clearing with its reminders of the family's life—wooden benches, a table, a fire pit, chipped enamel plates, a metal washtub, the jawbone of a moose, and the chalk-white skull of a wolf—she hadn't been able to imagine them living here.

Heimo ducked under the five-foot doorframe. "We got a lot of memories here," he said, stepping out onto the small porch. "That's where the girls liked to play." He pointed to a clearing at the side of the cabin. "When they were really young, we'd tie bear bells to their clothes so we knew where they were. When they moved, it sounded like a sleigh."

Aidan was still scanning the cabin yard. Heimo pushed her shoulder. "What's the matter? Didn't you think it would look like this?"

Aidan shook her head. "I don't know what I thought. Maybe I didn't think it would look so much"—she paused—"like home."

DOWN AT THE river we loaded the supplies—a fifty-five-gallon steel drum, which Heimo would use to keep food safe from the bears; a sack of flour and another of rice; a Coleman cookstove; a tool kit; a shovel and pick; a rolled-up section of carpet; a gas can; some roof poles; and large containers of salt and pepper—into the canoe. The salt and pepper had sent our spirits soaring. We were out and we'd need something to spice up the grayling we were eating twice a day.

I secured both sides of the drum with pieces of wood. Though empty, it weighed forty-four pounds. If it rolled when we were on the water, it would tip us.

The weather had turned nasty. According to the thermometer at the cabin, the temperature had fallen to 40, a thirty-eight-degree drop in less than fifteen hours. The gray skies were spitting slanting, wind-driven rain that felt more like sleet.

Aidan blew on her hands while Heimo explained his plan for getting back upriver. Because the canoe was crowded with supplies, he wanted me to walk to the new cabin site by way of the old river channel, while he and Aidan motored upstream.

"We should be okay," Heimo said. "For some reason the motor does better into the current. Let's test it out."

Wearing my hip waders, I held the canoe in the water while Heimo primed the fuel line. "Remember," I told Aidan. "If you go in, keep your legs pointed downriver in case you hit a rock or a sweeper. If you can't find a gravel bar to get out on, bring your knees up to conserve heat."

Aidan gave me a look as if to say, "Dad, I don't even want to *think* about going over."

The effects of cold-water immersion are frightening but predictable. Water is twenty-five times more efficient than air at drawing heat away from the body. If the canoe were to tip, Aidan's life jacket would keep her warm for only so long. The key is not to panic. Fifty percent of people who fall into water colder than 59 degrees, including strong swimmers, die because they are unable to calm themselves. The first thing you experience upon going over is the cold shock response, an extreme psychological stress, followed by gasping and hyperventilation that makes it feel as if you're actually drowning. What most people don't know is that this response passes. If you can collect yourself, you can get your breathing under control. If you continue to panic, however, self-rescue becomes much harder. After more than ten minutes in the water, your core temperature drops and you become all but incapable of saving yourself.

When the priming bulb was hard, Heimo yanked on the engine's starting rope. The motor coughed to life and then quit. "Goddamn thing," he said. "If it don't work, we're gonna have to line the boat the whole way back."

Lining is a critical skill in the Alaskan bush. You grab the bowline and the stern line, hold them over your shoulders to form an isosceles triangle, and walk along a gravel bar or in the shallows, all the while trying to balance the boat so that the bow tracks into the current. Against a swift-flowing river, it's hard, wearying work.

After three more pulls, the engine finally caught and Heimo revved it. He motored along the riverbank while I walked holding the canoe's gunwale.

"Motor sounds good," he said. "Push us off."

I didn't have time to object. I shoved the boat into the current and watched it sputter upriver, recalling my bad dream about Aidan being swept away. When they rounded a bend and I could no longer see them, I walked through willows matted with cotton grass and branches deposited by the spring floods, trying to drive from my head the image of the fifty-five-gallon drum rolling and spilling the canoe.

All parents must overcome fears in the process of sending their children out into the indifferent, sometimes perilous world. We assess the dangers for our kids when they are young, and begin giving them the skills to make their own assessments as they grow older. But when they hit their teenage years, the rules seem to blur. We become less trusting of our instincts and acquired parenting skills, moving uncertainly between an urge to protect them and a desire to let them blossom. Adolescence is a dislocating time for parents and children alike. Unlike babies, who come squalling into the world in need of everything, teenagers bounce uncomfortably, and often angrily, between periods of adultlike self-sufficiency and childlike dependency. We, as parents, are equally ill-equipped to handle the fluctuations. Some parents respond to the inevitable clashes, and the resentments that follow, with avoidance, retreating from their teens. At the very moment they should engage, at the very moment their teenagers secretly want them to be involved in their lives, they pull back. I was determined not to do this.

By the time I got to the far side of the small island and laid eyes on the channel that was once the main river, my nerves had calmed. It had been eleven years since I slipped on my hip waders and waded into this portion of the Coleen to try my luck with my fly rod. Though it was 10:00 p.m., the sun was shining as if it were noon, and Bohemian waxwings feasted on mosquitoes just above the surface of the water. In the light of that Arctic night I had the sense that all things were possible, that much living was still ahead of me.

As I now waded into the unfamiliar channel of middle age, with my knobby knees and aches and pains, various financial concerns, and more responsibilities than I ever imagined, I understood that life is often nothing more than a slow accumulation of days, that middle age is about coming to terms with what life is and not what you thought it would be. I also knew my blessings were large. The daughter whose birth I had left the Arctic for eleven years earlier, rushing back home, worried that I would miss her delivery date, is a wonderful, strong-headed girl named Rachel. Our third daughter, Willa, eight years old, is funny and sweet-natured. All three girls are as different as the seasons.

A congress of ravens woke me from my reverie. *A kill?* I thought. It could only be a kill to attract that many ravens. But where? Suddenly all my senses were in overdrive. I scanned the riverbank and the willows and gauged the direction of the wind. It was out of the north. If a grizzly was feeding on a carcass upwind of me, it wouldn't smell me. If I startled it, it would be on me before I heard the "woof, woof" warning, the crash of brush and the clapping of its teeth. The words of writer and bear expert Doug Peacock, who has studied grizzlies in the wild for over two decades, echoed in my head. "Getting mauled," he writes, "is in the configuration of possibilities anytime one is in grizzly country." And most of those maulings are the result of "blundering upon a bedded or feeding grizzly." Although humans are the world's most successful apex predators, being in bear territory without a shotgun or a rifle to defend myself put me a notch below the grizzly.

I watched the ravens. In an effort not to surprise a bear, I sang a song in an off-key falsetto—the only one that came into my head: "In the jungle, the mighty jungle, the lion sleeps tonight." For the life of me, I could come up with the words to no other melody. Feeling ridiculous, I stopped singing, recalling Peacock's advice: always remain "calm and dignified."

As I got closer to where the ravens were circling I inspected the sand for a grizzly's pan-size tracks. Seeing none, I reminded myself that *most of* the bears, as Heimo had said, were up in the mountains. Nevertheless, I could feel the goose bumps rising on my skin.

The ravens were hovering like ospreys. Almost directly beneath them, I remembered the words of my old football coach: "Head on a swivel, Campbell. Head on a swivel." If a bear rushed me, I had virtually no plan other than to stand my ground or dive into the river and hope the swift current would deposit me downstream before the grizzly crunched on my bones. But grizzlies can run over thirty-five miles per hour and an oncoming bear would probably have scooped me up like a salmon before I was able to make it into the deep water.

Then it dawned on me that I was on a long, empty stretch of gravel bar with nary a willow for cover. If there had been a grizzly sitting on top of his kill, I would have seen him. Above me the ravens were still croaking as if they were at a Sunday barbecue, but ravens are sociable birds; I realized that they had perhaps not spotted a bear guarding his kill but rather decided to gather for a riverside picnic, despite the rain.

"Damn ravens," I said. "Scared the shit out of me."

I walked less tentatively, a skip in my step as the adrenaline slowly receded from my bloodstream. Nerves settled, I decided that, fear or no, I was glad to be in wild country where bears still had the run of the place.

It took me an hour and a half to get to the gravel bar by our campsite, and when I arrived, Heimo and Aidan were not there. Unbeknownst to me, they were fighting the river downstream.

I was sitting among the rocks when finally I spotted them. As soon as they neared the gravel bar I grabbed the bowline and pulled them ashore.

Neither Heimo nor Aidan was in a mood to talk. The cold drizzle had turned into a steady downpour and we still had to lug the supplies to the campsite and get them under the plastic tarp as soon as possible. We pulled the boat fifty yards up a side slough and tied it off near our campsite. I noticed that Aidan was shivering. I held her hands in mine.

"Ouch," she said. "They hurt from the rope."

I looked at them. They were red and chafed and ice-cold to the touch.

"Go get some dry clothes on and get in your sleeping bag,"

I told her. "Heimo and I will bring up the supplies." She didn't move. "Go," I said again. "You need to get warm."

An hour later, having transported everything from the canoe, I was standing under the semidry branches of a spruce tree, trying to change clothes without getting soaked by the cold rain. I was shivering when I crawled into the tent and into my sleeping bag.

"I can't get warm, Dad," Aidan said. "Will you put your arm around me?"

"Of course," I said, moving the stuff sacks that separated us. On our first day Aidan had divided the tent so we could each have our own space, but now I pulled her close.

"Dad," she said. "That was scary. Heimo was shouting but I could barely hear him. I thought we were going to tip, and all I could think of was Coleen."

She filled me in on the details.

Shortly after I left them, the boat motor had cut out again. Fortunately, Heimo was able to direct it into a calm, shallow area of the river. Aidan got out and steadied the boat while he jerked at the starter rope. When the engine caught, he revved it, yelled for Aidan to jump in, and guided the canoe into the churning current. As they rounded a bend, they lost all forward motion. Aidan paddled hard until she heard Heimo yell, "Don't fight it!" Heimo knew that it was better to let the river whip the bow back downstream than to get caught broadside to the current. After Heimo managed to beach the boat on a sandbar, Aidan looked around and realized that they were safe, but nearly back where they'd started.

"We gotta get the motor going," Heimo said. "Halfway up, we can line it. But there's nowhere to do it here. The banks are full of bushes and the water is too deep."

Heimo started the motor again and guided the canoe into the

current. In front, Aidan paddled as hard as she could. Her shoulders ached but the canoe seemed to be standing still. What she wouldn't give to be on firm ground, peeling logs and swatting the swarming mosquitoes. Suddenly the canoe lurched and the motor died. Up ahead Aidan saw a wall of small rapids. Now Heimo was yelling, "Don't let up. Paddle like hell." Though he was shouting, to Aidan his words sounded faint and far off. Thirty seconds later they were through the rapids. Aidan's arms were spent. Heimo was yelling, but, again, she could barely hear him. She turned slowly in her seat so she wouldn't upset the canoe and saw him pointing at a narrow spit of sand.

"Over there," he shouted.

When they hit the sand broadside, Heimo jumped out of the canoe and Aidan grabbed the bow rope and dragged the boat onto the bar. From there they lined it upriver. Aidan didn't care if the rope rubbed her hands raw. All she wanted was to be off the water.

When she finished the story, she was still shivering. "I want to sleep, Dad," she said. "But I don't think I can; I'm too cold."

Ten minutes later I heard her snoring softly. Searching for warmth, she pushed me up against the edge of the tent. I lay awake listening to the rain and the wild wind, hoping that summer would hold on long enough for us to finish the cabin.

CHAPTER 6

NEW RITUALS AND
THE RIDGEPOLE

WHERE IN THE HELL WERE you?" Heimo asked when I emerged from the woods.

"Down at the river."

"Where's Aidan?"

"She's down there."

"Alone?"

"Well, I'm here, aren't I," I said.

"Smart-ass," he fired back. "You know what I mean."

"Yup," I told him. "She took the shotgun and went on her own before I got up."

"Wow," he exclaimed. "Good for her."

When I woke that morning, I'd seen her note. "Dad," she wrote. "I'm fishing and washing up. I took the shotgun with me. Don't worry, I'll be okay. 6:15 a.m."

It was 6:45 when I read it. When I realized she'd already been at the river for thirty minutes on her own, I experienced a moment of panic. My first inclination was to rush down and make sure she was okay. But then I realized that this was exactly the kind of thing I'd been hoping for. Only a week ago she wouldn't even go down to get a tub of water on her own.

I took a deep breath and walked down to the river as calmly as I could. I soon saw Aidan out on the gravel bar. She was fly-fishing, and I could see that she was practicing her back cast. Her towel was spread across the stones to dry. She'd already bathed. The shotgun was close by, leaning against a trunk of driftwood.

I whistled so as not to startle her, and she turned. Her smile was as big as the sun.

"Aren't you impressive," I said.

"I'm going to do this every day," she said. "It was so nice to be alone, and so beautiful."

"You sure?" I asked.

"Yup," she said. "It will be my ritual. That way I won't have to listen to you and Heimo doing your goofy Cheesehead skits."

She hooked her fly into the corky end of her fishing rod.

"You don't have to quit," I said.

"No," she replied. "I'm ready to go back."

Then she picked up a willow stick. She'd run it through the gills of an especially large grayling, which she'd already cleaned.

"Breakfast," she said.

When Aidan returned to the campsite, Heimo was making pancakes. When he saw the grayling, his eyes lit up.

"Excellent," he said. "I'm hungry."

While we lingered over breakfast, Aidan and I talked about what we'd eat when we got back to Fairbanks. "Can we go out to dinner, first thing?" Aidan asked. Without waiting for an answer, she said, "I miss cheese, watermelon, avocados, grapes, and Thai food."

"All right," I said. "I'll play. I want a chicken burrito, cherries, and a big, thick chocolate malt."

Heimo had gone down to the river to fetch water. When he returned, he set down his bucket. "I heard that, you two. You guys got bush eyes, bad."

"What?" Aidan asked.

"Your heads are full of food," Heimo said. "You're dreaming of food you can't have. Happens all the time. You mean to say you want something other than fish, pancakes, and ramen? The girls used to get bush eyes. Before we went to town, Rhonda and Krin wrote out long wish lists. But they were in the bush for ten months eating almost nothin' but meat." Heimo paused. "Okay," he relented, laughing. "I want fresh veggies, Yukon River king salmon, and a liter of Diet Coke."

Then, as if to announce that our game was over, he glanced at his watch and grabbed the chain saw. "Let's get going." He took a few steps down the trail, but stopped in his tracks.

"Listen," he said. "Swainson's thrush."

I cupped my hand in back of my ear as my eighty-six-year-old father does when he wants to hear. The sound was like creek water moving over smooth stones.

We listened for a minute or two before Heimo took off again, saying, "Ridgepole. Make-it-or-break-it time."

I knew what the urgency in his voice meant. There had been frost on the fire logs that morning. Though it wasn't yet August, Heimo understood that snow could come soon. He knew, too, that setting the heavy ridgepole, the beam running along the peak of the roof from front to back, onto which we would nail the roof poles, wouldn't be easy.

Twenty-eight feet long, with a diameter pushing twelve inches, the spruce log that Heimo had chosen for the ridgepole was as big as any on this section of the river. It took Aidan two whole days to peel it. At one point, kicking the dirt in frustration, she swore, "I'm done, Dad. Somebody else will have to peel this stupid thing." But she kept peeling.

Just transporting the massive ridgepole would be a serious challenge; Heimo had been talking about building some kind of rolling ramp with which to move it to the cabin site.

We'd barely made it to the woods when we heard a plane.

"Rick," Heimo said. "Edna sent a message on the satellite phone saying he'd be coming up, but I didn't think he'd be here today. Damn ridgepole will have to wait."

Rick buzzed the campsite as we were putting on our hip boots.

"He'll have some drums of fuel that we'll have to move into the willows," Heimo said.

By the time we got to the gravel bar, Rick was already standing outside the plane. In 2001 and 2002 he'd flown me out to the river a few times, and I hadn't seen him since. He looked taller, thinner, and younger.

"Looking good, Rick," I said, shaking his hand.

He smiled. "Yup, Sheryl and I are on the Paleo Diet."

Heimo looked amused. "Sheeeit," he said. "I been doing the Paleo Diet before anybody knew what it was. That's the way trappers have always aten."

Vilhjalmur Stefansson, the Arctic explorer and ethnologist who spent more than a decade with the Inuit, had also thrived on what might be called the Paleo Diet. It was actually the Inuit diet, and Stefansson documented the fact that 90 percent of what the Inuit ate consisted of meat and fish. He observed them going six to nine months eating nothing else. He also found that he and his fellow explorers of European descent could eat like Inuits and re-main perfectly healthy.

The small talk didn't last long. We had fuel drums—Heimo's winter supply of gas—to wrestle out of the plane and cache in the willows. By the time I rolled a drum into a nearby thicket and re-turned for another, Aidan was standing near the wing. I grabbed another drum. As I rolled it in the direction of the willows, I turned back and noticed that Rick and Aidan were talking. By the time I returned Rick was ready to take off. Minutes later, the plane bounced down the gravel bar and Rick lifted it into the air with one hundred feet of runway to spare. As the sound died away, I asked Aidan what she and Rick had been talking about.

"Bear bells," she said. "He looked at my bear bells and laughed and said it was a good thing I was wearing them."

"Why?" I asked.

"He told me that they would be good for identification. When I asked him what he meant, he said that when they found the bells in grizzly scat it would be good because they'd know it was me."

"That's Rick," Heimo said, chuckling. "He was just givin' you a hard time." He picked up a cardboard box and shook it. "Good-ies from Edna," he said, smiling.

Heimo opened the box back at the campsite; we all looked in-side like kids at summer camp opening a care package from Mom. "Moose burger," Heimo said, holding up a square of butcher paper. "Taco shells, crackers, onions, tomatoes from Edna's gar-den, chips, a liter bottle of Diet Coke, a brick of cheese, and salsa from our cousin Renee in Texas." Heimo plopped down in his camp chair and opened the Diet Coke, followed by the jar of salsa and the bag of chips.

"What about the ridgepole?" I asked.

"Screw it," he said. "I've lived out here long enough to know you don't pass up surprises like this." Then he held up the cheese. "Aidan, looook what Edna seent uuuup."

Aidan was already cleaning the blade of her pocketknife.

"I'll slice up a bunch," she said, "and we can eat it with the crackers." Then she raised her water bottle. "To Edna."

"To Edna," we all said.

Like the animals of the Arctic binging during times of plenty, we gorged ourselves, calling it quits only when the chips and salsa were gone and Heimo had polished off most of his Diet Coke.

"I'm happy, but now I need a nap," Heimo said, tossing the plastic bag into the fire. I was also feeling sated and lethargic, but Aidan seemed revived.

"I'll get some wood for tonight while you old men sleep," she said.

I watched Aidan walk into the woods. After three weeks, she seemed changed, more confident and more at ease in a place that, early on, had scared the hell out of her. No longer did she imagine malevolent grizzlies hiding behind every tree. This made my life easier. When we first arrived I had had to accompany her wherever she went, standing guard with my shotgun while she peed in the bushes or collected dishwater or emptied the honey bucket. Now, she barely complained about the bugs, the rain, the mud, the dirt, the sap, the sweat, the stink, grayling guts, the screen tent, hauling water, scrubbing pots, or even the bear trail. She could clean a grayling almost as quickly as I could. I'd watched her run her knife just beneath the silver skin to slice open the belly, hook her finger in the lower jaw, and rip free the entrails before cleaning the bloodline, along the backbone of the fish, in the river until her hands ached with cold. She even ate the musky roe she'd once snubbed.

She'd become adept at building fires, too, and banking the fire so we'd have coals in the morning. And she could use an axe and a drawknife well enough that Heimo no longer asked me to spell her.

Just the previous evening, Heimo had taken me aside as Aidan was doing her nightly workout. "She's a hard worker," he said. "She's a good kid, too." From Heimo, it was the ultimate endorsement.

The lesson for me was clear—not to push. I had initially tried to coax her, and when persuasion didn't work, I became forceful, ordering her *do it or else,* as on the first day when she discovered how hard the peeling was. Encouraging words had sometimes worked, but anger never did. The first time I ordered her to set a dry spruce bough on top of still-hot embers and puff the fire back to life, she got a face full of smoke and ash and stomped away. The first time I sent her to get firewood, she came running back, saying she'd heard a ruckus in the forest, and vowed that as long as she was in Alaska she would never get firewood again on her own. Although her learning curve had not always been as fast as I thought it should be, I had discovered that when I left her alone she did things with little fanfare. A small "good job" from me was enough. What seemed most satisfying for her was her newborn confidence, the kind of self-assurance that I'd seen glimpses of at home, but nothing like I'd witnessed here.

It was 2:00 p.m. and I had just awakened from my nap. Heimo, who had also been dozing, sat up suddenly.

"Smell that?" he asked. I shook my head, thinking that he had just awakened from a dream and hadn't yet cleared out the cobwebs.

"No, really," he said. "I smell bear shit."

I laughed. "You can smell when a bear shits in the woods?"

"I can," he said.

He sniffed at the air like a bird dog. After almost four decades in the woods, Heimo's senses are attuned to sounds and smells I would never notice. He got up, took his .44, and walked into the woods. I grabbed the shotgun. Ten minutes later, he returned.

"See anything?" I asked.

"No tracks," he said. "But I smelled something. That's for sure." Without pause Heimo picked up the chain saw and bounded off toward the new cabin site, his mind once again on the ridgepole. Aiden and I caught up to him standing in the middle of Aidan's peeling area, eyeing the large log. At twenty-eight feet, it would span the length of the cabin and then some.

"We're going to have to use two of the roof poles as pry bars to get the ridgepole off the ground. Once we get it set crosswise on top of two logs, we can try to lift it. Then we can carry it to the cabin." Aidan watched as we torqued on the poles and sweated and cursed until, finally, we had the ridgepole resting perpendicularly on the logs, a foot off the ground. We sat down to catch our breath.

"I'll take the heavy end," I said.

"Suit yourself, Superman," Heimo said. "I'll help you get it to your shoulder. But, remember, if it's too heavy, let it roll off and get the hell out of the way."

Heimo took a slug from his water bottle and went off to the bushes to pee. "I don't want to burst my bladder lifting that thing," he said.

When he was out of earshot, Aidan said, "Dad, are you going to be okay?"

Although I'd watched her since arriving on the river—like a hawk, early on—she was now the one watching me. "Remember what Mom told you," she reminded me. "Don't try to be a hero."

Heimo returned and slipped on his work gloves. Then we both

stood over the log, summoning our strength. "It's a heavy bastard," he said. "Don't blow a nut. Okay, on three. One, two." On three, we jerked the front end of the log to our waists. Heimo held it while I positioned myself underneath.

"Hurry up," he barked.

I rested the ridgepole on my right shoulder, straightened my back, stuck out my sternum, and braced myself. Then, as though at the squat rack, I pushed up with my legs. As Heimo let go I absorbed the full weight of the log. My shoulder felt as if it would break in two.

"Can you hold it?" Heimo asked.

"Yes," I said, gritting my teeth. As soon as I uttered the word, my left knee wobbled.

Heimo saw me falter and grabbed for the log. I regained my balance and locked my knees again.

"Are you okay, Dad?" Aidan asked.

"Shh," I replied, barely able to make a sound.

Heimo said to Aidan, "Come here and give me a hand."

When I heard Heimo grunt and felt the log move, I knew he had hoisted his end of the ridgepole to his shoulder.

"Let's move," he said hoarsely.

We took a few steps, and I staggered.

"Stop," I hissed.

Heimo heard me. I moved the log closer to my head and neck and repositioned my feet. Then I nodded to Aidan.

"He's ready," she told Heimo.

We shuffled our feet and settled into a rhythm. When I saw the cabin site I felt like a horse ready to break for the barn. All I wanted to do was to drop the ridgepole. Twenty feet more, I told myself. But my legs were burning.

Heimo saw me stumble. "Don't lose that fucker," he yelled. "We're almost there." Finally I heard him say, "Let it go at three."

At three I pushed the log as far away as I could. As soon as it left my shoulder, I heard it hit with an earth-rumbling thud. Feeling faint, I put my hands on my knees and steadied myself. Heimo sat against the wall of the cabin, panting.

"Jesus," he said. "I didn't think we were going to make it."

Aidan handed me a water bottle. I splashed my face and took a long drink.

"Nearly killed me," I said.

"Me, too," Heimo answered. "Gettin' too old for this shit."

No one said another word for a few minutes. All of us were dreading the next step: getting the ridgepole to the top of the wall and then up on the roof gable.

We did it incrementally, raising it onto the protruding logs of the front and back walls, and resting it on each one until we regained our strength. It was slow work, but half an hour later we had it lying on the highest log of the cabin wall. Next we had to move it up to the top of the angled gables at the front and back ends of the cabin. This was the dangerous part. The gables were triangle shaped, formed by four successively shorter logs that determined the pitch of the roof. If, as we moved the ridgepole higher, it rolled back, and one of us got caught in its path, we could be hurt—badly.

"Squish you like a sardine can," Heimo said. "If that happens, the satellite phone ain't gonna mean shit."

Heimo climbed to the top of the back wall and I climbed the front. "Not much room for error," he said, examining the staggered step-up to the top of the gable.

When I got the ridgepole to the first log of the gable, I held it there while Heimo pushed up his end. We got it up to the second step and, to preserve the momentum, moved it to the third one without stopping. Just as I relaxed, the log slid back.

"Look out," Heimo yelled, and I was off the wall and rolling on the ground before he finished shouting "out." When I got to my feet, I realized that I'd landed almost headfirst. My right shoulder had absorbed most of the blow, and it throbbed. I saw that Heimo, too, had jumped from the wall. He was dusting himself off. Having tumbled down the gable like a rock rolling down a hill, the ridgepole had somehow lost its momentum and stalled out at the wall's edge. We'd gotten lucky.

"Jesus Christ," Heimo said. "That was close. You okay?"

I nodded, despite my shoulder. We both climbed the wall again and pushed the ridgepole safely onto the cabin's top log.

Back on terra firma, Heimo said, "Wow, I ain't got my strength. I need a break. How 'bout you?"

"Yeah," I said, rubbing my shoulder.

We both sat against the front wall of the cabin. Aidan pulled a PowerBar from her pocket and sliced it with her jackknife. Heimo popped a piece into his mouth.

"I hope these things work," he said.

I ate mine, gulped down a half bottle of water, and tried to figure out whether or not I'd separated my shoulder. Five minutes later, it was still hurting but the pain had lessened.

"Sure you're okay?" Heimo asked.

I nodded again. "A little sore, maybe."

When Heimo walked to the side of the cabin, Aidan elbowed me gently. "Dad," she whispered. "I saw you fall. It didn't look good. I'll take your place."

"Not a chance," I told her, getting up.

"I'm serious," she said.

"So am I," I answered. "I don't want you anywhere near that ridgepole."

I joined Heimo at the side of the cabin.

"What you got in mind?" I asked.

"Just trying to figure out if we should rig up the come-along to a tree over there and winch that son of a bitch up," he said.

A come-along is a hand winch that works by means of a lever, a pulley, a cable, and a ratcheting wheel. Heimo's idea was to attach one end of the cable to a tree on one side of the cabin and the other end to the ridgepole on the opposite side. Using the winch handle, we'd raise the log to the apex of the gable. The problem, as Heimo soon discovered, was that when we made our supply run, we'd forgotten to put the come-along in the canoe. We'd have to use brute strength.

Luckily, the rest had paid off, and thirty minutes later the ridgepole was sitting at the tops of the gables with support wedges nailed in to keep it from rolling. We'd done it all without killing ourselves.

"Whaddya say we call it quits for the day and celebrate," Heimo said. "Gonna be moose tacos for supper tonight."

HAVING EATEN ALL the moose meat, tomatoes, onions, and most of the cheese, Heimo, Aidan, and I sat around the fire holding our bellies. For the first time in three weeks, I was actually full.

Heimo was relaxed now that the ridgepole was no longer haunting him. Leaning back in his camp chair, he asked Aidan if she was going to miss being in the bush. Aidan didn't answer right away. I was pleased to see that she felt comfortable enough with Heimo to consider his question, instead of blurting out the kind of answer she thought he wanted to hear.

She looked at her gloves, full of holes, and slipped them off. Her hands were scratched, her fingernails chipped and broken. Her pants were sticky with pitch and stained with dirt and ash. But the job that at one time had seemed insurmountable was nearly done. In a day or two, the cabin would be livable.

Aidan poked at the fire with a stick and laughed. "Peeling, no way. I won't miss that. But, yes, some things, I'll definitely miss."

CHAPTER 7

CLOUDBERRIES

I T WAS MIDMORNING AND AIDAN and I had already finished chinking the cabin, packing insulation and moss in the
cracks between the wall logs. We now were peeling the last of the
roof poles that we'd cut and dragged out of the woods. Heimo was
on the roof, straddling the ridgepole, nailing up new poles and the
ones we'd salvaged from the lower cabin. The plan was to get all
of them up and then lay down the Visqueen, a large polyethylene
sheet that would serve as the weather, or vapor, barrier. Heimo
and Edna would cover it with moss in September.

"Veracious," I said to Aidan, continuing the word game we'd
begun the previous day to pass the time.

"Heimo has a veracious appetite," she replied. Then she giggled. "No, no, that's voracious, isn't it?"

"Yup," I answered.

"I don't know," she said a minute later, laying down the drawknife.

"Okay," I said. "Were you being veracious yesterday when you said that you'd miss this place a lot?"

"Truthful, that's it," she said. "Yes, I was. I really was. I even think I'd like to come back. Maybe in fall or winter."

Looking at her, I knew she was serious. Before leaving home we'd talked about the prospect of making more than one trip to Alaska, and had agreed to see how the first one went.

"I feel so alive up here," she said, picking up the drawknife.

A minute later she stopped peeling again. "Dad," she said, "promise me that you'll try to live as long as possible?"

BY NOON THE poles were up and Heimo and I were nailing down the last corner of the Visqueen sheet. When we finished, he decided that instead of putting in the window and hanging the door, we'd dig the outhouse hole.

He chose a spot about thirty feet from the cabin, protected by trees and not in the path of the prevailing winds. I began by cutting out the moss and sod with an axe and used a pick and a shovel to loosen and scoop the dirt. Heimo put the dirt in a pail and dumped it at the cabin, where Aidan spread it out along the lowest wall log to patch the openings between it and the ground. Back at the outhouse hole, I hit large rocks two feet down and stopped to dislodge them. As I dug deeper, the rocks turned to smaller stones and then to sand and gravel from what was likely the old riverbed. After a few more swings with the pick, the gravel turned to permafrost.

"That's deep enough," Heimo said. "Let's go get some berries."

Soon we were paddling downriver on our new expedition. The wind was strong out of the south and the sky was an electric blue. We floated past the old cabin and turned up into a side channel.

As the water got shallow, we jumped out, took the rope, and lined the boat up to a gravel bar. Aidan beached the canoe in a patch of sand and cotton grass.

"Wait till you taste them berries," Heimo said, making a bee-line for the tundra.

Two hundred yards from the canoe, he stopped. "Did anyone bring the mosquito dope?" he asked.

"I don't need it," Aidan said. "Unlike you two, I brought my head net."

We both looked at her.

"You're kidding," she said. "You guys don't bring your head nets and you forget the mosquito spray, and I have to go back and get it. Dad, you'd scold me for being irresponsible."

She stomped away. It was a short walk back to the canoe, but it was the principle of the thing that she objected to.

"She's really mad, isn't she?" Heimo asked.

"Yup," I answered. "She really is."

When Aidan returned, Heimo put an arm around her shoulder and pulled her close.

"Thanks," he said. He took a granola bar from the pocket of his flannel shirt and handed it to her. "I know you're hungry."

We followed a feeder creek, along which I noticed that the blossoms of the fireweed were nearing the ends of their stalks. Fireweed blooms from the bottom up, and when the blossoms reach the top it's a sign that summer is almost gone. After nearly a mile we climbed a steep riverbank and looked out onto a sea of tundra stretching south and east toward the Strangle Woman Mountains, as far as the eye could see.

If Aidan was mad, she'd forgotten all about it. "It's so beautiful," she said. "It's how I imagine the African savanna looks."

Though beautiful from afar, up close the tundra was a marsh teeming with floating clumps of dirt and grass—muskeg tussocks, or "niggerheads," in the vernacular of old-time Alaskan trappers—interspersed with small, muddy puddles that made the footing difficult for Aidan and me, but not for Heimo. He had been walking in hip boots across tundra like this for decades. While we stumbled, he cruised. By the time we found ourselves in the middle of a football field–size spread of bushes, bursting with blueberries and cloudberries—or salmonberries, named for their bright pink-orange flesh—Aidan and I needed to catch our breath. We found a dry patch and sat down to enjoy the breeze and the blue sky.

Aidan broke the silence. "Do you feel it?" she asked. Without waiting for an answer, she took off her head net. "No bugs."

"Man, did we luck out," Heimo said, standing above us. "If it was still, the bugs out here would eat us alive. But right now, I ain't got time for lying around. I got berries on my mind."

Wandering among the dwarf birch and blueberry and cloud-berry bushes, we picked a container full of cloudberries for Edna—they're her favorite—and then we ate to our hearts' content. "The cloudberries taste almost like yogurt," Aidan said. "They're rich. And the blueberries are so sweet."

"Yup," Heimo said. "They've been soakin' up the sunshine. Eat up," he added. "You won't be gettin' anything this good at any of the grocery stores in Fairbanks."

We dined like grazing grizzlies for the next hour, until our bellies were bulging.

"I can't eat any more," Aidan said. "But we don't have to leave yet, do we?"

"Don't worry," Heimo replied. "We ain't got nowhere to go." Then he spread his arms out wide in a gesture that I'd come to recognize as one of pure joy.

Each of us found a few dry mounds of dirt and grass, and we lay back in the clean light of the drifting sun. The silence was as wide as the sky.

IT WAS THE morning of our final day in the bush. Aidan and I had lugged the last load of supplies from the campsite to the cabin, while Heimo, whom we would drop off in Fort Yukon en route to Fairbanks, finished screwing a thick piece of plywood over the roughed-out door to keep out the animals. Then Aidan packed the leftover food into the fifty-five-gallon drum while Heimo and I mounted the canoe on a tree platform where the grizzlies wouldn't be able to reach it. Then we heard the plane.

"That's him," Heimo said. "Let's get down to the river."

We ran back to the campsite and gathered our gear.

"Take a last look, Aidan," Heimo said. "Few people in the world will ever set foot in this country, and you just spent almost a month here."

Aidan took it in. Then, as Heimo walked over to the bear trail to take down the clothesline, she said to me, "I'm not ready, Dad. I'm not ready to leave."

"I know," I told her. "That's the way it always goes."

Twenty minutes later we were barreling down the gravel bar. We took off into a headwind with considerable runway to spare. As Aidan pointed north at the rocky peaks of the Brooks Range, blotched white with snowfields, I thought of a line from John Muir's book *My First Summer in the Sierra*: "We are now in the mountains and they are in us, kindling enthusiasm, making every nerve quiver, filling every pore and cell of us." I could only hope that the wilds of Alaska had touched my daughter similarly.

We were following the Coleen River south when Aidan tapped

me on the shoulder and drew my attention out her window to a moose that had waded out into a tundra lake.

An hour and a half later we landed in Fort Yukon. Edna was there to greet us.

"Specklebelly for dinner," she said. "Got it in the slow cooker."

Heimo picked her up and kissed her. "Specklebelly goose. Edna sure knows how to treat me."

Edna walked over to Aidan and me and handed us each a Coke and a store-bought Rice Krispies bar. With the markup at the Alaska Commercial Company store, our welcome-out-of-the-bush surprise probably cost her fifteen dollars.

"A little treat for your hard work," she said.

"Yup," Heimo said, shaking my hand. "I couldn't have done it without you and Aidan."

He pulled Aidan over to him and gave her a hug. "You're a good kid," he said. "Come up any time you want."

Then he walked toward the beaten-up truck that he used to run errands during the summer. "Added incentive, Aidan," he shouted. "Next time you come up, you won't have to shit in a bucket."

CHAPTER 8

WHEN THE
MOUNTAIN IS OUT

AFTER CHECKING IN TO OUR hotel and loading everything that needed to be washed into my oversize backpack, Aidan disappeared into the bathroom. I read in bed, occasionally checking my watch. Ten minutes went by, then twenty. Thirty-eight minutes later, Aidan emerged.

"Dad, how does my hair look?"

"Nice, Aidan," I said. "But how in the world can you spend forty minutes in the bathroom?"

"What do you mean 'nice'?" she asked, ignoring my question. "Seriously, how does my hair look?"

"Pretty. But your hair always looks pretty."

"Dad," she says. "You're not really looking. You're answering absentmindedly. And my hair doesn't always look pretty. It looked like crap on the river, or didn't you notice?"

This was a no-win situation. I looked again, reminding myself to take more time to answer. Be sensitive, I told myself. "I like your hair, Aidan," I said.

"Thanks," she replied, still dissatisfied with my answer.

She flopped down on her bed and turned on her computer, which we'd left with the hotel before flying out to the Coleen. I soon heard her typing at the speed of sound. I had to give her credit. She'd hung around two stinky, middle-aged men for three and a half weeks, listened to stupid Cheesehead skits, bad language, all while doing the work of a man, and now she was transitioning seamlessly to her former life.

"Facebook?" I asked.

"Yup," she said. "Snapchat, too. I have lots of messages. I'm sooo *pop*ular."

An hour later, she closed her computer and jumped out of bed. "Dad," she said. "I'm going for a run. She pulled a map of Fairbanks out of her backpack. "I think I know a good route." She spread the map out on the bed.

"Show me," I said.

She traced a path to the university and back. "Should be about six or seven miles."

Then, once again, she disappeared behind the bathroom door. When she came out, she was wearing a skimpy running outfit.

"You're not running in that, are you?" I asked.

"Dad," she said, "cut it out. This is what everyone runs in."

"Not me," I said.

She chortled. "That's funny." Then she was out the door.

"Be back in forty-five minutes or I'll worry," I yelled after her.

I fell asleep and woke to the sound of her knocking on the door.

"Forty-five minutes exactly," she said. "Wow, it felt good to run. I felt strong, too." Then she made for the bathroom for her second shower in two hours.

Ten minutes later, she came out dressed for dinner. She was wearing a halter top. "Check out my guns," she said.

Her biceps bulged. "Wow," I said. "You're a lean, mean fighting machine."

She smiled gleefully. "Say that again."

"All right," I complied. "You're looking pretty buff."

I wasn't flattering her. It was true; her arm and shoulder muscles rippled. She went into the bush strong, and after three and a half weeks of peeling, she came out even stronger.

"Ready to go?" she asked.

I hoisted the backpack loaded with our stinky clothes. Our intention was to hit the Laundromat before dinner and eat during the wash cycle.

"With all those muscles," I said to Aidan, "you should be the one carrying this."

We were standing at the corner of one of Fairbanks's major thoroughfares when a VW bus, loaded with young men, stopped at a red light. Aidan and I walked by. I watched them out of the corner of my eye. They practically climbed out of the windows to get a look at my just-turned-fifteen-year-old daughter. When one of them whistled, Aidan blushed.

"Boys should get a job," I said, channeling my dad.

Aidan was still blushing. Had she been with her girlfriends she might have enjoyed their attentions, but with her old man at her side she felt embarrassed. We were across the street when the light turned green; the driver of the bus lay on his horn to show his enthusiasm before driving off.

"It's the beginning of the end," I said, hamming it up for Aidan.

"Yup," she replied, playing her part. "I guess you're gonna have to get used to it."

By the time we got to College Road, near the university, Aidan had been leered at or catcalled at least half a dozen times. The last one, a gray-haired old-timer in a Mercedes-Benz, was almost more than I could take. As we walked into the Laundromat I said, "That's it. We're taking the bus or a cab back."

We stuffed our clothes into two industrial-size washers before the stench could fill the room and walked across the street to what we'd been told was Fairbanks's best Thai restaurant. We were both famished and ordered fish soup and spring rolls with peanut sauce for appetizers and two curries for our main dishes. We drained our soups fast and Aidan said, "Let's eat slowly; I want to savor every bite." She looked around the restaurant as she smothered her spring roll in sauce and chili peppers.

"See that table over there? See that guy in the middle? He's cute, isn't he? You can look, but don't be too obvious."

Before taking my next bite, I turned my head. On the far side of the room, four guys in their early twenties were sitting at a large table. Two were clean-cut. The other two were bearded with long-ish hair.

"You like the tan one?" I asked.

"Well," she hesitated. "Yeah, the tan one with short hair and the muscles."

"Not me," I said. "If I were a girl, I'd go for the two that look like they just came out of the mountains."

Aidan snorted. "This is crazy," she said. "Checking out guys with my dad."

We finished our dinner, took a parting look at the table of young men, nearly fell out the door laughing, and crossed the street to Hot Licks Homemade Ice Cream. While Aidan ordered two choc- olate malts, I walked over to the Laundromat to throw our clothes into the dryer.

It was still daylight when we walked back to our hotel. Aidan announced that she was going to watch something on Netflix.

"All right with me," I said. "I'm tired."

I woke at midnight, roused by the sounds of cars, sirens, and late-night revelers. Aidan was asleep. As if unready for the sudden move from the woods to the city, my mind raced. In Alaska, the bush plane functions as something of a time machine, transporting one, in a matter of hours, from a place where a sensitive ear can hear a moose crossing a river in the middle of the night to a place where the cacophony of modern civilization becomes a kind of white noise.

I made a list of chores I wanted to do when I got home: finish the chicken coop, lay down plywood sheets in the barn's hayloft, train my pup to hunt, do target practice with my bow before the upcoming deer season, put another super on my beehive, plant more apple trees, and learn to make plum jam from my mom.

I was scribbling in my notebook when Aidan screamed and jumped out of bed. She was standing with her hands on the wall. I wrapped my arms around her. "Aidan," I said, trying to wake her. "You had a bad dream."

"Oh, Daddy," she mumbled. "I had a dream that our bush plane was going to crash."

"That's all it was, Aidan," I said. "Just a bad dream. You're safe."

She lay back in bed and I pulled the covers around her. When she was little and had a nightmare, I would lie next to her and sing. Her favorites were "Kentucky Babe" and "Down in the Valley." I would sing verse after verse until I felt her body twitch and then grow quiet. Now, instead of lying beside her, I sat at the edge of the bed: "Fly away, fly away, fly away, Kentucky babe, fly away to rest . . ."

WE WERE ON a six-seater bus on our way to the funky mountain
town of Talkeetna, 275 miles south of Fairbanks via the George
Parks Highway. One of only two routes south from Fairbanks, the
road was remarkably free from cars.

We arrived in Talkeetna in the late afternoon. Home to almost
nine hundred people and a three-block downtown listed on the
National Register of Historic Places, it reminded me of some of the
tiny mountain towns above Boulder, Colorado. To Aidan it was
reminiscent of Cable, Wisconsin, the starting point of the Birke-
beiner, or Birkie, as it's known, North America's largest cross-
country skiing marathon. Instantly clear to both of us was that
Talkeetna is the kind of end-of-the-road place where we could get
comfortable. It has a brew pub, a music venue, restaurants, and
coffeehouses, along with some of the finest hunting, fishing, rafting, hiking, and mountain biking in the country.

The name Talkeetna comes from the Dena'ina Athabaskan
word for "river of plenty" or "place where food is stored near the
river"—K'dalkitnu. The village is situated at the confluence of
three glacially fed rivers: the Susitna, Chulitna, and Talkeetna.
Concerned residents are fighting plans by the Alaska Energy Au-
thority to build the country's second largest dam on the Susitna.

The reason we had stopped here, before heading to Palmer,
Alaska, to visit my friend Dave and climb glaciers, was to see
Denali. This was easier said than done. The mountain can be
shrouded in clouds for a week or more; many who come to see it
are denied the privilege.

As we walked the railroad tracks to our hotel—Latitude 62, a
humble place that reputedly served good food and was the water-
ing hole of choice for the town's characters—I suddenly gritted my

teeth. On the final fourteen-mile leg of our bus trip, from the Parks Highway down the Spur Road to town, my stomach had knotted up, and after a beer and a burger at a local restaurant my intestines felt as if they were being torn apart.

"You okay?" Aidan asked. "You sound like you're having a heart attack."

"I don't know what's wrong with me," I said. "I wonder if I have giardia."

I had barely gotten the words out of my mouth when Aidan exclaimed, "God, Dad. You gotta see this."

She was standing in the middle of the tracks, facing town. I looked up and followed her extended arm. There in the distance was Denali, set against a flawless blue sky. I watched as Aidan closed her eyes, trying perhaps to draw out the moment, to hold on to the awe of it. Before his death, Alaskan poet John Haines lamented that Americans had lost their "capacity to see the world." In the presence of Denali, it was impossible to imagine this could be true.

I'd told Aidan on the bus ride down from Fairbanks that we would be able to see Denali only from afar. Thanks to the cost of aviation fuel and steep price hikes for bush pilot services, we'd blown out our travel budget flying to and from Heimo's. But I knew the moment I laid my eyes on the mountain that we had to see it up close.

In the sacred stories of the Koyukon Athabaskans, Denali means "the High One," or "the Great One." At 20,237 feet, it is the tallest mountain in North America, and at 63 degrees north latitude, one of the coldest. Five major glaciers flow off its granite peaks, including the Ruth Glacier, a 40-mile-long, 3,800-foot-thick river of ice.

The following afternoon we arrived at the Talkeetna Air Taxi (TAT) airstrip for the last flight of the day and saw the mechanics readying the de Havilland Turbo Otter. As we'd hoped, the clouds had burned off, and, according to the woman at the front desk, the mountain was out. Visibility was as good as it had been in weeks. But she warned us that Denali and the other pinnacles of the Alaska Range—a rugged, four-hundred-mile-long chain of snowy peaks, where winds had been clocked in excess of 120 miles per hour—made their own weather. Fair skies could last for days or mere minutes.

I opted out of the tour, as I'd told Aidan earlier that morning I might. I was disappointed, but money, or the lack of it, was an issue. I was also convinced that I had giardia and was worried about my touchy stomach. "Airsickness bags," as a bush pilot friend once told me, "are hard to shit into." Aidan was disappointed that we wouldn't be seeing Denali together, but she also saw it as an opportunity to assert her independence.

The prospect of sending Aidan up alone with a bunch of people she'd never met before made me uneasy, but I had consulted the travel record for TAT online; it was excellent. I had emailed an old Alaskan friend, too, who said they were the best in the business, but then added, "Hope the weather is good. Flying the mountain is a life-changing experience—unless you run into the mountain, then it's a life-ending experience." In a follow-up email, he wrote, "Don't worry about the local air taxis, they haven't had an incident since Tuesday."

I don't mind dark humor, but when it involves my children I usually write the jokester off as an asshole. In this case, however, we had a long-standing friendship. What my buddy was referring to was the crash of a similar plane just the month before in Soldotna, on Alaska's Kenai Peninsula. The aircraft, operated by an air charter company, was flying two families, parents and children, to a fishing lodge when it struck the runway and burned shortly after takeoff. All ten people aboard had died.

Aidan had also heard about the crash, but if she was anxious about the flight she didn't show it. Walking to the plane, she made a half turn and waved good-bye. There was an extra seat on the tour; I had to restrain myself from running into the office and buying it at the last minute. Later it would strike me as melodramatic, but as I watched her move away I wondered if I would see her again.

As the plane sped down the runway I realized that I, like many others, craved the illusion of control, the belief that I could exert influence over every aspect of Aidan's life. I also realized that I was a hypocrite, plain and simple. Months before, I'd accused my wife, Elizabeth, of "catastrophizing," of imagining the worst. Now, here I was, consigned to her role of waiting and worrying, allowing dark thoughts to fill my head. And yet, as the pilot lifted the Otter over the trees, I asked myself a simple question: what could I do if the pilot encountered a violent storm or high winds? The answer, of course, was not a damn thing.

Two hours later, I heard the Otter's engines. The plane touched down and the pilot taxied over to where I was standing. Aidan was one of the last people to exit, and when she did, a smile lit up her face. She practically bounced over to me.

"It was amazing, Dad, beyond anything I ever imagined. I wish you could have been there, too."

On the way into town she was manic, stumbling over her words, trying to find the language to convey what the experience meant to her, talking at a decibel level that might have made the scree tumble from the nearby mountains. She was joyful. She was not just counting her blessings, she was shouting them to the world.

She turned and spun around with her arms outstretched. "I know why he does it now."

"Who?" I reply.

"Heimo," she said. "He feels it."

I looked at her, trying to follow, and she frowned. "The bliss," she said. "Up there, flying close to the mountain, I felt like I was filled with nothing but joy. And I still feel it." She ran away like a colt bolting across a meadow of spring grass.

"Hey, Dad," she said, sticking her head in the belly of a plywood bear cutout. It read, CATCH 'EM IN TALKEETNA. "Take my picture. Who says I'm afraid of bears?"

It was a cheesy tourist's photo, the kind that normally wouldn't interest me. But Aidan was grinning from ear to ear, looking freer, fresher, and perhaps happier than I'd ever seen her.

PART II

>>>>>>>>>>>>>>>>>>>>

CHAPTER 9

FERNWEH

WE HAVE A TRADITION IN our family. After supper, while sitting around the table, each of us writes down on a scrap of paper what we're grateful for. It can relate to something that day, or be about gratitude in general. On our first night back I watched Aidan, with her paper and pencil, look around the dining room, happily taking everything in. While we were gone she'd talked about home almost every night before falling asleep, filling the vacancy with fond thoughts and memories. After a few nights back, however, her look of savoring was gone. There was no more empty space. There was only the humdrum reality, the anticlimax of coming home.

Elizabeth said that Aidan had left a portion of her heart in Alaska. Since returning, it was almost as if she'd been inhabited by an alien being. She was disengaged, disenchanted, disinclined. It was as if our life here in the hills of Wisconsin, the one

she'd professed to love when we were gone, was suddenly suffo-
cating her. Polar explorer Ben Saunders calls it "post-expedition
blues." It was what I had hoped for—that she'd come to love
Alaska. But now she was like a migrating bird that had lost its
way. She was caught between two worlds, the familiar one she
inhabited before and after our trip, and the new, more beautiful,
more thrilling one she'd left behind in August. It was not just
the physical place of Alaska that fascinated her but the psychic
space the trip occupied in her head. Home, it now seemed, was
too close to home.

The signs were there even before we left for Alaska. She'd written an essay for school that she titled "Stuck in Lodi Again," after
the Creedence Clearwater Revival song. It began:

> I have been stuck in the same small town for much of my
> life. Twelve years ago, my father, a native of Wisconsin,
> and my mother decided to come to Wisconsin and settle
> down. In Lodi, they found a promising trout stream, a park
> with hundred-year-old shagbark hickories and a free public
> pool, and a half dozen hiking trails just a mile out of town.
> The downtown was tiny, but it also had character. No café
> in Wisconsin sold better coffee than Lodi Roasters. No de-
> partment store in the entire Midwest still had clothes from
> the 1940s hanging in its window. And no butcher sold bet-
> ter meat than the local Sausage Company. Lodi was unique,
> it was interesting, and, for a while, it seemed like the perfect
> home. I didn't even envy my cousin who lived in Chicago
> and talked about how lively it was. Why would I want to live
> in Chicago, when I could see the stars through my window?
> But gradually, as I grew older, the magic began to wear off

and I dreamed of moving, of leaving behind my old house, my friends, my school, and especially, my town.

After reading Aidan's essay, I emailed her a quote from Wendell Berry: "If you don't know *where* you are, you don't know *who* you are." Berry was writing about his place in the world, a farm on the banks of the Kentucky River. It is a piece of land that he belongs to, as much as it belongs to him. To Berry's quote, I added: "You cannot live a grounded life without being grounded in a place." Later, Aidan and I talked about her feelings of being trapped. I told her I understood her restlessness, but one of my hopes for her was that after seeing how much Heimo loved the Coleen River valley, she would return home inspired by his example and make a commitment to this place, and the daily chores that commitment entailed. Almost as soon as the words left my mouth, I realized how unrealistic that hope was. Aidan was living in a no-man's-land. She'd seen the world, and now she wanted more of it. She had tasted adventure, and now she wanted to live a life of adventure.

Even my mother and father noticed her discontent when we went to visit them on our first weekend home. Is Aidan okay? my mom wanted to know. When I explained Aidan's mood to her, I told her that the only thing I could equate it with was perhaps the heartache of a teenage girl's first breakup.

My mother didn't hesitate. *"Fernweh,"* she said. My mother is German. The German language, it seems, has a phrase, or a word, for everything.

"What?" I asked, not sure I heard her right.

"Fernweh," she repeated. "There's no English word for it. It's the opposite of *Heimweh,* homesickness. It means a longing for new places. *Ich habe Fernweh.* Literally 'farsickness.'"

"Wanderlust," I said.

"Not really," she answered. "They're not the same. *Fernweh* is more." She paused. "Emotional, a yearning. An aching." She paused again. "You know where she gets it, don't you?"

IT WAS A hot, humid afternoon, and Aidan—who still smelled faintly of woodsmoke—and I were walking through the back field with our German wirehair pup, Calhoun. The late August heat clung to our limbs.

"I missed home when we were in Alaska," Aidan said. "You know I did. But when people ask me if I'm happy to be back, I don't know what to tell them beyond the obvious. Do they really want to know that I feel changed, that I'm a different person than I was before we left? I feel like I'm home, but I'm not back."

Unwittingly, I did the right thing. I said nothing at all. I resisted the parental temptation to try to make everything better, which usually means making things worse.

Flowers were sprouting on the back prairie, purple and yellow coneflowers, bee balm, and brown- and black-eyed Susans. I pointed them out but Aidan just shrugged her shoulders. Some teenagers have the apathy act down to a science, but Aidan wasn't one of them. My mother once called her a "breath of fresh air," but now she was restless and disgruntled.

Maybe it was as simple as the change in landscape. Unlike Alaska, South Central Wisconsin is a place of subtle beauty and sharp boundaries—a checkerboard of farms and red barns, rolling fields, small marshes, and woodlots with shagbark hickories, black walnuts, and burr oaks. If the cause of Aidan's funk was a longing for a less domesticated landscape, I understood. Elizabeth and I had left the mountains of Colorado, where I had lived for five years and she had lived for over a decade, to return to the Midwest. Our Colorado friends questioned our sanity. I joked that we were swapping mountains for molehills and marshes. But the truth was a part of me craved the landscape that I'd grown up with. Elizabeth, on the other hand, never felt the pull. Her place was Colorado. At eighteen, she had fled Chicago's northern suburbs, where she was raised, and had no desire to return. She agreed to give Wisconsin a try because she loved me. Fortunately, the wrinkled hill country along the Wisconsin River appealed to both of us. We could live just twenty-five minutes from the city of Madison and still be in the country. Plus, we would be near family, so that as ours grew our children would come to know their grandmas and grandpas, aunts, uncles, and cousins.

Aidan and I continued walking. I could hear our neighbor's horses snorting. Over at the fairgrounds to the south, people were getting ready for the night's tractor pull. By the time the sun set, revving engines and a cheering crowd would drown out the sound of eager crickets fiddling in the grass. After the contest, a cover band of questionable talent would ascend the stage and blast songs from the seventies and eighties late into the night, while appreciative partiers ate brats soaked and boiled in Miller Genuine Draft and sipped their beers from plastic cups. The air would be thick with mosquitoes and moths.

It had been a dry summer. The grass was withering and corn leaves were twisting up. Wells across the state were running dry. Even on our little piece of land the signs of drought were everywhere. The leaves on the fifteen apple seedlings that Elizabeth and I and the girls had planted the previous fall were curling. The back pond was choked with cattails. The wooden house we'd built for nesting wood ducks was lying in the dogwoods where I'd left it before going to Alaska.

"I wanna get that duck house up while it's still warm," I told Aidan. She kept moving as if she hadn't heard a word, and was still walking away when I spotted ten-year-old Rachel, daughter number two, riding her bike back from soccer practice along the trail through the wild plums. When she saw me, she whipped her bike around.

"Wanna go swim in the creek?" she asked, skidding to a stop. She was sweaty, red-faced, and happy.

"Do you want to join us?" I shouted to Aidan.

"Nah," she shouted back. "Not interested."

Rachel pedaled to the house and was already waiting with her towel when I got there.

"Where's your sister Willa?" I asked.

"She ran off crying before I went to soccer," Rachel informed me.

"Willa," I shouted. "Willa."

"She must be in her tree," Rachel said.

Ten seconds later, I heard, "Over here."

We walked to the red maple at the edge of the yard. It was a perfect climbing tree and Willa was fifteen feet up, sitting in a crotch between two branches.

"We're going swimming. C'mon," I urged her.

Willa had forgotten whatever had upset her. She climbed to the lowest branch, swung to the grass, and dashed for the house. Minutes later we were walking through our neighbors Ted and Shirley's yard to access the creek. Ted had kindly cleared a path for us through his thorny blackberry bushes. The girls loved this stretch of stream across the road from our house, the way it wound its way purposefully through the meadow. There was a public pool in town, but the girls usually wanted to swim here.

The trail led through the thick marsh grass, which sizzled with the sound of mosquitoes, to the edge of the creek. A trout rose. Ten feet from the bank Rachel took a running jump.

"Cannonball!"

Willa went next, imitating her older sister.

"Get in, Dad," they both shouted.

I was sticky with summer sweat, but I hesitated. Fed by a spring that originated outside of town, the water was cold, very cold, and tannin-stained.

"Chicken," the girls yelled.

I waded in and dove under. We lolled in a four-foot-deep pool upstream, and by the time we left, the mist was moving in off the marsh. Dozens of bats and swallows were flitting just above the water. Soon fireflies would light the lawn and the party at the fair-grounds would be going full blast.

I HAD DECLARED that today would be a workday and I asked the girls to be dressed, fed, and out of the house by 9:00 a.m. It was 9:15, and I was alone in the garden, weeding. The hoe I was using was one that my dad gave me. It was at least forty years old, its handle smooth and soft from the accumulated oil of many hands. But the blade was still sharp, thanks to my dad, who cares for his tools as a millionaire tends to his investments. As kids we often heard his Depression-era motto: "Use it up, wear it out, make it do, or do without."

I finished hoeing by ten o'clock and went back to the house. Willa and Rachel were up but Aidan was still sleeping. I walked upstairs and was ready to knock on her door when Elizabeth tapped me on the shoulder.

She shook her head. "She needs her sleep."

At 11:00 a.m. Aidan finally showed up outside. Rachel and Willa had already staked and tied up some of the tomato plants and were now helping me build the chicken coop. Their job was to shovel and wheelbarrow away the dirt that I pulled out of the ground with the posthole digger.

"Grab a shovel," I told Aidan. She looked up, but didn't say a word. I followed her gaze. Above our heads in the rafters of the long barn I could see mud dauber wasps flying in and out of their nests.

"They won't bother us," I said. "Grab a shovel."

Aidan stood there, as if she hadn't heard me. I asked her if she'd left her brain in Alaska.

She snapped out of her daze. "I did," she said, "and now I'm back, and I don't like it." She stomped off, shouting back to me, "Just so you know, Dad, your disapproval only strengthens my resolve."

Rachel looked at me and shrugged her shoulders.

When Rachel, Willa, and I walked to the house for a late lunch, Elizabeth was in the kitchen. "Where's Aidan?" I asked. Elizabeth pointed upstairs.

I walked up and knocked on her door. I waited and knocked again. Then I opened the door a crack and saw that she was wearing headphones and had her eyes closed. I entered and rapped my knuckles against the footboard of her bed. She looked up and took off her headphones.

"Yeeessss?" she said with a kind of mock politeness.

I sat down at the end of her bed. "I know it's not easy being home."

She interrupted me. "I already told you it wasn't."

"Yes, you did," I said, trying not to take the bait. "I know. And I get that. But I need you to change your attitude. I really don't want to butt heads for the next few years."

"Neither do I," she said.

"I know you have big dreams," I continued. "And I know Lodi isn't part of that, but I need you to be here. And I need your help."

"Yeah," she said. "I'm here whether or not I want to be." Then she softened. "It's not that I hate it here. I don't. I just want to see and experience things."

"I know," I said. "I get that." Then I told her about the moment when I knew for the first time that Wisconsin couldn't hold me. I'd grown up hunting with my dad and my uncles, who first introduced me to the woods and taught me how to pay attention to the land. My favorite mornings were when my dad would come into my bedroom to wake me while it was still dark. "Son," he'd say in a near whisper, standing at the foot of my bed. "It's daylight in the swamp." Not long after, I'd be sitting in the station wagon listening to my uncles and dad talk over the crackling radio. There was something about the tone of their voices that I loved. They didn't try to hide anything from me; for a while, I was one of them. The dogs were bedded down in back, and I felt like the luckiest kid in the world. Soon we'd be roaming a thick forest or a field of high grass. Until I was twelve, I walked behind, carrying only a BB gun. But when a grouse or pheasant flushed, I, too, pulled the trigger. My uncles and my dad were the best woodsmen I knew. They could find their way through solid trees stretching from one section-line road to another or through a cattail marsh knee-deep with muck and water while only occasionally glancing at their compasses. Though I admired and loved them, at some point I recognized that my life and adventures would take me far beyond the forests, fields, and swamps of my home state.

Before standing, I squeezed Aidan's hand three times—*I—love—you*—as I had done in Alaska. Then I got up and walked out of her room. My tendency was to lecture her, which meant our talks rarely had the outcome I desired. But this time I decided that less was more.

What she had been trying to tell me, I think, was that she could no longer tolerate living for the promise of a glittering tomorrow. At home, she trained dutifully, hoping that college track or cross-country ski coaches would single her out as an athlete with the talent and discipline it took to make it at the next level. She studied late into the night, hoping for the possibility of securing a rare academic scholarship.

I had never before heard her question her goals or motivations or the circumscribed nature of her life. It was what ambitious high school students did, especially these days; they worked hard, forfeiting sleep and social events to make it into a top-tier college, where they would again fasten their dreams to that distant day when they could land the perfect job or get accepted to the best graduate school.

But Alaska had changed that. She had seen life's possibilities, and now she was less willing to defer exploring them. Like Thoreau, she now wanted to "live deep and suck out all the marrow of life." Unlike Thoreau, however, she would not be content with a little pond or a small stretch of woods. Her dreams were now as big as the Arctic and as pressing as Heimo's need to finish the cabin before winter came.

An hour later, Aidan joined me at the chicken coop. She was at least willing, if not eager, to pitch in. She helped me set the posts and dig the foot-and-a-half-deep trench in which we would bury the chicken wire to keep out predators. When we were done I asked her to give me a hand with the bees. I needed to add another super, a shallow box that contains the frames in which the bees build and fill their honeycombs, to my hive.

"Sure," she answered. She'd always enjoyed helping with the bees.

Our hives are tucked in a small grove of trees near the front prairie patch. In spring, after a friend and I built them, Willa and Rachel painted the hives light blue, yellow, and green instead of an ordinary white. After two days of much-needed rain, it was hot and sunny, and the bees were taking advantage of the good weather, darting through the air in every direction. (One colony will fly fifty thousand miles to make just one pound of honey.) Aidan lifted the bricks from the hive cap. Although she knew the routine, when she heard the hum of fifteen thousand bees, she stepped back.

"It's okay," I said. "Just move slowly. Use the smoker so they don't get too riled up." She squeezed the bellows of the small handheld smoker, beginning at the bottom of the hive and moving up. Soon it was surrounded by a small cloud. Contrary to popular opinion, smoke doesn't really calm honeybees. When bees become alarmed they give off an odor, a signal to the guard bees to defend the hive. Smoke just helps to hide the warning scent.

I lifted the hive cap to see if the bees were building comb and making honey. When they became agitated, Aidan added a few more puffs from the smoker. Using my hive tool, nothing more than a crude metal lever with a blade, I pried up one side of a frame and broke the honey seal, then did the same on the other side. Then I reached with my gloved hands to lift the frame out of the super. I brushed off the bees with the soft bristles of the bee brush and showed Aidan how the female worker bees were building honey-comb. Then I took the hive tool again and popped the wax caps on a small portion of the comb. It oozed honey. Some of the bees had already returned to the frame. Aidan wasn't wearing gloves, but she slowly wiped her index finger over the broken comb and put the honey to her tongue.

CHAPTER 10

THE PULL

I T WAS SEPTEMBER 9. AIDAN and I had been home for almost a month when Heimo called by satellite phone in the middle of *Monday Night Football*. I gave him the update on the Washington-Philadelphia game just to get a rise out of him. He hates organized sports of any kind, but football most of all. Growing up in Wisconsin, where almost everyone is a Green Bay Packers fan, Heimo defined himself as someone who was proud to tell people that he didn't give a shit about the game. As a teenager he was a promising catcher on his Babe Ruth League team but abandoned baseball to hunt, fish, and trap during every spare moment he had.

Heimo suffered my teasing good-naturedly before moving on to something he really cared about—the weather. He gave me an update: it was 32 degrees and Bear Mountain was already half-covered in snow. I could see it in my mind—the massive peak, treeless, snow-covered and white, set against a sky the color of a robin's egg.

After a few seconds of silence, I blurted out, "What if Aidan and I were to come up again?" I wasn't sure what impelled me to ask. I hadn't uttered a word to Elizabeth.

There was hardly a pause. "Sure," Heimo said. "Come up. November, December. You can help me clear trail, and Aidan can go with Edna on the trapline."

I hung up feeling proud, knowing that Aidan had passed muster. Heimo never would have invited us back, especially in winter, if he had thought she couldn't hack it. I bounded up the stairs to tell her the good news, and then I reconsidered. Before I got her excited about going back to Alaska, I needed to talk with my wife.

The following morning, when I told Elizabeth I wanted to discuss something, she knew it was about Alaska before I said a word. "You were gone for so much of summer," she said, preempting my question. "I worried about you and Aidan every day, and I missed you—a lot. And now you're asking me to go through all that again? We have only two more years with her before she goes to college. I don't want her to be gone for another month, especially in winter. It could be fifty below. That scares me."

Stupidly, I hadn't thought about what her concerns or objections might be and didn't know how to respond. She walked away.

I tried again that afternoon, opening with "We need to talk about this."

"What's there to talk about?" she shot back. "I always knew you might be going back, but what I really want to know is how long you've known you wanted to."

"I'm not sure," I said.

"I don't believe it," she said. "I know you. I bet you've been thinking about it since you left Heimo's. This isn't just about you;

this is about Aidan, too. It's about her safety and it's about the time I have left with her before she leaves the house. Why didn't you at least talk to me?"

"Maybe because I knew you'd be unhappy," I replied.

"Well, I am," she said. "I am unhappy."

After dark, I went to the garage attic with my headlamp on to search through my boxes marked "Alaska." In one I found my journals from my previous trips. I sat down and read my notes from my January 2002 adventure, and the memories of the Arctic winter came flooding back: the murmur of the river beneath the ice; the cold creak of the cabin door; the loping track of a wandering wolverine; the thin, crackling haze above a spring-fed pond; wolves running like shadows; and winter coming on like death.

That night I tossed and turned in bed, wondering if I was being selfish for wanting to go again, if I'd be endangering Aidan's life by taking her to the Arctic in winter. Alaska had been good to us. However, it was entirely capable of being something else, especially in winter. The following morning after breakfast, I told Elizabeth that I'd done a lot of soul-searching and had decided that I wanted to take Aidan back, that I wanted her to see the Arctic in winter, but that I would not go without her assent.

Apparently, she'd been thinking about it, too. In her quiet way, she'd decided to let us go. But whatever it was that had convinced her, she didn't say. "You and Aidan should go," she said calmly. "But you better keep Aidan safe. If anything happens, you won't ever be able to forgive yourself."

Two days later, I decided that I needed to talk with Aidan about the possibility of going back. I knocked on her bedroom door.

"Come in," she said, and then without missing a beat, she growled, "God, I hate physics, Dad."

"Do you want me to try to help you?" I asked.

She laughed, knowing that my brain had turned physics into neural trash decades ago.

"Uhhh!" She closed her textbook. "So, what's up?"

"Do you wanna go back to Alaska?" I asked.

"When?"

"Winter," I said. "We can help Heimo and Edna hunt and lend a hand on the trapline."

"Seriously?" she asked.

"I talked with Heimo," I said. "He wants us. But the question is: can you do it? Realistically, will you be able to handle being away from school for a month? That's a lot of time to miss. And what about the cold? You've never had to deal with that kind of cold."

"Yeeesss!" Aidan exclaimed.

"Okay," I said. "But Mom doesn't like the idea. She's worried about you. And she's worried about your studies. You're going to have to prove to her that you can work it out with your teachers."

"I know I can do that," Aidan assured me.

"You're certain?" I asked.

"One hundred percent," she said.

It was a warm evening in mid-September, a week after Heimo's call, and Aidan and I were in Madison attending a class called Hunting for Sustainability, offered by two friends who work for the Wisconsin Department of Natural Resources.

It was butchering night. Keith Warnke and Mike Watt had supplied two field-dressed whitetail bucks, with their bellies slit from rectum to diaphragm and organs removed. The deer hung upside down from a hoist and gambrel, attached to a beam of Watt's children's swing set, the idea being that if you're going to hunt, you ought to know how to use a butcher knife, too.

Aidan had already helped skin one of the deer and cut off its shoulder, and now she was up to her elbows in the gut cavity, slicing out one of the tenderloins—that prized piece of meat that runs on either side of the spine from the rib cage to the pelvic bone. Her shirtsleeves were smeared with blood. Warnke, the father of two daughters, encouraged her.

"That's a nice job, Aidan," he said. "Follow the spine with the knife and it should just peel out."

It was not an experience that Aidan had been looking forward to. She hadn't liked the idea of butchering a large animal. Too much blood, guts, and stink. But she understood that it was the price she had to pay for returning to Alaska—a skill she would likely be called upon to use at Heimo and Edna's. The real work in hunting is not in shooting an animal but in field-dressing and butchering it, especially at 30 or 40 below. And as it turned out, if Aidan was repulsed by the experience of nearly crawling into the deer's gut cavity, she hid it well. Once she peeled out the tenderloin she laid it on a table next to a variety of other cuts. Here, other students trimmed off the fat and the silver skin, the layer of whitish connective tissue about as edible as an old bike tire.

By 8:30 much of the butchering and processing was done and Aidan was back in her street clothes. When Mike Watt handed her six good-size tenderloin medallions wrapped in butcher paper, a reward for her hard work, she was delighted. As we pulled into our driveway thirty minutes later, we caught sight of the rising moon, a waxing gibbous, emerging from behind a thicket of clouds.

In the kitchen, I tore off the masking tape and folded back the butcher paper. Then I melted a quarter stick of unsalted butter in a small frying pan, laid in the venison, ground in a bunch of pepper, sprinkled some sea salt, and pan-seared the medallions until they were medium rare. I dropped three pieces on Aidan's plate.

"Your reward," I said, and she smiled. Over summer, she'd

bought an "Alaska Chicks Rock" hat, and now that she'd helped butcher a deer, she knew that she was one step closer to being the real Alaskan thing.

I called upstairs, and Elizabeth came down to enjoy the last three pieces. Ten minutes later, she and Aidan were snuggled together on the couch. I was struck by the image: our five-foot-nine, fifteen-year-old daughter, tucked happily into her mother's arm.

TWO WEEKS LATER, our dog, Calhoun, and I were greeted by fall's first frost. The grass in the meadow was white and brittle and cracked when it rubbed against my overalls. In the early-morning light, I could see the leaves of the black walnuts yellowing and spotting black. Somewhere off in the woods a pair of crows were berating a red-tailed hawk. Though I'd always enjoyed watching the hawks hunt, the way they soar and slip the wind, I was grateful for the crows' vigilance. The hawks, I knew, had taken an interest in Willa's kitten, Midnight, which roamed the yard and woods unaware of the danger.

Our neighbors Vince and Judy had discovered Midnight in their yard. She was about eight weeks old and severely undernourished when Willa adopted her. Willa named her Midnight and set out to nurse the black kitten back to health. She never went anywhere without her cradled in her arms. When she rode her bike on the grassy trails around the land, Midnight rode in the basket on the handlebars.

As Calhoun plunged into the cattails in our back pond, a woodcock, dining on worms in the soft soil, flushed and screeched. Watching the woodcock fly low over the hayfield, I was grateful that I would be home for fall in Wisconsin, my favorite season. I would be on hand to pick the last of the broccoli and the sweetening cabbage heads and to plant garlic cloves; to bed the bees down for a long, cold winter; and when the tamaracks turned a dusty gold, to hunt the nearby marshes for ducks and pheasants.

I heard Calhoun thrashing through the pond, and suddenly he bounded out, hard on the scent of a rabbit or a running pheasant. I let him go and I picked a handful of wild plums. The plums had ripened—the harvest moon in Wisconsin is sometimes called the wild rice or red plum moon—and their flesh was sweet and their skin no longer bitter. The girls would be excited by the news.

I stepped out from behind the cover of the tree line and felt the northeast wind turning cold. In less than two months, Aidan and I would be going north as a portion of the animal world was heading in the opposite direction. Just days before, I'd spotted a large group of monarch butterflies hovering over the stubble of the fresh-cut bean field. In spring, I'd seen their caterpillars on the milkweed stalks in our back prairie, and, now full-grown, they were gathering in preparation for their long journey to the jungles of Mexico. The barn swallows were doing the same, leaving their nests in the eaves and crossbeams of the barn, getting ready to head south.

October whipped by like a banner of windblown mallards. The pie apples we'd picked and stored in boxes in the basement were growing soft and fragrant. In the back field, the dogwoods and alders had shed their leaves, and the golden tamaracks were dropping their needles. The burr oaks would hold on to most of their leaves through the winter. The bucks were in rut, testing the breeze with their noses and rubbing their scent glands against the staghorn sumac and aspen popples, scraping patches of ground down to the dirt before urinating on them, and eating the windfall plums. The humidity was gone from the air now, and the sky was a slate gray, that strange and lovely late-autumn color when the angle of light is so perfect that time seems to stop.

As our departure date approached, I wondered if Wisconsin was always this beautiful in fall, or if I was noticing it only now that I was leaving. One night we were on our way home from a cross-country meet and I let Aidan know that it was not too late to change her mind. Perhaps she sensed I was having second thoughts. She reminded me how hard she had worked to make the trip possible; she had done much of her schoolwork in advance and had met repeatedly with her teachers to discuss what she could do to keep up while we were gone.

"No way, Dad," she said to me. "We're going. I'll drag you, if I have to."

Hearing her certainty, I remembered Elizabeth's words. Suddenly I was thinking about winter bears, too much darkness, skin blistered with frostbite, and falling through the ice. What if I couldn't keep her safe?

CHAPTER 11

BACK TO THE BUSH

I T HAPPENED AT THE SAME time. Aidan and I exited the Fairbanks airport terminal and were overtaken by coughing fits like coal miners stricken with black lung.

"The air is so cold it feels like it's burning my lungs," Aidan told me. "It's hard to breathe."

We loaded our gear into a taxi—two backpacks, two duffels, and Aidan's cross-country skis—and got in as fast as we could.

"Damn, cold," the driver drawled. "Came up from West Virginia. Been here for five years and I still ain't used to it. Where y'all from?"

"Wisconsin," I told him.

"This ain't so bad for y'all then," he said.

"I'm not sure we're used to *this* kind of cold," I replied. "Got any idea what the temperature is?"

"Thirty below according to that sign back there. Where y'all off to with all that gear?"

"The bush," Aidan answered.

"Ha!" he snorted, as we pulled into the hotel parking lot. "Good luck."

After we got to our room and got situated, I suggested to Aidan that we put on our winter gear and head outside to test it.

"Really?" she asked.

"Better to know now," I said.

In the Arctic, little errors can lead to big ones, and I wanted to be sure that Aidan's boots and down mitts were warm enough. All suited up, we walked down Airport Way. When we turned north on University Avenue into a bitter wind, our eyelashes iced up. On the bridge over the Chena River I heard the snap of ice expanding or contracting in the darkness below. Above us the moon was sharp and clear and I could see the gray-black features of its mountains and valleys with a startling vividness, as if I were looking through a high-powered telescope.

We walked down to College Road a mile or so from our hotel and decided to stop for something to eat. We entered a restaurant and sat down in a booth. I took off my hat and face mask, but kept my layers on until I could feel the cold leave my body.

"The gear held up, huh, Dad?" Aidan said. "It's not the easiest stuff to walk in, but I stayed warm."

Aidan and I ordered a large pizza, which we ate quickly. Then Aidan sampled the restaurant's gelato selection. "Heimo told me that I had to put on some fat," she said, returning to the booth with a cup. We shared it and lingered for a while before we struggled into our gear again.

We exited the restaurant into a storm. It was sleeting sideways, small, mean pieces of ice. Aidan and I lowered our heads and trudged off. Forty minutes later, we arrived at the hotel. This time Aidan's eyes were so iced up she could barely open them.

Stupidly, I'd left my expedition mitts behind, and now my fingers were so cold I couldn't grasp the card to get into our room.

"I need your help," I told Aidan.

She opened the room door, and, as I walked in, I told her, "Good lesson for both of us. If your hands get too cold, they're worthless."

I turned on the news. The local weather report called for thirty-knot winds in Fairbanks and sixty-five-knot wind gusts over the White Mountains, which we'd have to cross to reach the Coleen. Realizing that our flight out would likely be delayed, I called Daniel Hayden, the bush pilot who'd taken us out in the summer, and we made plans to talk the following morning. Daniel was headed up to his family cabin on the Sheenjek for a week of trapping and offered to fly us out to Heimo and Edna's.

I slept fitfully. Throughout the night, the wind pounded and shook our hotel room picture window. When Daniel called at 6:00 a.m., I'd already been awake for two hours.

"Doesn't look good," he said. "I think we can get out of Fairbanks, but I'm worried about the mountains and the winds in the [Yukon] Flats. I'll check with Fort Yukon later in the morning."

Aidan and I used the delay to sort through our survival gear—food, warmers, emergency blankets, signal flares, and a sealed sandwich bag containing a supply of paper, a magnesium fire starter, matches, and four lighters, overkill perhaps—making certain it would be accessible in the event the plane went down. Two hundred and fifty miles of wilderness separated Fairbanks and Heimo and Edna's cabin, and there was no telling what could go wrong.

At 9:00 a.m. Daniel called again. "We have a window," he said. "How soon can you be ready?"

"Now."

When he arrived thirty minutes later, I looked back and forth between his compact car and our gear, certain we were going to have to leave something behind. Aidan knew what I was thinking. "Uh-uh, I can't leave my skis, Dad. I have to train."

"Then we'll tie 'em down to the roof if we have to," I told her.

Fifteen minutes later Daniel's car was so full that once we crammed ourselves in we could barely close the doors. Aidan's cross-country skis ran the length of the car from the rear window to the back of the dashboard.

When we got to the airport, Daniel and I hustled to pull the insulated warmers from the plane's wings and its nose. Then we removed the chocks from behind the wheels and turned the plane in the direction of the runway. The plane was surprisingly light—nothing more than exterior skin sheets riveted to a body made of aluminum alloy. Once we got it pointed in the right direction, we chocked the wheels again and started the hard part: packing. In addition to our backpacks, duffels, and Aidan's skis, we were bringing in boxes of food for Heimo and Edna—a Thanksgiving turkey and ham and as much fresh produce as we could load into our two shopping carts. Somehow we managed to get everything in. Bush pilots are master packers, able to use every square inch of space in their planes.

Minutes later I was crammed into the front seat, trying to keep my feet off the pedals and my knees from hitting a switch. I prayed that my legs didn't cramp. Turning my head as far as I could, I removed my headset and asked Aidan, who wasn't wearing one, if she was okay, but the sound of the plane's 230-horsepower engine drowned out my voice.

Soon we were high over the hills of Fairbanks, which I could hardly make out because of the ice fog that hung over the city.

Daniel was punching coordinates into his handheld GPS when we hit an updraft. Aidan, who was using the plane's thermal covers as a seat, smacked her head on top of the plane. "Ouch," she shouted loud enough for me to hear through my headset. And then it came back to me. The previous night in our Fairbanks hotel, I'd dreamed that our bush plane's back door popped open high over the White Mountains. Aidan cried out for me, and, despite my shoulder harness, I torqued my body around and grabbed for her fleece jacket. As the wind threatened to suck her out of the plane, I woke with my heart feeling like it was going to rip out of my chest. And then I heard Aidan snoring faintly in the bed next to me, my brave fifteen-and-a-half-year-old daughter embarking on her second trip to the Alaskan wilderness, this time in the dead of winter.

"We're bucking headwinds," Daniel said over the intercom. "I think I can get you to Heimo's, but it's gonna be a long, bumpy ride. Three hours, maybe more."

By the time we got to Fort Yukon, Daniel elected to fly farther east, following the Yukon River until we hit the Porcupine. Paralleling the Black, the river the Gwich'in call the Draanjik, we flew northeast in the direction of Old Crow, through the Yukon Flats, its meadows pockmarked with frozen ponds. Then, near Graphite Lake, we turned north using the Porcupine Mountains to shelter us from the wind. In summer, we'd flown up the Porcupine to the mouth of the Sheenjek and then jumped over to the Coleen, but Daniel thought this route would be safer.

By the time we got to the Coleen the wind was just northeast of our nose and ice crystals were pelting the plane. The windshield was almost completely fogged over. Daniel cranked the defrost and lowered his head, as if he were ducking bullets, to peer out a semiclear section of acrylic plastic no bigger than a grizzly's paw.

Watching him, I recalled an article I'd read on the life expectancy of Alaskan bush pilots: they're thirty-six times as likely to die in a given year as the average U.S. worker.

Though I couldn't see her, I knew that behind me Aidan was anxious, and I reached back for her hand. I squeezed it three times.

"Gotta take her up," Daniel said, and I heard the plane grinding for altitude. "See if we can get above this storm."

As he said this, I noticed that our airspeed was fluctuating between sixty and sixty-five miles per hour. The plane was laboring in the big wind. Above the clouds, at fifty-two hundred feet, the sleet let up, but the wind still battered us. I felt like I was on one of those amusement park rides where the bottom drops out. The plane cruised and then fell in a downdraft. The altimeter was bouncing all over the place.

"Gotta get back down," Daniel said. Bush pilots are the coolest customers in the Arctic, but I thought I detected a tenseness in his voice.

We lost almost five thousand feet and were soon cruising just below the clouds and just above the river, barely higher than the tallest trees. We could see where caribou had crossed the ice-bound Coleen and scaled the bank. Aidan spotted them in a copse of black spruce and shook my shoulder to make sure that I saw, too. When they heard the plane, the caribou ran. Usually their large hooves act as snowshoes and prevent them from sinking in, but the snow was drifted up to their bellies and they made little progress. I scanned the open tundra, wondering if wolves were following them. In winter, wolves depend on caribou for more than food. Caribou blaze trails for them through deep snow and pack it down with their hooves, allowing the wolves to access terrain they wouldn't otherwise be able to reach. Ravens, in turn, follow the wolves; wolves mean food.

Farther upriver we flew over a trapper's cabin, the first sign of human life in almost an hour. I saw a sizable woodpile, meat hanging from a rack, and blue-gray smoke rising from a chimney, and I knew that whoever lived here had taken a midday break from his trapline and stoked the fire in his stove. Perhaps someone was inside warming his hands and feet and drinking tea. Seconds later, the cabin door opened and a man came out and looked up. I waved, but if he saw us he chose to ignore the greeting.

"That's Bob Harte," Daniel said. Our airspeed was holding at ninety-eight miles per hour and the sleet had stopped. I could hear that Daniel's tone had changed. "Heimo and Edna's place is about sixty miles north. Harte has been out a long time, too." Just then, Daniel motioned out his window at a moose bedded down in the frosted willows.

Fifteen minutes later, I saw Heimo's snow-machine trail on the river. Soon afterward I spotted the winter runway on the gravel bar that we'd fished from during the summer. Heimo had flattened it with his snow machine, removed the big rocks and the logs, and marked its borders with spruce boughs. We flew over the top and then circled back. Daniel was unhappy with the wind. He had been hoping for something out of the north or the south, but what we had instead was a strong and dangerous crosswind, the kind that could flip a plane.

As we flew over I caught sight of Heimo and Edna standing at the edge of the runway, facing into the wind gusts that rustled up small clouds of swirling snow. Daniel made another pass and I felt the plane pitch. Being in a tiny aircraft brings a whole new dimension to flying—you know you're at the mercy of Mother Nature.

"Gonna try it this time," Daniel said, sideslipping the wind. I took off my headset and turned to Aidan. She put her ear as close to my mouth as she could.

"Hold on," I said. I wondered if she'd heard until I felt her grip the back of my seat.

As Daniel brought the plane just above the runway, he throttled down. The plane pitched and Daniel steadied it. I felt the wheel skis touch, and Daniel taxied to the far end of the runway before cutting the engine. Edna stayed at the snow machine while Heimo popped open Aidan's door and then mine. Aidan and I wriggled out as quickly as we could.

Heimo was dressed in canvas pants, thick beaver mitts, a canvas parka with a wolverine ruff and seams held together by dental floss, and boots, called *kamiks* or *mukluks,* made of moose hide with wolf trim and sealskin liners. It was the same outfit he wore a dozen years ago when I flew in to the Korths' cabin on the Old Crow River. With his long, full beard and faint mustache, he looked like an Amish farmer.

At 28 below there was no time for formalities. Heimo and Edna knew that at this temperature the fresh fruits and vegetables would freeze in minutes. Daniel, too, was eager to be on his way to his family cabin before he lost light.

While Heimo and Edna made a trip to the cabin to drop off the food, I helped Daniel gas up the plane. He climbed up onto the wing and I handed him the gas can, which he grabbed barehanded. Then he twisted off the top and poured the gas into the funnel. All around us the air was sparkling. I turned my attention to Aidan, who was facing north, watching as November's last light cast the windswept slopes of Bear Mountain in a delicate, rose-gray glow. In a matter of an hour the light would grow pale and fade.

The wind was raw, and Aidan slipped on her face mask and pulled her badger-fur hat as far down as she could. As beautiful as

Bear Mountain was, she turned and walked over to us and stood with her back to the north and her arms wrapped around her as if she were an underdressed child waiting for the school bus.

When Heimo returned, Aidan lugged our baggage over to the snow sled. Heimo lifted each piece into the sled without urgency. He had saved the fruits and vegetables and was likely looking forward to a feast of fresh produce for supper. Daniel finished gassing up the plane and we made plans for his return.

"Let's just watch the weather," he said. "Give me a little window, a few days maybe." We said quick good-byes. Once in the air, Daniel banked the plane, passed overhead, and tipped his wings. Although Aidan and I would be here with Heimo and Edna, it was hard to escape the weight of loneliness.

"There goes civilization," I said, trying to sound as if it didn't matter.

Heimo chimed in. "Yup, there ain't no goin' back now." Then he trudged over to the snow machine, a big Arctic Cat. "Let's go, Aidan. You can kneel in the sled and make sure the bags don't fall off." Then he turned to me. "You can walk back. You remember the clearing."

When I made it to the cabin, Heimo was introducing Aidan to the Arctic oven: a ten-foot-by-ten-foot, double-walled, fire-resistant polypropylene tent outfitted with a small woodstove, which sat about forty feet from the cabin door.

"It's your home away from home for the next three and a half weeks," he told us and laughed. "I keep the Arctic oven as a backup in case the cabin burns down." He showed her the vents at the front and back of the tent. "These here are so you don't die of carbon monoxide poisoning in your sleep. Make sure they ain't clogged with snow or ice."

Heimo took her to his woodpile, where he had his winter's supply of cordwood neatly stacked. Nearby was a meat rack, from which two front quarters of a caribou and two rear quarters of a mountain goat hung. Boreal chickadees casually pecked at the meat, leaving a dusting of reddish brown flesh on the snow.

"We don't have much meat," Heimo said. "We need to kill something soon."

Then he pointed to the woodpile on top of which sat the head of a caribou and a number of frozen king and silver salmon.

"This wood's gotta last the winter," Heimo said, "so you gotta cut your own. Better get to it while you still got some light. I'll show you a tree you can cut. There are some bear tracks back there. I'll show you those, too."

I'd been hanging back, but I could see that it was time to step in before Aidan was overwhelmed. She'd been in the Arctic for less than thirty minutes and had discovered that she might be asphyxiated, that the severed head of a caribou, whose frozen eyes had turned to ice, would be staring at her day and night, and that there was a winter bear lurking near the cabin. I could see her sizing up the tent, wondering how quickly a winter bear could rip a hole in the polypropylene walls. Although largely the stuff of legend, winter, or ice, bears are rare but real. One had killed the Korths' dog in 2006 and nearly killed Edna, too. While most grizzlies take in enough calories to den up for four to five months in a sleeplike state, metabolizing their own body fat, the winter bear is forced out by hunger to wander in a desperate search for food.

Heimo heard me coming and turned around. "I was just telling Aidan about the wood."

"I remember your rules," I said.

"You'd better," Heimo threatened. "I shoot firewood thieves."

Heimo walked to the cabin, saying something about making himself a salad. When I heard the door open and slam shut on its tight spring, I stole a few logs of wood.

"To get our fire started," I said, winking at Aidan.

I unzipped the Arctic oven and Aidan walked in with her headlamp on. With a cot on either side of the woodstove, it was smaller than I remembered, and smaller than she'd imagined. "This is it?" she asked, judging the nine square feet of floor space. Resigned, she stood in the middle. "Not bad," she said, using her hands to measure the distance between the top of her head and the tent's peak. "But where are we going to put all our stuff?"

"We'll have to arrange our clothes under our cots."

"Did you bring any string?" she asked, eyeing the tent.

I took a ball of string from the outside pocket of my pack and handed it to her. She took her jackknife, pulled out the blade, cut two long sections and then ran them diagonally between the corners of the tent.

"We can hang clothes for a little extra room," she said. "And we'll dry 'em here if they're wet."

"Good idea," I said. "You unpack, and I'll cut some kindling and get a fire going."

Outside I grabbed Heimo's axe and a spruce log and cut kindling sticks. At minus 28, the wood split with little effort. I could tell, too, by the crisp sound the axe made when it entered the wood and cleaved it apart, that Heimo had recently sharpened the blade. I gathered the kindling, which even in the brittle cold smelled faintly of pitch, and unzipped the tent flap.

"Hurry up," Aidan said. "I'm freezing. I wouldn't call this the Arctic oven. I'd call it the Arctic icebox."

"It's the same drafty woodstove I used over ten years ago," I told her. "When the fire goes out at night and you're freezing in your sleeping bag, you're going to need to know how to do this." As I said this, the memories of that winter visit came back to me. On my first few nights, I slept through the fire's fading embers and woke colder than I'd ever been in my life. Those first nights were hell, but gradually my internal clock adjusted to the demands of the fire. I woke every two hours or so, in time to catch the coals while they were still glowing.

Aidan interrupted her unpacking for my primer. I got the fire going. It smoked until I opened the vents wide and stuffed tinfoil in the gaps between the door and the stove's belly. Only then did it draw like it should. Despite the cold, it took only a few minutes before the small space felt like a sauna. I shut the stove's vents and Aidan unzipped the tent flap and threw open the polypropylene door.

"That's crazy," Aidan said. "It's almost thirty below and we're baking in here."

When the tent cooled, I zipped up the door and closed the damper on the stovepipe, remembering how hard it was to regulate the tent's temperature. Rarely was it just right.

After settling in, Aidan and I bundled up to go cut more firewood, and Heimo came out as if on cue to show us which trees to cut. He noticed the smoke already coming from the Arctic oven's stovepipe.

"You dirty SOB," he said, smirking.

CHAPTER 12

THE REAL WORLD

BRING BACK MEMORIES?" HEIMO ASKED, pointing to the clearing where Aidan had peeled poles during the summer. "I bet you missed it, didn't you, Aidan?"

She didn't respond. Heimo was fond of teasing her, and she knew it. Besides, she had only one thing on her mind, and that was getting firewood. Nightly temperatures would run between 25 and 45 below. Although she'd brought along two minus-20-degree sleeping bags, keeping warm at those temperatures would require lots of wood.

Dragging the sled, we crossed a creek bed and Heimo showed us his water hole. Stuck into a nearby snowbank was a heavy-duty chisel, which he used daily to punch through the accumulated ice.

"This is where I get my cooking and washing water," he said. "Drinking water I get from the spring."

Fifty feet in back of the creek, Heimo showed us a stand of dead trees. "Take any one of these," he said. "After you chop it down and Aidan limbs it, I'll help you drag it out to the trail. We can cut it up with the chain saw by the clearing where Aidan left the sled."

We had brought two axes, one to fell a tree and a smaller, two-pound axe for limbing. When the tree was down and Aidan had taken off the branches with the small axe, Heimo and I hauled it out of the woods. "Damn," I said. "This is harder than I thought."

"It ain't easy movin' in all those clothes, is it?" Heimo agreed. "You better hope we don't break down when we're on the trapline. It'll be a long snowshoe to get back home."

By the time we got to the clearing Aidan had already walked to the cabin to get the chain saw. Thirty seconds later, Heimo heard Kini, the Korths' half-Akita, half-husky, barking, and hustled back. I grabbed the big felling axe and followed Heimo, thinking that a moose might have wandered into the cabin yard or, maybe, there really was a winter bear roaming the river. Behind the cabin, Kini was straining on her picket chain, pawing the snow. Heimo and I looked around to see why she was so excited, and I spotted Aidan by the toilet. Just then, she looked up.

"Sheesh," she said. "Is she going to sound the alarm every time I want to use the outhouse?"

We laughed, and then I picked up the chain saw and walked back to the clearing.

Minutes later, Aidan joined me. "Dad," she said, "you know that hole you dug for the outhouse? Well, it's still just a hole. Heimo forgot the house. All there is is two spruce poles over an open-pit toilet with a wood seat shaped like a triangle. The pit is full of rock-solid poop. A mountain of it. I think I'd rather use the bucket."

By the time Aidan and I finished cutting, hauling, and splitting the wood, it was 4:30—suppertime. Both Heimo and Edna eat big breakfasts, but neither eats lunch, so by late afternoon they are often famished.

Aidan added two logs to our fire and we both walked toward the cabin. Ten feet away, we stopped and stepped back to admire it and to feel a bit of pride that we'd had a hand in creating it. At the door I scraped my boots on the snow.

"It's called the Eskimo shuffle," I told Aidan. "You do it to announce yourself."

We ducked in through the low-cut door and banged our boots against the doorsill.

"Hurry, hurry, hurry," Heimo said.

After we'd entered, he tacked a wool blanket over the entrance to keep in the heat. Aidan and I took off our boots. We'd barely said more than hello to Edna since we arrived. She came over and gave Aidan a hug.

"It'll be nice to have you here," she said.

"Forget that stuff," Heimo said, as we sat down on old camping chairs. "I'm hungry." He licked his lips. "Specklebelly goose and spuds and a salad with lettuce, carrots, tomatoes, and peppers you brought from town. God, it's been so long since I've had fresh veggies."

Heimo gave me a plate with some salad, ladled out potatoes, and plopped down a piece of goose smothered in Edna's gravy. He did the same for Aidan.

"Eat," he said, and he watched to see her reaction. Aidan had had goose many times before, but never specklebelly. She took a drumstick in her hand and bit into it with relish, wiping the grease from her chin. Heimo slapped his knee. "I told you. Ain't nothin' better."

It was true. The greater white-fronted goose, known colloqui-
ally as the specklebelly, is a dark meat with the texture of grass-fed
beef and a wild taste. Edna's secret was to let it sit in a slow cooker
at low heat for hours on end.

After serving Edna, Heimo buried his own plate in potatoes,
goose, and vegetables until there was no blue enamel showing,
and dug in like a ravenous wolf feeding on a kill. As a young man
Heimo had drunk hard, but it had been over thirty years since he'd
tipped a beer or thrown back a shot. The wilderness and drink,
he realized, didn't mix, and now that booze was no longer a part
of his life, he reserved his considerable appetite for food. Heimo
doesn't just eat; he sucks every last morsel of flesh, fat, and cartilage off every bone and then he licks his fingers—why use a napkin
when you don't have to? he says—so he doesn't miss out on a drop
of gravy or grease. And he doesn't waste any time talking; eating at
the Korth cabin is not a social occasion. By the time I finished my
plate, he was well into his second helping.

When he was finally done he pushed his seat (a five-gallon pail)
under the table, plopped down on his plywood sleeping platform.
"For supper tomorrow," he said, holding his belly, already planning the next meal, "it's gonna be bunnies or seal. What do you
think, Aidan?"

"Either," Aidan said noncommittally. In Fairbanks I'd given
her a talk about finishing everything on her plate, even if she had to
choke it down. To snub an Eskimo woman's cooking is the worst
kind of insult. Edna, I told her, was especially proud of her skills.
Specklebelly goose, rabbit, caribou, ptarmigan—I knew Aidan
would willingly eat all of those. But seal? Even Heimo considered
seal an acquired taste. The meat is dry, and thick-fibered, so dark
red in color that the Eskimos call it black meat. Only the blubber
makes it edible.

Heimo was digging at his teeth with a toothpick. "Look around, Aidan," he said. "Can you believe you helped build this?"

Though Edna was still in the process of decorating the walls and making shelves, the cabin was comfortable and homey, and smelled sweetly of pitch. Although the thermometer outside the window read minus 31, inside it was as warm as a house with a modern furnace, despite its seven feet, six inches of headroom. Unlike their other cabins, which had lower ceilings, Heimo wanted this one to feel spacious, so we'd built the ceiling more than a foot higher. After we were gone, Heimo had added a vertical support beam to help support the roof when it was two feet deep in snow. Except for the higher ceiling, with its peeled poles, which glowed orangish red in the light of the flickering fire, the cabin was a model of economy and efficiency. Next to the beam, a Coleman lantern hung and hissed from the ridgepole. Above my head and to the left, closer to the stove, Heimo had rigged up a spruce pole and suspended it by wire from the ceiling. Plastic hangers, draped with damp hats, gloves, and socks, hung from the pole. Heimo had also run lines, equipped with wooden clothespins, along the ceiling. Aidan had clipped her gloves, socks, and badger-fur hat to the pins in the hope that they would soon dry. In back of me, piled onto wooden pegs, was an assortment of outdoor gear—parkas, pants, hats, and mitts, and a small window. Over the door, whose edges Heimo had lined with fur for insulation, rested a number of rifles and shotguns. In the cache above the sleeping platform was enough ammunition to last the next few years.

To the right of the door was Edna's kitchen, with a south-facing window looking out onto the cabin yard. Edna had built a counter and shelves, which she was eager to decorate with the adhesive paper we'd brought from Fairbanks. Above the counter, she'd nailed up plastic milk crates as cupboards to hold spices, plates, bowls, and utensils. Under the counter sat two five-gallon buckets, one for drinking water and one for dish and cooking water, and two plastic tubs. Just a few more steps back into the cabin was the large quarter-inch-steel stove a friend had fabricated and welded. Next to it was the wooden folding table the Korths used for meals, and over it a big, west-facing, double-pane window. Farther back, in the cabin's northwest corner, Edna had built a shelf unit to hold toiletries and other items. A radio hung on the wall next to the shelf.

During my visits in the early 2000s, every evening the Korths would tune their radio to KJNP, a religious station out of North Pole, Alaska. For bush families, KJNP's *Trapline Chatter* was the only regular connection to the outside world. Relatives from the Lower 48 sent holiday and birthday greetings, gossip, everyday news, and weather updates, which the station's Bev Olson read over the air once or twice a day. Thanks to the satellite phone, and now satellite Internet, which has finally—despite Heimo's reluctance—made its way to the Coleen River, nightly KJNP updates are largely a thing of the past at the Korth cabin.

After dinner, we tried to access the Internet signal because Edna was hoping to Skype with her granddaughter, Rhonda's daughter, Coleen. Two weeks before our arrival, Heimo had rigged up the dish on the cabin's roof but now he was grumbling about not needing any "damn Internet." He didn't like the idea of the Internet to begin with. What he liked even less was trying to locate the satellite signal. Clear skies or not, he couldn't seem to get the dish in the right position.

Heimo powered up the generator and plugged Edna's computer into it. Then we set up something of an assembly line. Aidan stood inside the cabin near Edna, while I positioned myself at the cabin door. Heimo was up on the roof, where he'd be moving the dish to get the best signal. I held the door open a crack and heard Aidan shout something to me.

"What?" I yelled over the sound of the generator.

"Three bars," she shouted louder.

I closed the door and stood at the bottom of the ladder that Heimo had fashioned out of spruce poles. I could hear him swearing to himself. We needed at least four bars of service for Edna to be able to Skype. Heimo looked down at me while holding on to the satellite dish.

"Hurry up," he said. "It's cold as shit up here."

"Still three bars," I told him.

As he made a minor adjustment to the dish, I heard Aidan and Edna shout, "Only two bars now."

I walked to the bottom of the ladder, chuckling to myself because I knew how mad Heimo was going to be when I told him the news.

"Two bars now," I yelled.

"Goddammit," he cursed. Then he moved the dish ever so slightly, as if he was sighting in his rifle and adjusting the scope one click to the right. Again, I heard shouting from the cabin. By the time I got to the door, Aidan was there.

"Perfect," she said. "Five bars."

I dashed to the ladder. "Hold it right there," I said. "Five bars."

Heimo was blowing on his bare hands. They were chilled, but because of what is known as the hunter's response, they were not so cold he couldn't use them. (Because he has so often worked gloveless when setting traps at 30 and 40 below, the surface capillaries in his hands periodically allow warm blood to pass into them, elevating his skin temperature.) Nevertheless, Heimo was happy to get off the roof. He stepped carefully onto the icy ladder, making sure he didn't lose his footing. When he was halfway down, I saw Aidan at the cabin window. I opened the door and poked my head in.

"Only two bars now," she said.

Heimo was standing at the bottom of the ladder and I was laughing so hard I could barely get the words out. "Shiiiiiittt!" he said, starting to climb back up before I finished my sentence. "This thing is nothing but a clusterfuck. I hate this damn Internet." When he reached the roof, he drew a wad of phlegm from his throat and spat. He failed to achieve the velocity he needed and hocked all over his beard and canvas parka. Bending his head back, like a wolf howling at the moon, he screamed, "Dammit! I hate technology." He stayed there watching the night sky, as if contemplating the immensity of the universe.

Half a minute passed before I heard him growl. He took off his beaver mitts, pulled out the wood shim, and adjusted the dish. Aidan was back at the window. "Perfect!" she shouted.

Heimo heard her and slid in the wood shim. "If we lose it this time," he said, "I'm done."

He climbed down the ladder and stomped past me, walked inside the cabin, took off his kamiks, and pulled a bucket next to the stove. "I was shivering up there," he said.

I tried to cover up my laughter by coughing instead. He caught me. "All right," he said. "You go up there next time and freeze your ass off, dipshit."

When Edna and Aidan laughed, he got up, grabbed two logs from a cardboard box by the door, threw them into the stove, and slammed the door shut. "I'm cold," he said, spreading his fingers to absorb the fire's warmth. "I didn't dress for that crap." Then he smiled, the warm stove working its magic on his mood. "Sheeiit," he said. "Go ahead and have a big laugh if it makes you feel good."

Edna announced that she and Heimo were ready for their computer tutorial. Aidan had promised to help them set up Skype and email and teach them some basic computer skills; I wondered if she was regretting it now. At home she gets frustrated with my ineptitude, and Heimo's and Edna's knowledge of computers was even more rudimentary. She'd have to summon a river of patience to teach them.

I stood by watching and could see Heimo's irritation building. Edna was asking smart questions and making a concerted effort to learn, but Heimo's attention was drifting. "I gotta pee," he said, standing up. He opened the door, walked out in his T-shirt, but then stepped back into the cabin. "I don't get it," he said. "This world outside is real. Email and Skype, that's make-believe."

Before Heimo returned I crept outside and made a beeline for the tent. I didn't want to be around for the rest of the lesson, listening to Heimo grumble. I went to use the pit toilet. In the distance, I heard the river ice moving and moaning like a wounded animal. Before heading back to the tent, I saw a pale light coming from the cabin window and the chimney puffing smoke, and it occurred to me how remarkable it was that Heimo and Edna were still here.

A decade ago, Heimo and Edna had decided to move to town so that Rhonda and Krin could get a high school education. I'll never forget the day Heimo told me they were leaving the bush. They had come to Fairbanks for Christmas and Heimo had called me.

"We're leaving the . . . bush." He tried to say it as matter-of-factly as possible, but he could barely force out the words. He paused for a long time to compose himself. Then he continued,

"Yeah, Edna and me talked it over. One day, we hope to move back out."

As Heimo finished, his voice grew stronger, as if by uttering the words "We're leaving," he was one step closer to accepting the reality of his decision, however painful it was. When I asked him if he was okay, he said, "Yeah, I guess. I don't like it, but it's the only way. The girls need to know how much we love them, that we're willing to do anything for them, even if that means leaving. This is our dream, not theirs."

I wagered then that they'd never return to the bush, that they'd grow accustomed to the comforts of town. But, in defiance of the historical trend that saw longtime bush families say good-bye to the woods in favor of lives that were neither as beautiful nor as hard, Heimo and Edna came back to the land they'd always considered their home.

I returned to the tent. An hour and a half later, when Aidan came in, I was tucked deep inside my sleeping bag, reading a book.

When she saw that my headlamp was on, she mumbled, "You ditched me, Dad. Thanks a lot. That was hard work. Heimo barely listened. He did crossword puzzles the whole time."

I poked my head out of the top of my bag. "I'm sure Edna appreciated it," I said. "And at least the tent is nice and warm."

"Yeah," she said. "But I have to go back out to brush my teeth and pee." At that, she unzipped the tent and dashed into the cold as if she were taking a quick dip in an Arctic river.

I waited for her to return. "Brrrr," she said, jumping in.

"Cold out there?" I asked.

"Yeah," she said. "And quiet. Not a sound. I saw the northern lights, too. There were these whitish green bands moving across the sky."

"Aurora borealis," I said. "Some believe they're a gift of light from the dead to lift the gloom of a long winter."

Aidan agreed. "It was like spirits flashing across the sky."

TWO HOURS LATER I woke shivering, despite all the layers I'd worn to bed. I turned on my headlamp, which I had dangling from my neck while I slept, and saw that the fire was out and the coals were dead. It was what I'd been dreading, having to relight the fire in the middle of the night. I shone my light on Aidan. She was tucked so deeply into her sleeping bags, I wasn't even sure she was there. I struggled out of my bag and cursed. I'd forgotten lesson number one: always keep a supply of kindling and firewood under my cot. But there was no time for regret; the tent was cold and getting colder, the kind of subzero temperatures that could freeze the life out of Aidan and me. I slipped on my stiff boots and realized that I'd not even had the good sense to put wood just outside the tent.

I groaned, exited the tent, walked over to our woodpile, grabbed an armful of logs and some kindling, and stuck it through the two-foot opening I'd left in the tent flap. Then I cut my light. When I did, I could see that the sky was clouding over. There was no moon, only a broad darkness as black as a cave. In the woods behind me a tree popped from the cold. *Crack!* It shattered the hard silence like a rifle shot.

Back at the tent, I stepped inside onto the icy floor. I heard Aidan mumble something. Then she unzipped her sleeping bags only enough for me to see her face.

"I'm so cold," she said.

"Don't worry," I told her. "It'll be warm soon."

I tore some paper, balled it up and put it in the stove, and lay in some dry kindling that I'd cut as thin as stir sticks. I tried my lighter, but the butane was too cold to vaporize, so I reached into the pocket of my fleece pants and took out matches. The first match lit quickly, and fortunately so did the fire. I opened the chimney damper and the stove's vents and crawled back into my sleeping bag. Aidan whispered, "Thanks, Dad."

I pulled my fleece hat low over my ears, wriggled into my bag, and pulled it up over my head. I lay there listening to the sound of Aidan breathing and to the breeze sifting through the snow-weighted trees. In the distance, I thought I heard the howl of wolves.

CHAPTER 13

WOLVERINE AND WHALE

"YOU NEED A NEW WOODSTOVE in the Arctic oven," I told Heimo grumpily at breakfast. He'd made oatmeal with cinnamon and dried cranberries that we'd brought from town.

He looked at me. "Didn't sleep so good, huh?"

"Nope," I said, thrusting a large spoonful of oatmeal into my mouth. "The stove leaks like a sieve and coughs smoke. I had to relight the fire four times and twice I had to open the entire tent flap just to breathe."

"Did you clean out the stovepipe?" Heimo asked.

"You mean you didn't before we arrived?"

"Can't say as I did." Heimo chuckled in a mock Texas twang.

Edna was sitting in her customary chair between the woodstove and the table. She had her hand over her mouth, trying to keep from laughing out loud.

"Jesus," I said.

When I was done with my oatmeal, I pushed my chair back, offered a cursory thanks for breakfast, and announced that I was going to deal with the stovepipe. When I walked outside I heard Edna guffaw. I pulled the broom from a snowbank near Heimo's woodpile and walked over to the Arctic oven. I spent the next few minutes trying to wrestle off the top piece of the stovepipe, barehanded, my fingers aching on the now-cold metal, turning it clockwise and counterclockwise until it finally gave. I turned on my headlamp and looked into it. All clear. Then I stood as tall as I could and leaned into the tent to reach the other portion of the pipe. I stuck in the broom handle and worked it like a plunger, scraping soot from the pipe. Halfway down I hit what felt like a gooey glob of tar. Creosote! I'd found the culprit. I pushed the broom handle in hard and felt the creosote let loose and drop down the pipe. It sounded like scurrying mice. After fixing the stovepipe I jabbed the broom handle into the snowbank and walked toward the cabin. Looking up I saw that Heimo, Edna, and Aidan had been watching me. As they jumped back from the window, I heard laughter.

An hour later Heimo had the snow machine and sled ready to go. Aidan and I were dressed in our cold-weather gear for a day on the trapline. Heimo and Edna kissed outside the cabin, as if Heimo were some adman or accountant leaving to catch the train to work. It was a sweet ritual, one all the more surprising in light of the fact that they spend eight to nine months together in the bush before going to town. They have their differences, for sure, but they also have a deep affection for each other that allows them to endure and, most of the time, to enjoy the kind of close-quarter living that would turn many couples into homicidal maniacs.

Heimo's plan was for Aidan to ride behind him on the Arctic

Cat while I bounced along in the sled. Once we got upriver we'd leave the machine behind, put on our snowshoes, and climb one of the wind-blasted mountains to the west, checking Heimo's traps as we ascended.

Heimo asked Aidan if she remembered the story he had told her over the summer about Herman, the old Eskimo hunter from St. Lawrence Island. She pulled a sealed plastic bag from her pocket, containing a needle and thread, and swung it back and forth, as if to say, "Yuuup." Heimo smiled. "You learn faster than your old man."

We pulled out of the cabin yard and moved north along the trail. Heimo stopped periodically to point out marten, snowshoe hare, and mink tracks. After last night's snow the tracks were unreadable to me, like the rising of a small trout in fast water that catches the attention of only the most seasoned angler. A little farther down the trail, Heimo stopped to study the rounded pad of a "link," or lynx. Instantly, he became a predator. The animal, he said, was likely a female, moving east from the forested hill to the alders along the riverbed.

"How can you see all that?" I asked him. Trancelike, his eyes followed the tracks, and half a minute passed before he addressed my question. "After almost forty years, I don't even have to think about it," he said, shrugging his shoulders. "It's second nature."

We continued north through a maze of whiplike willows that slapped and clawed at my face. So many times Heimo had spent his days alone in the snow and cold, flogged by the numbing wind, leaving the cabin early and returning late in the gray, dusky light, with no reward for his efforts, save a frostbitten ear or heel. But today would be different. Half a mile upriver, he stopped to celebrate. "Yes!" When I saw the saucer-size prints in the trampled ground, I knew he'd caught a wolverine. With its front foot held in the trap's steel jaw, the big male was straining at the end of the trap chain. In its struggle it had clear-cut every bush within reach.

At first Aidan didn't notice it, but when she got off the snow machine and walked in the direction of the "catch circle," she was hit by the stink, the pungent musk expelled from the wolverine's anal glands, and asked, "What's that smell?" Then she saw the wolverine and jumped back. It glared at her, and she stepped back farther. "Can I stand behind you, Dad?" she asked.

From behind me, she studied the animal, its short legs, long snout, bushy tail, enormous paws, almost nonexistent ears, little eyes, and small, rounded head, which held a viselike jaw. It looked like a cross between a weasel and a grizzly bear. When Heimo approached it, it lunged at him, snarling and tugging at its chain. Like Heimo, wolverines are drawn to remote and inhospitable places. Once common in the Rocky Mountain west, the Sierras, and the Cascades, the wolverine has seen its range shrink considerably. In Alaska, for trappers, hunters, pilots, and ecotourists, seeing wolves and grizzlies is a far more common experience than sighting a wolverine. Ernest Thompson Seton, a famous naturalist and one of the founders of the Boy Scouts of America, saw only two during his entire time in the field in the Canadian Arctic in the late 1800s, but his description is especially vivid: "Picture a weasel . . . that little demon of destruction, that small atom of insensate courage, that symbol of slaughter, sleeplessness, and tireless, incredible activity—picture that scrap of demoniac fury, multiply that mite some fifty times, and you have the likeness of a wolverine."

Hyperbolic though Seton's portrait is, the wolverine's reputation for ferocity is well deserved. Early French trappers in North America called it the devil bear. Though less than one-half the size of an adult wolf, pound for pound the wolverine might be the strongest mammal in the Arctic. Wolverines have been known to scare off bears and bring down caribou and Dall sheep; their jaws and teeth are capable of cracking through frozen meat and bone. And their hunger is legendary. They are both insatiable scavengers and top predators, eating everything from carrion to small animals and birds, berries and insects. Unlike wolves, which can go days between meals, the wolverine is always in search of food. Some Eskimo groups refer to it as *gulu gulu,* the glutton.

The wolverine hunkered down as if it was about to pounce on one of us. "Can it get away?" Aidan asked, noticing its long, sheet-metal-sharp claws and sizable canines. Heimo told us to step back, and positioned himself close to the animal.

"You might not want to watch this," I told Aidan. She turned her head just in time. Heimo shot it through the heart and lungs.

In the Alaskan bush, there is no escaping death. To preserve their historic way of life, and to scrape by, Heimo and Edna must trap. Without the small income they make from selling furs, they could not live here. Flying in supplies and gas a few times a year isn't free. Without trapping, the Korths would be forced to take menial jobs in Fairbanks or another town. And without trappers, the Alaskan wilderness would no longer be a place for people living close to the land in what John Haines, Alaska's onetime poet laureate, called the "old, independent ways." Not living off the land, as Haines said, fundamentally changes the nature of the experience. Backpackers, big-game hunters, and rafters pass through. To live as Heimo and Edna do binds one to a place.

The wolverine's death was quick; it didn't writhe or twitch or gasp for air. By the time Aidan heard the echo of the pistol and turned back, Heimo was already kneeling beside the animal, removing its foot from the trap. Aidan squatted next to him, slipped off a glove, and ran her bare hand over the wolverine's lush, brown fur. The soft-point bullet had barely even made a hole.

"Did it feel pain when it was in the trap?" she asked Heimo.

He was silent for a while. "I can't judge an animal's suffering," he said. "But I try to keep it to a minimum."

I could see Aidan thinking. "Is it ever hard for you?" she continued.

She'd asked me the same question about an animal's death in Fairbanks before we came out to the river. I didn't have an answer for her, so I told her the story of the Micronesian turtle hunters I sailed with in the Caroline Islands of the western Pacific. They were bold and proud men whose lives depended upon their hunting and fishing skills. Every spring, they set out from isolated atolls onto the ocean in their rustic sailing canoes to search for sea turtles near the turtles' nesting islands. There, in the shark-infested waters, they harpooned the two-hundred-pound animals and dragged them to land. Using knives and rope they punctured and tied their fins together, turned the frantic turtles onto their backs, and floated them out to their sailing canoes, while sharks, attracted by the blood, swam close by. Then, rather than kill the turtles, they kept them alive to preserve the meat while they sailed back to their islands. Sometimes the trip home took days. They tethered the turtles and pulled them through the water or left them on deck in the baking sun to wheeze and gasp for air for the entire journey. The hunters paid tribute to God, or their gods, for the bounty, and most took only what they needed to feed their people, but to an outsider like me the spectacle was hard. When I asked one of the hunters if the suffering of the turtles bothered him, he told me, not quite comprehending my question, that hunting sea turtles was the way of his people and that some of the turtles had to forfeit their lives so his people could live as they were meant to live.

There are certainly those people who don't believe that Heimo and Edna belong out here. Earlier in the day, Aidan had reminded me of a discussion we'd had with a friend after returning from our summer cabin-building trip. He had insisted that Heimo and Edna had no right to live, hunt, trap, or build a cabin on federal refuge land. His opinion was that it was there for the animals and for the ecotourists—and perhaps, begrudgingly, for the big-game hunters—who observed a leave-no-trace wilderness ethic. It was just the three of us talking on our screened-in porch, and Aidan and I defended their right. Why, we wondered, did his notion of the "wilderness experience" exclude people like Heimo and Edna? Our friend argued that the Wilderness Act left no room for what he called the Korths' "obsolete" way of life. He reminded us that it defined wilderness as "an area where the earth and its community of life are untrammeled by man, where man himself is a visitor who does not remain."

This issue had become very important to Aidan, so much so that she'd written a paper for school about it. She quoted Wendell Berry to make her point. Berry wrote, "You can't save the land apart from the people, to save either, you must save both." Then she told our friend about Heimo's relationship to the land, his love for it, about how he and Edna live a seminomadic life, moving each spring to one of their three cabins in the Arctic National Wildlife Refuge. She explained that they did it as a form of stewardship: to let the land rebound from their presence.

Heimo scooped up a handful of snow and rubbed it over the wolverine's fur to soak up the blood. Then he turned to Aidan. "Does it bother you?" he asked.

She hesitated and I wondered if she would be truthful. "Yes, I guess it does," she said.

He softened. "I can understand that," he said. "For you, for city people, it might be difficult. But I'm a hunter and a trapper. Death is a part of my life. Sometimes, it ain't pretty. But I love this land and I love the way of life. I hunt and trap hard, but I know how important it is to leave seed. You trap out a country, and it takes a long time for the animals to come back. As for their pain, pain ain't new to them; they live with it. And so do I. I've frozen nearly every part of my body. I've almost drowned and almost been aten. Some people might call me a killer, but most of them just leave the killing to others."

Aidan examined the wolverine's claws and then touched and admired the wide band of white—the "diamond"—that runs from the wolverine's front shoulders to the base of its tail. She wanted to know how much a wolverine fur is worth.

"Three to five hundred dollars," Heimo told her.

"Five hundred dollars," she repeated, contemplating the sum.

"Sure," Heimo answered. "Wolverine fur is the finest there is. Because it don't mat or freeze to the skin, Alaskans like to use it to make hood ruffs or trim for their parkas. It sounds like big money," he continued, "but it ain't much when you figure all the time I put into it. I break the trail, and every time it snows or the wind blows it over, I have to break trail again. And it's not as if I catch a wolverine in every set. This might be the only one I get this winter. Plus, it will take me at least eight hours to prepare the fur. I treat it good."

I helped Heimo put the wolverine in a large flour bag, which he laid at the front of the sled. "Try not to rest your feet on it," he said. "I don't want you damaging the fur."

Aidan jumped on the snow machine behind him. "You know," he said, turning to her, "a wolverine is a survivor. I respect that."

We traveled another five miles upriver and then we parked the Arctic Cat, put on our snowshoes, and prepared to check a line of traps that Heimo had laid out on an unnamed mountain.

"It's good marten country," he said, looking forward to the prospect of finding more fur and, at the very least, of climbing a pretty mountain.

"Marten?" Aidan asked.

"You know pine marten," Heimo said. "It looks like a fisher, but smaller and lighter in color."

"A fisher." Aidan said it as a statement, but Heimo could hear the uncertainty.

"Just wait and see. Maybe we'll get one."

Aidan walked off in the direction of the mountain.

"You better get rid of some of your gear," Heimo called after her.

She turned. "At twenty-seven below?"

"Trust me," Heimo answered. "You'll be sweatin' in no time."

Aidan and I took off our parkas and laid them in the sled next to our bulky snow pants. Underneath were layers of microfleece.

"You're smart to layer," Heimo said. "That's the key in this country."

Heimo's trail went straight up a steep hill. He reached the top and waited for us and heard Aidan huffing and puffing. "Move slow," he said. "You don't want to sweat too much."

When Heimo stopped at his traps to dust the snow from the trap pans, Aidan and I kept climbing. As we walked, we reviewed basic compass skills: how to adjust for the difference between true north and magnetic north—what's called magnetic declination; how to shoot an azimuth and follow a line of travel; and how to account for the kind of lateral drift that makes walking a perfect compass course impossible.

When Aidan and I reached the top, we stopped to watch the way the afternoon's pale light spilled over the mountain. We knew that in late November the sun would begin its two-month hibernation. Then daylight would be an occurrence that happened somewhere else, farther south, and this far, frozen place would surrender itself to the blue shadows of twilight.

When Heimo approached, Aidan noticed that he was carrying something in his hand.

"Got a marten in the last pole set," he said. "The others were empty." Then he turned to Aidan. "This is a marten. See the fur and the orange on its neck and shoulders. Lush, huh?"

"It's bigger than I thought," Aidan said. "Bigger than a mink."

"Yah," Heimo said, as if Aidan has just made the most transparent observation ever.

Finding good marten country is the key to being a successful trapper. The other animals—wolverine, wolf, lynx, fox, otter, mink, weasel, beaver, and muskrat—are what Heimo calls "gravy." They're what enable him and Edna to set a little money aside for emergencies and for the possible day when neither of them is up to the physical demands of this way of life. Heimo wasn't the only trapper to swear he'd never live in town. He knew a lot of them, once strong, tireless men, who were forced to leave the bush when their bodies broke down.

"Help me get this in," Heimo said, handing me the marten, which was frozen stone-stiff. When I got it in his pack and cinched the top, he turned to admire the view. The sun lay low in the southeast, in the direction of the Strangle Woman Mountains, and reddened the river valley.

"Look at it," he said, "fighting to shine."

"Are you going to miss it?" Aidan asked.

Heimo shrugged his shoulders matter-of-factly. But the truth is that no one ever gets used to the darkness. December and January challenge even the strongest psyches. People who live in the bush start preparing for it as early as August. When the willows and balsam poplars yellow, the bearberry blazes a bright crimson, the alders turn a muddy brown, and the first killing frost comes, they know that winter is just around the corner.

On our way down the mountain Heimo stopped at the first pole set to show Aidan how he builds a trap for marten.

"You might have to know how to do this one day," he said.

First, he showed her how he located a dead, seven-to-eight-foot spruce tree, about as thick as a man's arm, close to his trail. Then, using his axe, he cut the tree three feet from its base. Next, he notched the top of the stump, carving a groove, into which he laid down the rest of the tree—the pole—at a 45-degree angle, with the thin end pointed at the sky and the thick end resting on the ground. Again, using his axe, he fashioned an indentation at the thin end of the pole. Here, he placed a steel trap—a No. 1 Oneida long spring—making a loop with the trap chain, which he put over the end. Once he pushed the loop to the middle of the pole, he secured it with bailing wire, so a struggling marten couldn't drag the trap through the forest. Then he used a piece of string and tied it off to keep the trap in place. Finally, he attached another piece of string to the pole and tied the wing of a spruce grouse to the opposite end as bait. The bait dangled high enough from the ground that a marten wouldn't be able reach it. It would be forced to use the pole as a ramp and, in the process, Heimo hoped, would end up in the trap.

When we got back to the snow machine, we walked along a slough bed, where Heimo spotted a wolf track and scat packed tight with caribou hair. "Lone wolf," he said. "Traveling in the direction of the cabin. First time I've seen one here."

We followed the tracks until they cut into the thick woods and then we returned to the frozen slough. The wolf, Heimo knew, was built for long-distance travel even in extremely cold temperatures. At 40 and 50 below zero, it was able to preserve its core heat by restricting the flow of blood to its skin. The temperature of its footpads was just a notch above the point at which tissue freezes.

"Young male," Heimo said. "Next time we come up we'll see if he's still around. If he is, we'll set for him." He continued walking and then stopped. "Did I ever tell you about Rhonda and the wolves?"

By the time Aidan shook her head, not sure she wanted to hear, Heimo was already two sentences into his story.

He and ten-year-old Rhonda were on the snow machine tracking a small pack of wolves through a thick forest of low-cut black spruce trees when he heard them out on the tundra. He instructed Rhonda to get off and wait for him because he knew that they would be in for a rough ride over tussocks and he worried that Rhonda might not be able to hang on.

He had his 22.250 slung over his shoulder just in case he got close enough to shoot. Trapped or shot, wolf skins were bringing $250. The money would go toward a visit to the dentist when the family went to town in June. When Heimo made it to the tundra, he saw by their tracks that the wolves had doubled back. Then he heard them howl from the trees where he'd left Rhonda. He'd been around wolves long enough to know that hungry ones might attack a human, especially a child.

He opened up the snow machine full-bore, barely keeping his grip on the handlebars as he bounced across the tundra. When he arrived the wolves were gone, but so was Rhonda. For a few seconds, he panicked. Had they dragged her off? He was shouting for Rhonda when he spotted her tracks in the snow, which led to a tree. His little "woods girl" had heard the wolves coming and had picked the tallest, sturdiest black spruce in the forest to climb.

After Heimo finished the story he walked off to check two more sets on his own. I felt Aidan grab my elbow; I knew that Heimo's story had frightened her. She didn't like the thought of being without a weapon while a wolf roamed the woods. Growing up she'd loved Jean Craighead George's tales about Julie the Eskimo girl, who lived with the wolves, and George's later book about Amaroq, Julie's brother, and his adopted wolf pup, Nutik. But reading poignant stories about Eskimo children and being on foot in real wolf country were two different things.

"I'm scared, Dad."

"Don't worry," I said. "We'll be okay."

I knew that, despite Heimo's story, predatory attacks by wolves are rare. A government report published in 2002 found that since 1942 there had been just forty-nine documented cases of aggression toward humans by wolves in Alaska and Canada. That is less than one reported attack, or near attack, per year. But it laid to rest the fallacy that I grew up with: that wolves never, ever, attack humans.

We walked and talked, and by the time we reached the snow machine, Aidan seemed to have forgotten her fear and was eager to get back to the cabin so that she could ski. When she'd first brought up the idea of bringing her skis, I was skeptical, but then she reminded me how hard she had trained over summer even after long days of peeling poles. She promised me that the skis would do more than take up space in the bush plane or lean against the cabin wall, collecting snow.

LATER THAT DAY Edna and I stood on the ice. It was minus 25 degrees, and a north wind rushed down the river valley. Beneath us, the ice croaked, coughed, groaned, and wheezed like a living thing.

I'd just finished hand-drilling the last of five holes, and Edna was putting lures on her makeshift fishing rigs, which were nothing more than pieces of cottonwood wrapped with fishing line. Nearby, Aidan was skiing an oval track that Heimo, on his snow machine, had made for her by pulling me on a sled around the perimeter of the winter runway.

Edna stood over a hole and dropped in a small spinner and five feet of line. "I do it this way," she said, jigging the lure with short tugs so that it bounced off the river's gravel bottom. Twenty seconds later, she pulled up a small Arctic grayling with a shining green and turquoise tail.

Edna slipped the hook out of the fish's mouth, as Aidan called from the winter runway. I excused myself and walked over to her. Her eyelashes were almost frozen shut, and, thanks to the cold and the moisture of her breath, her face mask was nearly solid ice.

"Dad," she said, pulling down the mask to expose her mouth. "I'm not sure about this. It's rocky, and the snow's so cold it's like sandpaper."

"Your call," I said. "But we don't have enough time to make a trail somewhere else, at least not today."

"Aaaahh," she groaned. "I guess I'll keep doing it. Will you wave to me when forty-five minutes is up?"

She took off with a kick but got very little glide. I felt for her. She'd brought her skis so that she could get a jump on her cross-country season, but the conditions were anything but good.

Back on the ice, Edna wasn't having much luck, either. Three small grayling lay at her feet.

"These are for the dog," she said. "Not big enough for us."

As I drilled another hole farther out on the river ice, she joined me. "I grew up fishing with my dad," she said. "He taught me how to trap, too—mostly white fox—and hunt. He raised me with a gun and a trap in my hand. But he loved animals.

"I'm like him," Edna continued. "I trap, but I've always loved animals. People from the city would never understand that."

I cleared my throat to say something but swallowed my question. She was talkative and unguarded in a way I'd rarely experienced and I didn't want to discourage her.

"Trapping," she explained, "is our way of life. It's how people have always lived up here. I'll teach Aidan to be a wilderness woman, too. I'll show her how to hunt and track and trap."

Heimo pulled up on the Arctic Cat as Edna yanked another little grayling from the hole.

"I was looking for caribou downriver," he told us.

Edna looked at me. "We need meat. What we got ain't gonna last, especially with you and Aidan here." Then she trudged off, shaking her head. "Can't even get any good-size grayling."

I checked my watch and waved to Aidan, then helped Edna gather her fishing rigs and wipe off the ice that had thickened on the lines. Heimo picked up the four fish and stuck them in his pocket.

"Barely enough meat on these for Kini," he said.

On the river I'd turned my back to the mountains and the gusts, but as I walked over to Aidan I felt the knife slash of the wind-blown snow. My throat was raw and I worried about how Aidan would feel after nearly an hour of skiing.

"Skiing stunk," she said, still frustrated. "But don't tell Heimo. I know he took time to make the trail for me."

We walked off in the direction of the cabin. When Aidan got among the trees, she took off her hat. I was taken aback. Her hair was white with hoarfrost. I'd been given a glimpse of my daughter as an old woman.

By the time we got back to the cabin yard, her mood had improved. But then she realized that the Arctic oven was as cold as a deep freezer. Just as she was contemplating building a fire, Heimo called out the door, "Supper's ready. Hurry it up."

"Brrr," Aidan said, running past me.

I quickly cut a dozen pieces of kindling, laid the wood inside the tent, and noticed that the sky had not yet gone to stars. Inside the cabin, Aidan was sitting next to the woodstove, cradling a cup of tea that Edna had made for her.

"Your girl was ice-cold," Edna said. "Crazy to ski at twenty-five below. She needs someone to mother her."

"I can't think of anyone better," I replied. "Thank you."

"You know what we're having for supper," Aidan said to me in a dubious tone. "Whale. Have you ever had whale?"

Heimo and Edna broke out in laughter.

Aidan looked at them. "What? What!"

"Not whale," Heimo said, barely able to get the words out. "Seal. We're eating seal."

To Aidan, whale, seal, it didn't make a difference. One was as exotic as the other.

But Edna was still laughing. She cleared her throat enough to speak. "Wait till I tell my relatives in Savoonga. They sent the seal meat. They're gonna love the story."

Then Heimo shouted "whale," and he and Edna began laughing all over again. Aidan and I joined them.

CHAPTER 14

THANKSGIVING

W E WERE LISTENING TO THE weather on the radio. Just a week into our trip and the forecast for the southern foothills of the eastern Brooks Range called for temperatures to climb as high as zero, the result of a strong Chinook wind off the Gulf of Alaska.

"Gonna make the ice dangerous," Heimo said, shutting off the radio. "Never seen anything like it. The week before you and Aidan got here, it was fifty below."

Outside there was enough water dripping from the roof to make ice sheets at the base of the cabin. Inside, Edna was stanching tea-colored leaks with old rags. When she asked Aidan to lend a hand, Aidan was more than glad to put down her physics book.

Before coming up, Aidan had hoped to be able to email, or even Skype, with her teachers, but it hadn't taken her long to figure out that was a pipe dream. To conserve fuel, Heimo ran the generator only every third day for an hour or two in the evening, around 7:00 Alaska time, which correlates to 10:00 p.m. Central Standard Time—too late for Aidan to ask her teachers for help. Plus, the Internet connection was almost nonexistent, especially when there were clouds. This left Aidan teaching herself physics and calculus.

Heimo sat down to massage his moose-hide kamiks to keep them supple. They were his favorite boots, strong, light, and warm. When she couldn't find any more rags, Edna washed her hands and plopped two plump snowshoe hares into the slow cooker.

"Make 'em spicy," Heimo said, and Aidan made a slurping sound. She'd come to love the taste of fat, especially after a day on the trapline, and the rabbits, she knew, would be fat. Although at first she had wrinkled up her nose at the idea of eating seal blubber, the blubbery pieces turned out to be her favorites, as Heimo had said they would. When Heimo was satisfied that he had kneaded the stiffness out of his boots, he got to his feet. "Let's go," he said, pulling on his parka and putting a large hunk of bannock in one of the pockets. Bannock is a bush dweller's staple, much like hardtack biscuits were for sailors, cowboys, and Civil War soldiers. Bannock was introduced to Alaska by Scottish trappers working for the Hudson's Bay Company. Originally, it was an unleavened bread made from oat or barley, but Edna made hers with baking powder, flour, powdered milk, and water.

"Better grab one, too," Heimo said to me, pointing to the bannock in the cast-iron pan. "We're gonna be gone for a while."

Heimo's plan was to check one of his longer traplines, a trip that would take us three hours to the west over two drainages. When Heimo went out to prepare the Arctic Cat and sled for our trip, Edna followed him. I stayed inside with Aidan to remind her about the ice. She and Edna were going downriver, and I wanted her to be extra careful.

The night before, while lying in our cots, we'd discussed overflow and safety on the river. Even in winter, water flows beneath the river ice. Sometimes, it runs so hard that it builds and backs up until it finds a seam, a crack, or a break in the ice. When it does, it rushes to the surface as overflow and freezes again, though often not completely. If it gets covered with snow, the snow acts as an insulator, and much of the water underneath remains liquid. Even accomplished Alaskan woodsmen are afraid of overflow. They can distinguish it by its cloudy, yellowish brown color, but sometimes it can still surprise them. If you're far from the cabin and mistake it for solid ice, and fall in, your only choice is to build a fire or freeze to death.

"Keep an eye on Edna," I told Aidan. "She'll let you know what's safe and what isn't."

I gave Aidan a hug and wished her luck.

"You be careful, too, Dad," she said.

When I walked outside, Edna was saying good-bye to Heimo. "Be safe," she said, kissing him. "And if you see a caribou, bring home some meat for us."

I sat down in the back of the sled and Heimo slowly pulled out of the cabin yard. When he headed directly west, instead of wrapping around and going north up the river, I was relieved. I didn't like being in the sled on questionable ice.

Heimo picked his way through a dense spruce forest, leaning and dipping from one side to another, like a barrel racer at a rodeo. Every now and then he hit a limb weighted down with snow. He always escaped the avalanche, but I was not so lucky. I cursed him mightily whenever the snow spilled down on me, but because he had earplugs in, I was left shouting in the wind.

After a bone-rattling two-hour ride, we rose above the tree line. Heimo shut off the snow machine, pulled out his earplugs, and turned around on his seat. He didn't utter a word, but I knew the look. It was as if he was saying, "Beat that. Tell me there's anything in the world more beautiful."

To the north, high, whispery white clouds floated over Bear Mountain, and the whole river valley was awash in a rose-colored light that seemed too delicate to be real. The wind was doldrums quiet, and we sat in silence for a minute or two before Heimo hit the starter switch. We were off, but not for long. The north winds had battered the mountain, obliterating his trail with snow. Now, it was my job to break a path through the hard-crusted snow, while Heimo followed on the snow machine.

I jumped from the sled and started out strong, but after a hundred meters I was barely able to lift my legs. The snow was nearly hip-deep.

"C'mon," Heimo shouted. "Just a little bit farther."

Heimo followed me until we reached the end of the meadow, where the land dipped into the trees and the next drainage, and his trail was largely clear of drifted snow.

It took almost an hour on the winding trail to get halfway down the mountain. We picked our way slowly through the trees as the trail grew steeper. At one point, the Arctic Cat felt like it was going to roll and I stuck out my foot to push off against a small tree. For a moment we were suspended in midtip, and my foot was jammed in the machine's Kevlar track. As I struggled to get it out, I saw Heimo reach for the throttle.

"Wait!" I yelled. "My foot."

Heimo jerked his hand back. "Jesus Christ," he gasped, "I was going to gun it. That track would have ripped your foot right off, easy, and I couldn't have did jackshit to save you." He paused to inspect the track. "Can you imagine me having to call up Elizabeth or your mom and dad and give 'em the news?"

"You would have had to leave me here bleeding to death while you checked the rest of your traps," I said.

"Hell, yeah," he responded. "No sense in wasting a day."

We continued down the trail, slower than ever. In the last two hours, I hadn't noticed one sign of life, not even the sound of a distant raven. Finally, as a thicket of head-high black spruce trees gave way to a small field, I saw some tracks.

"Marten?" I asked.

"Yup," he said. "See that? He's chasing a bunny. My first set is a quarter of a mile from here. Maybe we got him."

I looked down the trail at the featureless forest, which stretched for hundreds of miles in every direction, and wondered how Heimo had any idea where his traps were. If pressed I could find my way back to the cabin, but I could not have located even one trap in this landscape of white and green.

"How do you find your sets?" I asked. "You have a mental map?"

"No," he said. "It's just, what would the word be—intuition?"

We moved farther down the mountain, and Heimo checked eight pole sets, all of which ended up empty. He came to a stop at a fork in the trail.

"Stay here," he said. "I have two more sets down the west fork. I'll be back in ten minutes or so. I'll leave you the axe so you can build me a pole set."

And he was gone. As I looked for a tree near his trail, I spotted the perfect spruce and whacked it with the axe. I limbed it and then set out to build Heimo a pole set. Minutes later, as I was wrapping the chain of the trap around the pole, I looked up—a sixth sense, perhaps—and spotted movement in the trees in a valley to the near north. Suddenly I felt the surge of stress hormones flooding my body. Though I couldn't make out a form, whatever was down there was brown and big. Despite all my reassuring talk with Elizabeth about grizzly density in the Arctic—approximately two bears for every fifty square miles—and my calm dismissal of Aidan's fears of a winter bear, I felt it again, the same as I had experienced on the river in summer when I spotted the circling ravens: fear.

The slight wind was out of the north, so whatever large animal was down there wouldn't pick up my scent. I told myself that as long as I kept still and quiet, I'd be okay. For the next five minutes I didn't take my eyes off of it; it moved little. Then, in the distance, I heard the Arctic Cat approaching. The animal did, too. It appeared from behind the trees and walked slowly and lankily north, high-stepping through the snow. I could see it now—not a winter grizzly, but a moose, not one, but two. From where I was, they looked huge, as big as a well-stacked woodpile, and perhaps seven feet at the withers, near the base of the neck, with horns nearly as wide as one of the small spruce trees was tall. They stopped for a moment to browse and then they walked across a lowland meadow in the direction of a stand of willows.

Heimo spotted them when he pulled up. "Get on," he said, and we headed for the valley.

At a hundred feet from the moose, he stopped. "I almost lost my head," he said. "We need meat so bad, I was ready to shoot an old bull. Plus, the season ain't even open."

It was true, when Heimo caught sight of the moose, I saw that he had nothing but meat on his mind. But about the last thing he and Edna wanted was a rutted-out bull without an ounce of fat on him that had been bawling for cows and rolling in his own piss. He and Edna would be eating gamy boot leather for a whole winter.

We got off the snow machine and walked closer.

"Be careful," he said. "If they charge us, dive behind a tree."

I immediately looked for the closest tree with a trunk thicker than the handle of a hammer. I chose one about twenty-five feet away and wondered if I could get to it before a charging moose could get to me.

"Look at the left horn on the far one," Heimo said. "Must have broke it off fightin' for a cow."

I held an imaginary rifle to my shoulder and looked down the barrel through the iron sights.

"You could take 'em easy," Heimo said. "We could butcher him in thirty minutes, but we'd have a helluva time gettin' him back home."

The moose seemed indifferent to our presence, and we watched them for another five minutes. Slowly they melted into the woods. "Next week, the December [rural resident] season opens," Heimo reminded me. "Then we'll really be looking to hunt."

HAVING HEARD US coming, Edna and Aidan were outside waiting when we pulled into the cabin yard that evening.

"You look pretty," I said to Aidan as Heimo shut off the Arctic Cat. "She does look pretty, doesn't she?" Edna agreed.

Aidan brightened. "Edna and I washed our hair today. She brushed and braided mine and she made me these." Aidan pushed her hair back to show me a pair of earrings that Edna had made her from walrus ivory.

"The earrings are beautiful," I said.

Edna smiled almost shyly. Then she turned to Heimo. "We were getting worried about you two."

"About what, Mom?" Heimo asked.

"I was starting to think maybe you broke down," Edna told him. Then she looked at the empty sled. "No caribou?"

"Nope," Heimo said. "But we did see two old bull moose. I'll tell you about it at suppertime. Jimmer and I gotta go get water."

On the way to the spring, Heimo was practically running. "Bunnies tonight," he said. "Mmmm-mmmm."

When we got back to the cabin, Heimo recorded our catch for the day—0—on a calendar and entered 0 into his trapping logbook. The logbook went back decades, and allowed him each October to plot his trapping strategy for the upcoming year and to assess its success each spring, when the season ended.

"I think Aidan is my good-luck charm," he said, closing the book. "Tomorrow I'm taking her with me."

"Not tomorrow," Edna said without looking up. She was inspecting a sealskin, which she hoped to tan and make into a vest. "Nope, tomorrow's Thanksgiving."

"Ahhh, I almost forgot," Heimo grumbled.

I knew Heimo wouldn't take more than a few bites of domesticated meat. He'd eat vegetables and leftover bunny while we dined on the store-bought turkey, ham, and pumpkin pie that we'd brought in, per Edna's request, from Fairbanks. Thanksgiving was Edna's tradition, one she'd begun decades before, when Rhonda and Krin were little girls. A family friend from Circle, a small community more than a hundred miles to the south, had decided he'd fly in dinner for the Korths one Thanksgiving Day. It was a trip he continued to make, reliably delivering the goodies each year for Edna's fete. This year, it was our turn.

By late morning on Thanksgiving Day the cabin yard smelled of food. Edna heard us outside and poked her head out the door. Dinner, she said, would be ready by 4:00 p.m. Aidan and I were already hungry. Since breakfast, we had hauled water from the spring, cut wood, cleaned the stovepipe, and gone down to the river with our binoculars to glass Mummuck Mountain for caribou.

When we walked inside the cabin, we almost bumped into Heimo, who was working on the wolverine he'd caught. He was dressed in a plastic butcher's apron and wore latex gloves. Skinning an animal and fleshing it, the act of removing the fat and muscle from the skin, can be a messy job, and he was mad because this one had fleas. Periodic infestations are one of the drawbacks of living in a trapping cabin.

Heimo made a few last knife strokes, and some fat shavings fell on the pile at his feet. I smelled the sharp odor of fur and flesh. He made a small cut on each ear and turned them inside out. Then, using pushpins, he tacked the fur skin-side out onto a five-foot stretching board shaped like the head of a spear. I helped him lift the board onto a hook suspended from one of the ceiling logs. There were a few drops of blood on the floor, which Heimo used an old rag to wipe up.

"Watch out for it when you come and go," he told Aidan, who had a look on her face somewhere between curiosity and disgust. "It has to dry for a few days like that. Then it has to hang for a while fur-side out."

Heimo winked at me, as if to say, "Pay attention." Then he said to Aidan, "Next, I'm going to skin out and flesh a mink. I use the tibia bone of a moose to flesh it. Maybe you wanna give me a hand, huh?"

Edna chimed in, unaware that Heimo was baiting Aidan. "You'll be a real wilderness girl, if you do that."

Heimo watched Aidan squirm. He let her suffer and then mercifully he gave her an out. "Or would you rather go down to the river and sight in my 22.250 with your old man?"

"I don't know," Aidan answered. She appealed to me. "Dad, what do you think?"

When I told her that I could use her help, she looked at me with relief and gratitude. On the way to the river, she said, "Thanks, Dad. I didn't want anything to do with that mink. They stink so bad, and I can't even shower up here. I couldn't stand the thought of having that smell on me."

When we reached the winter runway and searched for a place to shoot, Aidan spotted a twelve-inch-by-twelve-inch bare area of dirt on the snowy bank across the river. "What do you think, Dad? Is that about right for a target? Heimo wants it zeroed in at a hundred yards."

To my surprise, Aidan seemed excited by the prospect of sighting in the rifle. There was a time when she handled all guns as if they were poisonous snakes. Our shooting sessions usually ended with her stomping away and calling me "impatient." These might have been the only times in my life when I wished that I'd had boys, or at least one boy, instead of girls. Most boys naturally gravitate to guns. It's not that I want her to become a shooter or a gun lover. But my fondest boyhood memories are of hunting with my father and uncles, and I simply hoped that she would learn how to handle a gun safely and responsibly so that occasionally she could hunt with me.

She wanted me to take the first shot, while she watched through the binoculars.

"Low and to the right," she said, after I pulled the trigger.

I ejected the shell and showed her how to use a dime to make the elevation and horizontal adjustments on the scope, one click at a time. By the time we got to the fourth elevation click, and our fourth shot, I knew that the rifle was close to being zeroed in, and asked Aidan if she wanted to take the telltale shot.

When I gave her the rifle, she stood with her hips slightly forward, left elbow resting against her body, feet about twenty inches apart with her back foot at a 90-degree angle to the target, and the front foot turned a tad in the direction she was shooting. She adjusted her weight and pulled the trigger.

"Try another," I told her. "You jerked on that one."

She went through the same motions, but this time I saw her take a breath and pull the trigger only as she exhaled.

"Almost," I said. "Just a little low."

I could see that she hadn't braced her elbow against her side and knew that the rifle likely felt heavy. But I didn't dare to correct her and ruin the moment.

"A few more?" she asked.

"Sure," I said, "as long as you want."

I watched her closely. She pulled back the bolt and ejected the round, put a new one in the breech, pushed the bolt forward, and closed it. Then she tucked her elbow in tight and narrowed her stance. Seconds later—*craaack!*

With the binoculars I could see the sand and dirt pop. "Dead-on!" I shouted. "Excellent."

She shot twice more and then we heard Edna's voice behind us. Edna had been making her daily rounds, scanning the river and the bald hilltops with her binoculars, searching for a moose or caribou like a farmer, watching the sky, waiting for rain.

"I'll teach you how to shoot from the knee," Edna said, walking up to us. "That's how I like to do it."

I left Aidan with Edna and walked back to the cabin. By 4:00 p.m. sharp we were all seated, Heimo and Edna at the table, Aidan and me sitting on our buckets, holding our plates in our laps, licking our lips, ready to dig in to organic (though farm-raised) turkey, ham, potatoes and gravy, green beans, and a salad, all brought in from Fairbanks for the occasion.

"To your first Thanksgiving in the bush," Heimo said, raising his water bottle. "Dig in!" And then he added, "I'd rather have bunnies any day."

I WAS SOUND asleep when Heimo's voice startled me. *Winter bear,* I thought. *There's a bear in the cabin yard.* My heart racing, I jumped out of my cot. Then I heard Heimo's scratchy whisper: "Get out here. You gotta see these northern lights."

Seconds later I was outside, looking up. Rivers of green light whirled and shimmered across the night sky. I stood there watching, so immersed in the moment that I forgot about Aidan.

"I came out to pee and looked up," Heimo said, breaking my trance. "Incredible, huh."

"Aidan," I said loudly. "Come look."

"Whaaat, whaaat," she answered, mostly asleep.

"Get out here and look at the sky," I said again.

She stumbled out of the tent. It was 3:00 a.m. and Heimo had already gone back inside the cabin.

Aidan rubbed her eyes and looked up. "That's so beautiful."

Her voice had a serene quality. "Beautiful," she said again, and then she walked back into the tent without saying another word. I heard her crawl into her sleeping bags and zip them up.

"Good night, Aidan," I said.

"Good night, Daddy. Good night, Heimo."

CHAPTER 15

THE LIFE THEY LOVE

THE THERMOMETER THIS morning read 36 below, but Heimo was still worried. A warm-up is always dangerous, but the last one, because it was so dramatic, had created numerous leads and holes in the ice. Heimo pointed them out as we followed the riverbank north. The flat, gray light didn't help. It distorted depth perception, making it hard for him to identify the trouble spots.

Fifteen miles up, he stopped the snow machine. "You check the ice over there, and I'll check it over here," he said. "Make sure to shuffle your feet. And be real careful near the bank. If you go through, the current will suck you right under the ice. You're a goner then."

I needed to be attentive, but my mind kept turning to Aidan. It was the first day of moose season, and she and Edna were planning to hunt along the river ice.

I was halfway across when I heard Heimo yell, "Shit!" I saw him jump back. He was waving to me and shouting. I couldn't make out what he was saying, but there was something in his voice. I didn't know whether to move forward or go back. All my worrying about Aidan, and here I was stranded on the river ice too scared to take a step.

When I saw Heimo move in the direction of the snow machine, I decided that I needed to retrace my steps, too. I was in the middle of the river, halfway back to the bank, when I heard Heimo yell, "Bad!"

I felt like I'd just gripped an electric fence. I stood as still as I could, wondering if the whole sheet of river ice was suddenly going to drop out from under me.

Heimo was screaming now and gesticulating. "Stay!" he shouted. "Don't move!"

I watched as he shuffled his feet and made his way over to me. He was moving slower than I'd ever seen him, testing the ice as he approached. When he got to me, he said, "Grab the back of my coat and follow me."

I did as instructed, and, when we finally made it to the riverbank, he blew out the breath he'd been holding. "Shit," he said. "That was close. There was nothin' but overflow with a thin layer of ice underneath. If you would've fell through, we never woulda found your body."

We got back on the Arctic Cat and moved north, stopping periodically to inspect the ice. Three miles up, Heimo cut the engine. "We gotta cross soon," he said, "or we ain't gonna be able to. You stay here. I'll check it out."

Heimo zigzagged to the far bank and then walked a straight line back. "Ice is better here," he said, "but I ain't gonna take any chances. I'm going to gun it across. You'll have to hold on."

I grasped Heimo's parka as tightly as I could. When we hit the bank and dipped down, Heimo cranked on the throttle and we whipped across the river. At one point we hit a patch of pale-green overflow slush and I was pelted by tiny shards of ice. Heimo stopped on the far bank.

"You get hit?" he asked.

My face felt like I had rolled in a patch of stinging nettles.

"Sorry about that," he said. "The windshield saved me."

If Heimo was worried about me, his concern didn't last long. He had lots of traps to check, and we'd lost valuable time trying to cross the river.

We traveled up a narrow creek bed. The banks were steep, and I was bending and shifting my weight. On an especially treacherous bank, Heimo and I leaned as far out as we could to counter the tilt of the machine. Still, it began to roll, slow-motion style. When it reached the tipping point, Heimo hit the kill switch, pushed himself away, and ended up waist-deep in a drift. I wasn't so lucky. The bulky Arctic Cat landed on top of me. Heimo grabbed me under the arms and, after a few minutes, managed to pull me away.

"You're a heavy son of a bitch," he said when I was finally out from under the machine.

Our troubles had just begun. Before we could go anywhere, we needed to get the Arctic Cat upright. We leaned in with our shoulders and lay on our backs, pushing with our legs. Nothing seemed to work.

"Shiiiiit!" Heimo said. "I never should have bought that stupid, heavy snow machine. We coulda pushed my old one out easy."

We spent the next ten minutes shedding our parkas and outer layers as we tried to right the machine. At 40 below, I was dressed, above the belt, in a single layer of polyester and a fleece pullover. When we finally got the Arctic Cat back up, we knew the engine would be flooded so we didn't waste our time trying to start it. First, we'd have to pull the spark plugs and dry them off.

"I'm hungry," Heimo said. "Might as well eat."

He broke the bannock in half with his bare hands, his fingers large and swollen from decades of freezing and thawing, and handed me a sizable piece. If he'd been upset, now he seemed entirely relaxed, as if we'd had a banner day. What I called hardship was for him nothing more than the usual stuff of life. While we rested and ate, the orange light of the sun, which sat just below the horizon, filled the valley.

After a while, Heimo rocked himself off the snow machine and pulled out his tool bag. Getting to the spark plugs wasn't easy; we had to take off the side panels and then the cowling. At these temperatures the plastic pieces didn't have any bend in them, and our fingers hardly worked, either. Heimo dropped the socket wrench in the snow three times and had to dig for it. On the third time, his hands were so cold he asked me to search for it. I plunged my arm in up to my elbow. I could hardly feel anything, much less a cold piece of steel. But my hand touched something and I closed my fingers. When I pulled up, the wrench hung loosely from my pinkie.

Heimo poked his head into the engine, maneuvered the wrench inside, loosened the first plug, and handed it to me. I could smell the fuel on it. I dried it in my handkerchief and then held it in my bare hand. I dried the others, and Heimo placed them back in. After we put on the hood, he stood over the start cord.

"If you're gonna say a prayer, now's the time," he said.

He pulled, and the Arctic Cat responded with a robust rumble and then conked out. He tried again and got another encouraging rumble. On his third attempt, the engine turned over.

Aidan at home testing out her backpack. *Elizabeth Campbell*

Heimo and I preparing to build the gables. *The James Campbell Collection*

Aidan and I in front of the almost completed cabin. *The James Campbell Collection*

Arriving on the Coleen in November 2013. *The James Campbell Collection*

Aidan in front of our home-away-from-home, the Arctic oven. *The James Campbell Collection*

Heimo on the trapline. *The James Campbell Collection*

Aidan on Denali's Ruth Glacier. *Aidan Campbell*

Butchering the caribou. *The James Campbell Collection*

Aidan fixing supper, a day's paddle north of the gorge. *Chris Jones*

Lining the worst section of the gorge. *Chris Jones*

Aidan at camp #3 on the East Fork Chandalar River. *The James Campbell Collection*

Me trudging toward Guilbeau. *Aidan Campbell*

Dave and Chris on a crag overlooking the Hulahula. *Dave Musgrave*

A polar bear on Arey Island. *Aidan Campbell*

Group photo in front of a windbreak on Arey Island. *Dave Musgrave*

A rare warm and sunny day near the headwaters of the Hulahula. *Chris Jones*

The riverbed snaked back and forth as we continued toward the refuge's wilderness boundary. At nearly 68 degrees latitude, well above the theoretical line called the Arctic Circle, this is the northern limit of the world's forests. To the south, the trees grew bigger—balsam poplar, referred to as cottonwood, and stands of white spruce that reach up the waterways like God's fingers. But, here, the only trees were centuries-old black spruces and head-high willows and alders with trunks no thicker than the shaft of a canoe paddle.

Half a mile later, we reached the white, windswept tundra.

"I wanted you to see this," Heimo said.

I pulled down my frozen face mask, felt the twinges of frostbite on my face, and looked north. The wind was so cold that the skin on my face felt as if it was being torn by a dull axe. But I could not take my eyes off the tundra or the bare, treeless peaks that rose behind it, gleaming and white.

"This is where I want Edna to put my body, if I go first," Heimo said, staring north, his forehead, face, and neck completely exposed. "Those are my funeral plans."

Heimo had mentioned this place before, but I'd never seen it. Now, I imagined what the scene might look like, his body lying on the wild, windblown tundra. Wolves would likely find his carcass first, and they would tear away at his flesh. Perhaps an Arctic fox would strip his bones clean. Then maybe a wandering raven would find a few scraps that the wolves and fox had left behind.

"It's a good place to be dead," I said.

BY THE TIME we made it halfway back to the cabin, we'd reset and rebaited over two dozen traps, including two wolf sets, which

Heimo prepared with great care. Trapping is a battle of wits that the animal often wins, especially if it's a wolf.

We were moving slowly in the day's last light, watching the river ice for overflow and weak spots. As we came down off the top of a hill, the Coleen River valley spread out below us. The stooped, snow-covered black spruce trees looked like weary, white-robed pilgrims worshiping December's new moon.

We finally pulled into the cabin yard as the evening's first planets appeared. I was cold, bone-wearingly tired, and glad to be back. I wondered how many times Heimo had experienced the exact same emotion—returning, achy and exhausted, but overjoyed by the smell of woodsmoke, flowing blue-white from the stovepipe, and the sight of the cabin, tucked in the trees.

Aidan and Edna hadn't come out to greet us; it was too cold. Inside, Aidan was sitting next to the woodstove studying physics, popping salmon eggs like Jujyfruits, and, oddly, still wearing earmuffs. Edna was sitting on the sleeping platform with a headlamp on, sewing lynx fur onto an Eskimo slipper. The Fort Yukon station was playing Athabaskan fiddle music.

"She got frostbite," Edna said about Aidan's ears. "The bottoms were white. They might blister. We had warm compresses on them."

Gently I lifted the earmuffs and saw that underneath the skin on her ears was raw and fire red. I touched one and she jumped.

"They're so tender," she said.

Heimo took a quick look. "That don't look too bad," he said. "I've seen a person's skin turn black and fall off before."

"Don't say that, Heim," Edna scolded him. "You're gonna scare her."

"Okay," Heimo said. "Sorry. What's for supper?"

"Caribou steaks," Edna answered. "Aidan cut them with the bow saw. But that's the end of our caribou meat."

"Don't worry, Mom," Heimo said. "We've always been able to find food."

Ten minutes later, we were wolfing down our meals of caribou steak, brown rice and gravy, and bannock. After a long, cold day on the trapline, I was as hungry as I'd ever been. Apparently Aidan was, too. She finished her steak, chewed the gristle off the bone, and then opened her knife and used the blade to winnow out the marrow. Edna was clearly pleased.

"If we get a caribou, I wanna see you eat the organs."

Aidan didn't say a word.

"Them organs, they're what's really good for you," Heimo interjected. Then he launched into a speech on the benefits of eating grass-fed protein. Though he'd barely made it through high school, he sounded like a college biology professor, talking about rumination and how the caribou's four stomachs help unlock the energy of the grass and lichens it consumes. He explained to Aidan that eating the lean, protein-packed meat of the caribou is like tasting a piece of the Arctic.

When he finished, he announced that we had snowshoe hares to clean. I rose from my chair like an arthritic old dairy farmer struggling to reach the barn.

"You okay?" Heimo asked.

"Just tweaked my back a little today wrestling with that damn machine," I told him.

Once outside, Heimo picked up one bunny and I grabbed the other.

"Keep the guts and the hide," he reminded me. "I'll use 'em as bait."

When I finished, I wiped the blood from my hands in the snowbank and walked inside the cabin. The kettle was singing on the stove. Edna poured two cups of tea and handed one to Aidan.

"I should be taking care of you," Aidan said.

Heimo stepped into the cabin. "Why's that?" he asked, overhearing Aidan.

"No big deal," Edna said. "I fell in today and got a little wet."

"Upriver?" Heimo asked.

Edna nodded.

"You gotta watch out up there, Mom," Heimo warned her.

"I was cold when I got home," Edna said. "But not as bad as Aidan."

Edna sipped her tea and then pulled out the sheet of plywood from behind the parkas.

"Ready for some Sheepshead?" she asked.

"Not again," Heimo protested.

Aidan's eyes lit up. If anything was going to take her mind off her frostbitten ears, it was cards. It had become something of a nightly ritual. After supper, we let the cast-iron pots soak, and we played Sheepshead, or *Schafskopf,* a card game that originated in Central Europe and was brought to Wisconsin by German immigrants.

We played a few hands and quit early to scrub the pots and pans. When the dishes were done, I excused myself to check on the fire in our tent. Outside, the Little Dipper, Ursa Minor, burned brilliantly in a clear, coal-black sky. I followed its handle to its brightest star, Polaris, the North Star, which had helped orient Arctic explorers for hundreds of years. Inside the tent, I finished stoking the fire just as Aidan entered.

"My ears really hurt, Dad," she said.

I turned my headlamp to its brightest setting and inspected them.

"You got frostbite, all right," I told her. "They'll be okay, but now that they've thawed out, they're going to hurt for a while."

"I'm going to put Vaseline on them," Aidan said. "Will you wait with me while I do that?" As we sat there, Aidan recounted her day.

Edna had slung her .30-30 over her shoulder and announced that they would spend the morning hunting. They walked slowly downriver along the east bank. The breeze had stilled and they stopped periodically and listened for the sound of a moose browsing among the thick willows. Edna told Aidan she liked it best when there was a wind because she could track and stalk and get in close enough for a kill shot without a moose hearing her. But calm days could be good, too, she said. Sometimes it was so quiet she could hear a moose chomping on the willow branches.

A mile down, just past the old cabin, they turned back north and skirted the river's west bank. Three hundred yards up, Edna spotted a set of tracks, but she couldn't tell how fresh they were. She whispered to Aidan that it was likely a cow and a calf, or maybe two young bulls. Then she told Aidan to be alert. If a cow with a calf was nearby, and it sensed danger, it might attack and try to trample them both.

As they followed the tracks into the willows, ducking under low-hanging branches and crawling through narrow openings on their hands and knees, Aidan could feel her heart pounding. She tried to stay as close to Edna as she could. The last thing she wanted was to get separated. The willows got more and more tangled, so she and Edna retreated toward the river. At first, Aidan was disoriented and wondered if they were going in the right direction. Then she imagined what it would be like if she were alone. Could she find the cabin on her own?

When they reached the edge of the river, they stopped again until they grew cold. Edna said that they had to keep moving. In the Arctic moving is what keeps you alive.

Half a mile upriver, they crossed the ice to check Edna's bunny snares along a frozen feeder creek. Snowshoe hare tracks criss-crossed the creek bed, and Edna was sure she'd caught at least one. Aidan heard a sound. It was like a baby crying.

"That's a rabbit in a snare," Edna told her.

"It sounds so sad," Aidan said. Edna confessed that she didn't like it, either.

Aidan followed the cry, pulled back the branches of a bush, and saw a snowshoe hare with a noose of thin, No. 3 picture wire around its neck. It huddled in the snow as if trying to hide from a prowling marten or lynx. Edna knelt next to Aidan and pulled the picture wire tighter. "Suffocates the bunny," she said. "If it was a marten, I'd squeeze it to stop the heart."

For a moment the rabbit struggled, and then it went limp. Edna loosened the noose, pulled out the bunny, and gave it to Aidan, who held it by its back legs. As they walked up the creek to check the other snares, it swung back and forth in her hand.

Edna was upset when the other snares turned up empty. All those tracks and only one rabbit. Without a moose or a caribou, they would have to depend on fish and rabbits for food. And one snowshoe hare a day wasn't going to cut it.

Before leaving the creek bed, Edna and Aidan reset the guide sticks that steered the rabbits into the wire noose. They walked north again, past the cabin, to the foot of what Heimo and Edna called Guroy Mountain, a fat, rounded ridge that looked like the back of a bear. Years ago, they had placed a cross here for their daughter Coleen. *Guroy*, Edna told Aidan, meant "Piggy" in Siberian Yupik, her native language. It was the nickname that she and Heimo had given Coleen, because of the way she ate, with so much zest. Edna wiped at her eyes with the sleeve of her coat and admitted that even after three-plus decades, the memory still haunted her. Then Edna turned her back to the mountain.

"Let's go find meat."

They spent the next hour looking for moose tracks, but then Edna decided their time would be better spent doing chores around the cabin. They followed a slough back downriver. In the distance Edna spotted a bird perched on a high branch of a tree.

"Maybe a great gray owl," she said.

She told Aidan how her father had healing powers and how he took in injured animals and nursed them back to health. Once he adopted an owl with a broken wing. He put on a splint and fed the bird for weeks. Everyone in the village said he was crazy. Then, one day, he turned it loose, and the owl could fly. Its wing had mended. The bird was so grateful and so devoted to him that it flew above him everywhere he went.

Halfway back to the cabin they needed to cross a narrow section of the slough, where, because of the springs, there was still open water. They searched for a thick tree branch that they could use to walk across. Edna went first, using another branch to help her balance. When she slipped off, Aidan's first inclination was to rush out to her, but Edna told her to stay put. There was no sense in both of them getting wet.

The mud was deeper than the water, and Edna had a difficult time getting to the bank. When she did, Aidan helped to pull her out. Edna rubbed snow on her pants to soak up the water before it froze. Seeing her shivering, Aidan understood the true importance of Edna's earlier advice to keep moving and to get back to the cabin as fast as possible. To be wet at minus 36 degrees was dangerous. It was the kind of cold that could freeze the life out of a person.

By the time they started for the cabin, Edna's boots were like blocks of ice, heavy and slippery. Because it was hard for her to walk and carry the .30-30, too, she gave the rifle to Aidan, who slipped the sling across her shoulders.

"If we see something," Edna said, "you might have to take the shot."

When they reached the cabin, Edna wasted no time getting inside. While Aidan gathered wood, Edna sat as close to the stove as she could. She tried to remove her boots, but they wouldn't budge; they were frozen to her feet.

Aidan put two logs in the stove, adjusted the damper, pulled a chair next to Edna, and held her hands in hers. They were a man's hands, she thought. Hard, leathery, and accustomed to work. Then Aidan pulled off her hat and Edna saw her ears. Aidan hadn't noticed them going numb in the cold.

Having smothered her ears in Vaseline, Aidan was now ready to go back to the cabin to say good night to Heimo and Edna. I told her that I'd join her after checking the temperature.

At the far side of the cabin, there was enough light for me to see the thermometer without using my headlamp. It read 34 below. Kini lay curled up in the snow, her nose tucked under her tail. I knelt beside her. She was an outside guard dog disdainful of the cozy cabin. I petted her until I grew cold. As I walked toward the cabin I heard Eskimo music. Inside, the yellow glow of the lantern filled the room and Heimo and Edna were doing a traditional St. Lawrence Island dance. Mimicking the swelling and cresting of waves, Edna moved her arms in fluid arcs and Aidan joined her, while Heimo simulated thrusting his spear into a walrus. With each lunge, I heard him grunt.

In 2002, thirty miles east of here, near the Korths' cabin on the Old Crow, I first saw Heimo and Edna dance. I was delighted and joined Heimo, crouching like a wrestler and digging my imaginary spear into a three-thousand-pound walrus. In my excitement, I stomped a hole in the plywood floor, a faux pas that the family still talks about.

Over a decade had passed since that first visit. Rhonda and Krin were gone, building families of their own, harboring vague dreams of one day returning to the bush. Heimo was nearing sixty. His beard had gone gray. Though still strong, he felt the accumulated aches and pains that are the results of living such a raw, physical life. Edna, too, had slowed. Her back was shot and her eyes had begun to fail her. But they were still here, determined to live the life they loved, and sometimes to dance on a cold Arctic evening when stars filled the sky.

CHAPTER 16

WILDERNESS GIRL

I WOKE IN THE MIDDLE OF the night, turned on my headlamp, and pointed it at my watch: 2:00 a.m. The fire was out and the tent was cold and my back was spasming. I needed to relight the fire, but couldn't move.

"Aidan," I said. "Aidan."

She woke with a start. "What, Daddy? What?"

"The fire's out."

Aidan was sitting now with her feet on the floor of the tent, but she couldn't shake the sleep.

"I need your help," I said.

"What's wrong?"

"I need you to start the fire," I told her. "My back is screwed up."

"I'll get you some ibuprofen," she said, growing more clear-headed. "And then I'll get the fire going again."

She handed me three pills and the bottle of water she kept in her sleeping bag so it wouldn't freeze.

I could barely prop myself up on my elbow; the water trickled out of the side of my mouth and onto the floor of the tent. Aidan wiped it up and then stripped paper for the fire and opened the damper on the pipe and the vents on the stove. A minute later she had a small fire going. The tent warmed and I waited for the ibuprofen to take the edge off the pain. If I lay on my back without moving, I could avoid the muscle spasms that shot from my torso to my shoulders.

It was 6:30 when I heard Heimo outside the tent. "How's she going der, Jimmer?" he said, putting on a thick Wisconsin accent. "Today's the day. We're gonna go downriver and hunt hard for caribou."

I mentioned nothing to him about my back. When he left, I talked to Aidan, as I did each morning, to wake her. It took a full five minutes before she was lucid.

"How are you feeling, Dad?" were the first words out of her mouth.

"I don't know," I told her. "I haven't tried to sit up yet." Then I rocked forward and my back seized up.

"Oh, Dad," she said. "I'm worried about you." She handed me three more ibuprofens, put another log on the fire, and went to the cabin. She returned with a cup of coffee and a piece of bannock.

"What else can I get you?"

"A younger body." I grimaced as another spasm hit me. I threw my head back and clenched my teeth.

"You're not thinking of trying to hunt with us, are you?" she asked. "That wouldn't be smart."

"I don't know," I grumbled.

By the time I finished my coffee and bannock, the ibuprofen had taken effect and I was determined to walk to the cabin. Aidan offered her shoulder. Edna watched us from the window, and, by the time we got to the cabin door, Heimo was waiting.

"What in the hell?"

"I must have hurt it yesterday," I offered.

"Shit," he said, genuinely concerned. "Stupid snow machine. I don't think I could have got it out without you."

He held the door open for me. I stooped as low as I could and bumped my head on the frame.

"Shit," I said. "I can't bend."

Edna watched me try to duck into the cabin. "We're gonna have to leave you behind," she said, shaking her head. "We gotta get meat today, and you'll slow us down."

Though I may not have appreciated Edna's bluntness, her words underscored the reality of living in a place like Arctic Alaska. One hundred and fifty years ago, if I had been a member of a small wandering band of Gwich'in hunters, I would have been left behind to die. Modern times are gentler, but the fact remains: I'd be nothing but deadweight on a hunt, a liability to all, and a danger to myself.

After a breakfast of oatmeal and cranberries, Heimo announced that they would leave in thirty minutes.

"It's gonna be cold," he told Aidan. "Thirty-five, forty below, so dress warm and pack along some extra clothes."

There was something about Heimo's tone that made Aidan anxious. She jutted out her chin as if to say, *I can do this,* but her eyes gave her away; they'd lost their sparkle. When I saw that, my protective instincts kicked in. I struggled out of my camping chair and told her that I'd join her in the tent to help her pick out gear for the day. I glanced at Heimo, and he gave me a scolding look as if to say, "Let her go; she can dress herself." I stopped for a second, wondering if I should explain myself. But I kept moving. Yes, Aidan was here to learn self-sufficiency and independence, but 35 below was nothing to fool with.

Back in the tent, Aidan had layered up and stuffed her day pack with extra clothes. "What do you think, Dad?"

I took her scarf and wrapped it around her neck and face.

"I'm not in kindergarten anymore," she said.

"I know," I told her. "But you don't understand how cold it's going to be, especially in that sled."

On the way downriver, Aidan would be sitting in the sled for at least an hour or two, contending with the cold made even colder by windchill. Thirty-five below with a ten-mile-per-hour wind feels like minus 59. At fifteen miles per hour, it feels like minus 64. After nearly four decades Heimo and Edna had grown somewhat used to the cold, but, like most humans, Aidan was not designed for polar winters. Modern technology could provide her with the best cold-weather clothes designed to trap warm air close to the body, but evolution had equipped her only minimally. Quivering muscles and chattering teeth were poor defense mechanisms, and the body's main responsibility is a stark one: to keep the core warm at all costs, constricting blood supply to one's limbs, even if that means sacrificing them.

We exited the tent, and I noticed that Heimo was using a camp stove to heat the Arctic Cat's engine, the gas, and the oil pan. At these temperatures, the oil was as gummy as sweet sorghum syrup.

Edna appeared from the cabin with her moose-hide kamiks. "These will keep your feet warm," she said, handing them to Aidan. Then she walked over to me and gave me my kitchen instructions. My job was to make the bannock and to stir the broth that the specklebelly geese were soaking in.

"If Aidan can hunt," she added, "you can cook."

When Heimo was done heating the oil, I took him aside. "Please take care of Aidan," I said. "And be especially careful on the river ice."

"Don't worry; she'll be all right," he assured me.

When I asked him what time they'd be back, he shrugged his shoulders. "When? Not till we get a caribou."

I walked over to Aidan. My paternal instincts were kicking in and she knew it. "Don't worry, Dad," she said. "I'll be okay. You make sure to take care of yourself."

Heimo threw something to her. She caught it against her chest.

"Goggles," he said. "You'll need 'em to sit in the sled."

"Here, let me," I said, adjusting them around her eyes. She shook her head like a young horse unaccustomed to the bit.

"They're uncomfortable, Dad."

"You'll want 'em," I said, recalling my experience with over-flow and the sharp, sand-size pieces of ice that pelted my face and eyes. "Promise me you'll wear them."

Heimo and Edna were both sitting on the snow machine.

"Let's go," Edna shouted over the engine. "The caribou are waiting."

I cleared a spot in the sled for Aidan.

"Hold on to the sides," I told her.

I checked the cotter pin that fastened the sled to the Arctic Cat and then I walked up to Heimo, who grabbed the bone of his nose, turned, and blew. He wiped a glob of jellylike snot from a nostril and then looked at me.

"Look back to make sure she stays on," I reminded him.

Edna caught the edge in my voice. "Jim's like a mama grizzly," she said. "Don't wanna mess with his cub."

As they left the cabin yard, the trees swallowed up the sound of the snow machine. I spent the morning reading and listening to the scratchy radio and then, despite my back, decided to try to cut firewood and kindling. By late morning I returned to the cabin. The bannock had risen, and I stirred the broth again for the umpteenth time and read some more. Soon I was antsy again; popping three more ibuprofens, I took one of Heimo's shotguns and some bird shot and walked gingerly to the river to hunt the willows for ptarmigan. I looked for their tracks and listened for their ratchety calls.

I snowshoed north into what looked like a kind of spirit world. As the day's light dimmed, and the palette of colors that tinged the sky faded, I spotted a great gray owl—perhaps the one that Edna and Aidan had seen—at the top of a white spruce that looked west onto the river and east onto the tundra. I moved in closer until I could see its large, clownish head. Great grays are fond of hunting at dawn and dusk, but in December in northern Alaska there's little difference between day and night, so they turn diurnal, spending much of their time in pursuit of prey. This one, perhaps listening for a burrowing lemming or a hare, let me stand near enough to the tree that I was certain I could see its yellow eyes. We watched each other for a few minutes and then I turned south to investigate another willow bar.

I limped back to the cabin around 4:30. I'd overdone it and my back was sore again, but I brightened when I heard the sound of the snow machine. This time I was certain. It was not Heimo's flag fluttering or a bird's wings, but the sound of the Arctic Cat, still far downriver, but coming closer.

When they pulled into the cabin yard, it was all I could do not to rush to Aidan and hug her. I held back, careful not to let her—or Heimo and Edna—see my agitation.

"Welcome back," I said. "I see you got a caribou."

If they were relieved, or elated, to have killed a caribou, I wouldn't have known. Nobody said a word. They were chilled and covered in frost and dried blood and were eager to get into the cabin. But first they had to hang the meat. I helped Edna out of the sled—she had agreed to switch places because Aidan was so cold—and she handed me a cross fox.

"Put it over there," Heimo intervened. "I would have checked my other traps and set a bunch more, but I knew you'd be worried about Aidan, so we came back early."

I turned on my headlamp to inspect the fox. It was rock hard and its eyes were frozen solid, but its fur was full and beautiful. It had a dark stripe that ran the length of its back and intersected another stripe, forming a cross at its shoulders.

We hung the caribou meat and then everyone stampeded the cabin. I'd already brought in wood and water for drinking and dishes, so apart from gassing up the Arctic Cat for another day of hunting or trapping, Heimo's day was done. He pulled up a chair, joining Edna and Aidan at the fire. Edna had her hands against Aidan's cheeks, warming them. In the amber glow of the lantern, I could see the caribou blood under her fingernails and in the creases of her joints.

There was little space at the woodstove, and everyone was still too cold to speak, so I went outside to feed Kini. Excited by the commotion, she was barking. I petted her and gave her a can of slop made from rice, rabbit gravy, and a few pieces of fat. Then I went to the Arctic oven, knocked the frost off the walls of the tent, and grabbed a handful of kindling to build a fire. Aidan, I knew, would be grateful for the warmth.

I lay down in my cot to stretch my back until I heard Aidan call from the cabin door. Supper was ready. When I sat down everyone else had finished their plates and was back for more. I picked up a drumstick, sat back, out of the way, and marveled at the spectacle. They all ate like football players at the training table. Ten minutes later, supper was done.

Heimo and Edna were relaxing on their sleeping platform while Aidan, sitting at the woodstove, held a cup of tea in one hand and a goose leg bone in the other.

"Hey, old man," Heimo said, now eager to talk. "You would have loved it today. I got downriver and there they were, two caribou just standing there. When I got off the snow machine, they ran. I dropped the first one with one shot and was going to shoot the other, but my hands wouldn't work; they were so cold." He rubbed his hands together as if he was still trying to warm them. "Don't matter. I think we'll get another. It's good to know they're still around. Besides, we got about a hundred and twenty-five pounds of meat. That'll last us for a while."

"Should have saw your little girl today," Edna added. "She was cold and we were walking to get warm and she got stuck in a snowdrift. She had on so many clothes, she couldn't get out. I tried to pull her out, but I couldn't. So she had to roll out."

Having finished cleaning the leg bone with her teeth, Aidan laughed.

"She butchered good, too," Edna said. "Butchering that caribou was a good way for her to end her trip up here."

Edna's words startled me. I'd lost my sense of time. In the Arctic the rhythm of life plays out over seasons, not over a calendar's days, weeks, or months.

"Oh, yeah," Aidan said. "I forgot we're leaving. It seems so soon."

"You like it up here, don't you?" Edna asked, clearly pleased. "You like being a wilderness girl."

Just then, Heimo stood. "Gotta go gas up the snow machine

before I get too lazy. Why don't you guys tell Jimmer about the hunt today?"

Warm and well fed, Aidan and Edna were happy to oblige.

Aidan began by describing the trip downriver in the sled. As Heimo wound his way through the willow bars, the branches slapped at her like whips. She held tightly to the sled with one hand and covered her face with her other arm. After one section of densely packed trees, Heimo stopped, and Edna turned to check on her.

"You all right, Aidan?" she yelled back. Aidan gritted her teeth and gave her the thumbs-up.

Heimo navigated one more gravel bar and then gunned the snow machine for a straight shot south along the river. Aidan's goggles fogged up and her eyelids froze shut. Occasionally, when Heimo slowed, she could hear the sound of open water, where it ran blue-black over the ice. She knew then that Heimo was searching for a safe route. She clung to the sled and prayed the ice would hold.

An hour later, Heimo slowed and then turned off the snow machine.

"Caribou crossing," Aidan heard him say. "And the tracks look fresh. Wolves are after 'em, too."

Aidan took off her goggles and her layers of gloves and mittens. Then she held the insides of her gloves up to her eyes. When her eyelids thawed, she saw wolf tracks, their large, furred pads and spaced toenails, weaving back and forth across the caribou trail, predators following their prey.

"You and Aidan post here," Heimo told Edna. "I'll go downriver."

Edna was barely clear of the machine when Heimo took off.

Aidan laughed when she described how Edna had shaken her fist at Heimo's back and shouted at him.

"Yeah," Edna chimed in. "That damn Heim. Sometimes he's in such a hurry."

Thanks to a lesson from Edna, Aidan was able to identify the caribou tracks scattered along the riverbank. She could see their crescent-shaped prints and their straw-colored guard hairs among the lichens. Their sense of smell had allowed them to find the deep-buried grasses. Aidan also saw where the caribou had pawed away the snow to get at the moss and Labrador tea.

"Looks like they ate and moved on," Edna told her. "Maybe because of the wolves. Let's hope they come back." She and Aidan sat on a wind-hardened snowbank, with their backs to the trees to cut the cold, and in the muted light they watched the woods and the river. Aidan tried not to breathe; the air was so icy it hurt her lungs.

"Are you okay?" Edna asked. "Slow," she instructed Aidan. "Breathe slow."

Then she told Aidan how the caribou's nostrils are covered with short hairs that warm the air before it passes into their lungs. After more than thirty years, she said that she and Heimo were like the caribou. They had grown used to the cold.

Aidan practiced inhaling slowly. Ten minutes later, she felt pressure building in her bladder. Edna watched her fidget.

"What's wrong?" Edna asked. "You got ants in your pants?"

"I think I have to pee," Aidan said. "But I'm trying to hold it; I don't want to have to take off all these clothes."

"Try to think about something else," Edna advised her. "Maybe it will pass."

Twenty minutes later they heard a gunshot downriver.

"That's Heimo," Edna exclaimed. "I hope he got one."

Minutes later, Aidan saw Edna close her eyes.

"You can take a nap," Aidan said. "I'll wake you if I see something."

"No," Edna explained. "I was just listening. I think I hear the snow machine. Heimo's on his way up. That means he got a caribou."

Aidan heard nothing. "Are you sure?"

"Yup," Edna said. "Heimo's coming."

Aidan watched a raven circling upriver, soaring and dipping as if playing in the wind. Finally she heard the low rumble of the Arctic Cat's engine.

"He's almost here," Edna said, standing.

Edna and Aidan walked to the river's edge. Aidan spotted the snow machine with the binoculars. She could see a caribou in the sled, its long legs dragging in the snow.

"Yup, he got one," she told Edna.

"Get ready," Edna said. "We got work to do."

Aidan and Edna helped Heimo pull the caribou, a cow, from the sled. "Where's the bullet hole?" Aidan asked.

She knew that Lower 48 hunters liked kill shots through the heart and lungs—the "boiler room"—and double-shoulder shots, though they damaged more meat. But she knew that Heimo and Edna were fans of neither. They liked to shoot caribou and moose behind the ear or in the neck so that they ruined as little of the meat and vital organs as possible.

Edna showed her the hole behind the caribou's right ear—a perfect shot.

"Butcher it," Heimo said, bounding back to the Arctic Cat. "I'll try for another."

Aidan watched as Edna took off her parka and pulled up the sleeves of her wool sweater.

"Guess I might as well pee now," Aidan said.

"Yup," Edna answered. "You're going to have to take off some of those clothes anyway." Edna waited while Aidan undressed. "Man," she said. "You're bundled up warmer than a musk ox."

When Aidan finally got down to her fleece tights, she bared her backside to the wind and cold.

"What's taking you?" Edna asked.

"It's so cold, I don't know if I can pee," Aidan said, giggling.

As Aidan told me the story, Edna put down her tea and guffawed. "I thought her bladder had froze up until I saw the snow turn yellow."

Aidan's hands grew numb as she struggled to get her clothes back on. In the meantime, Edna sharpened her knife. She had butchered so many caribou that it was second nature to her. She would take the lead; Aidan's job would be to hold the animal and move it into different positions so she could make the cuts.

"We don't use no saw or a big knife," she told Aidan. "A small knife will do the job fine."

As Edna knelt next to the caribou, Aidan pulled up on the animal's muzzle and Edna drew her knife swiftly across its upper neck, severing the jugular and carotid vessels so the dark blood could drain without spoiling the meat. Edna cut more and then Aidan used all her weight and muscle to twist off the head. When it came free, she laid it to the side in the snow.

Next, Edna skinned the caribou. She cut the hide on one side while Aidan tugged at it and peeled it back over the dark red muscles and white tendons. Then Edna cut off the hind and front leg and repeated the process on the animal's other side. When all four legs were off, she moved to the intestinal cavity. Aidan watched as she made a shallow incision, taking care not to puncture the intestines and taint the meat. After opening up the gut, from the diaphragm down, and cutting out the bladder and anus, she handed Aidan the knife, pulled off her gloves, and put her cold hands into the steaming carcass.

They were wet with blood when she pulled them out. She shook them before putting her gloves back on, dotting the snow red.

"Are your hands cold?" she asked Aidan.

"Freezing," Aidan replied.

Edna pointed to the caribou. "Warm 'em up."

Aidan looked at the cavity, drew a deep breath, and thrust her bare hands underneath the intestines. It was thick and warm, and she kept them inside the animal's gut until she could feel her fingers again.

"Now for the brisket," Edna said.

Aidan withdrew her hands, and Edna cut out the chest and then reached inside and severed the windpipe and esophagus. When Aidan pulled down the large liver and the coil of intestines wrapped in their thin layer of caul fat, she heard a low slurping sound as they tumbled, steaming, onto the snow. Edna pushed the intestines away from the butchering area and handed Aidan the liver. Aidan was surprised by its heft. Then Edna dug out the still quivering, bright red heart and the hard, white omasum, or the Bible, one of the caribou's four stomachs. Aidan noticed that it was shaped like a football. Edna washed a small piece off in the snow, sliced it, and slurped it into her mouth like an oyster, tasting its wildness. She looked at Aidan. Aidan shook her head: *no thank you.*

Aidan tried to hide her distaste. She knew the Bible was a delicacy. Back at the cabin, Edna and Heimo would cut it open, clean out the moss and lichens from the stomach's layers—the Bible's pages—and eat the whole thing raw.

Edna severed the backbone where it attached to the rib cage and divided the caribou in two to make it easier to haul. Then she and Aidan put the legs, head, pelvic area, and ribs in a pile and lay the brisket and organs on the caribou skin. Edna reached into the pocket of her parka and removed a needle and thread. Aidan looked at her, bewildered.

"I'm going to sew up the hide with the meat inside so we don't lose any on the way home. Can you thread it? I can't see good."

Edna made her last stitch just as Heimo arrived.

"Any more caribou?" Edna asked.

"Nah, only one."

Edna and Aidan lugged the twenty-five-pound legs over to the sled, and Heimo slung the bulging hide over his shoulder. When he returned, he lay wolf traps around the gut pile. Satisfied with his set, he looked at Aidan and laughed.

"You should see yourself," he said. "All spattered with blood. It ain't easy up here, is it? If it was, everybody'd be doing it."

Edna put her arm around Aidan. "Don't tease her," she said. "This girl did good today. She don't get grossed out and she's a fast learner. If there's ever a caribou-butchering competition, I want her as my partner."

Heimo entered the cabin just as Aidan and Edna finished the story. We were all tired from the long day, so we cut the evening short. Edna was already curled up on the sleeping platform when we said good night. We shivered in the night air and ran to the Arctic oven, where, fortunately, smoke still rose from the chimney.

We grabbed our toothbrushes and dashed outside into the

bitterly cold air. We were done in less than a minute and jumped back inside.

"It's so nice to be warm," I heard Aidan say. Then she asked, "Dad, are we really leaving tomorrow?"

"Yes," I said. "I guess we are."

When I turned on my headlamp and fed the fire, I couldn't see her. Then I saw her face, half young woman and half little girl, peeking out from under her down sleeping bags.

CHAPTER 17

BIRTHDAYS AND BEAVER TAIL

I WOKE IN THE MIDDLE OF the night, awakened by the glow of Aidan's headlamp. "What are you doing?" I asked.

"Writing in my journal."

When I asked why, she told me that she didn't want to forget the details of the caribou hunt.

"It's the middle of the night," I reminded her.

"Yeah," she responded. "I know."

Half an hour later, I no longer heard the soft scraping of her pencil against the pages of her journal. Her headlamp was still on but she was asleep. I turned the lamp off without waking her. Returning to my cot, I fell into a deep sleep, until I was awakened by her scream.

"Caribou!"

I thrashed out of my sleeping bag and instinctively grabbed the skinning knife that lay in a sheath at the head of my cot. When I came to, I was standing in the middle of the tent with my knife, the blade still covered, in my hand. The stove was out and the tent was dark as pitch. My heart was beating like a surging river.

Aidan screamed again. "Caribou. I see caribou!" Then, in a quieter voice, she said, "Edna, look."

I went over to her and shook her gently. "Aidan, wake up."

"What, Daddy, what?"

"You had a dream," I said.

"What, are you sure?"

"You were dreaming," I said again.

"No, I wasn't," she insisted.

"You were," I told her. "You said something about caribou."

"Really?" she asked. "Caribou? That's funny." She giggled like an eight-year-old. Minutes later I heard her snoring.

I woke to Heimo's voice. "Rise and shine, Jimmer. We gotta drag the runway if Daniel's going to get his plane in today. Wind's up though. You could be here till January." Heimo walked back to the cabin. "Oh, yeah, oatmeal's on."

Aidan sat up in her cot, rubbing her eyes. "Did he really say what I think he said? January!"

"Yup."

Aidan growled. "I don't want to leave today, but I'm going to flunk physics if we don't get home soon. I haven't been able to email with my teacher at all."

When Aidan and I left the tent for breakfast, I could see the tops of the trees bending in the wind. Inside, Heimo was listening to the forecast on the radio: "Report for the eastern foothills of the Southern Brooks Range—*crackle, crackle*. Winds—*crackle*—out of the north gusting to thirty miles per hour. Freezing rain probable."

"Oh, well," Heimo said. "One thing you learn up here is that you can't rely on the weather. It does what it wants. We've waited weeks for planes. Gotta forget about it or you drive yourself crazy."

"I got an idea," Edna announced. "Aidan, how 'bout you and me decorate the cabin for Christmas?" Aidan agreed that it would be fun.

By 10:00 a.m., Heimo and I and Edna and Aidan had gone our separate ways. Edna and Aidan had taken the sled on the forest trail to the Korths' lower cabin, where Edna kept their Christmas decorations. Both were carrying rifles, Aidan the .30-30 and Edna the .30-06. Heimo and I were at the winter runway. Using the snow machine and the drag, weighted down with rocks, Heimo hoped to be able to smooth out a six-hundred-foot strip so that Daniel could put the plane down on wheel skis. The skis operate hydraulically, allowing pilots to take off on wheels from the airport in Fairbanks or the strip in Fort Yukon. Using a manual pump in the cockpit, pilots force their skis down under the wheels so they can then land on snow on remote runways.

While Heimo dragged, my job was to snowshoe the runway and stick in spruce boughs to mark the borders of the strip, which had been buried in snow. I'd already come to realize that routine and tedium are as much a part of life in the Arctic wilderness as they are anywhere else. The work here is often hard and repetitive: gather water, cut and split wood, hunt, trap, cook. It's one of the reasons I'd come to admire Aidan. She did the work, and each night she wrote in her journal, regardless of how tired or cold she was.

Heimo once told me that it was the starry-eyed poets who didn't last in the Alaskan bush. They came out imagining that they'd spend their days reading Thoreau and contemplating the meaning of life only to discover that being in the bush is often about nothing more than survival. Those who were willing to buckle down and work until their backs ached and their hands grew raw, and then callused, were the ones who made it. Surely, some of them were poets or philosophers or amateur naturalists, but they understood that words and big ideas take a backseat to the daily labor.

I began by walking north along the runway's eastern edge, placing fresh spruce boughs in the snow at sixty-foot intervals. The wind was surly and cold, but I soon realized that I was over-dressed. While I took off my parka and the fleece jacket I had on under it, I watched Heimo going back and forth. All I could see was his red, permanently frostbitten nose. It shone like a beacon.

It took me until the early afternoon to mark the perimeter of the runway. By the time I caught sight of Edna and Aidan coming up the river, I knew Daniel wouldn't be making it in. The wind swept down the valley, bringing with it freezing rain from the mountains.

I saw that Aidan was pulling a sled, leaning into the rope that she had wrapped around her waist like a sled dog straining at its harness. She had agreed to drag it to spare Edna's bad back.

"You look tired," I said, when they stopped at the runway. The sled was piled high with boxes.

"This stuff ain't light," Edna said. "You got one strong daughter, Jim." Then Edna turned to Heimo. "Wanna help us decorate?"

"No way," Heimo responded. "Jimmer and me will take your rifles and see if we can find a moose." Before Edna could ask Heimo pretty please, he was already walking downriver. I ran to catch up with him.

"Edna's crazy about Christmas," he said, shaking his head. "She decorates the entire cabin. Hell, the girls ain't even here. Who does she think is going to stop in? Carolers?" He continued, "Ah, well, if it makes her happy."

We climbed up the riverbank and walked west to investigate some moose tracks that we had seen days before. In the deep snow, it took us nearly an hour to get there. When we found them, Heimo was discouraged.

"Three-day-old tracks," he said. "No new ones."

We trudged around the woods for a bit longer and then we headed for the cabin. When we walked in the door, Aidan was stringing tinsel around the vertical log beam that supported the ridgepole. Edna was hanging cutout angels and putting figurines on shelves. Christmas music was playing on the radio.

"I love them," Edna said, holding an angel.

"No shit," Heimo mumbled in my direction.

"What did you say?" Edna challenged him. She came over and punched him playfully. Then she turned on the battery-operated lights for the final touch.

"There," she said, beaming. "Festive."

"Yup," Heimo added. "All those lonely Arctic travelers will appreciate it."

"I don't care if anyone sees it," Edna replied. "Me and Aidan had fun. Besides, it's Christmastime and I like it."

"I know, Mom. I know," Heimo conceded. "It looks nice."

THE FREEZING RAIN lasted for almost forty-eight hours, but three days past our assigned pickup date the sky was cloudless and clear with mare's tails high up. The wind off the Brooks Range was still strong and swirling, but the great blanket of gray that had settled low over the valley was gone.

We were sitting in the cabin eating breakfast. "Hey, did you know that today is my dad's birthday?" Aidan asked.

"No kidding!" Heimo exclaimed. "I can tell; he looks older," he said, looking at my beard, which had gone wild and gray.

"Yup," Aidan said. "December tenth."

Heimo jumped up from his chair and bolted out the door. From the window, I watched him throw the plastic tarp off the pile of supplies. A few minutes later, he walked back in, holding up a stick of butter.

"I found it," he said triumphantly. "The last one. Don't say I never did anything for your birthday." He handed it to me. "I know you love it with your bannock."

I set the rock-solid stick on a plate on top of the woodstove. Aidan was already licking her lips. She loves butter even more than I do. After five minutes, I took the plate away and slathered the now-soft butter over my bread. Aidan reached for it before I could hand it to her.

"True Cheeseheads." Heimo laughed.

"I'm going to make you a pie," Edna announced.

"Hell with it," Heimo interjected. "If we're going to have a birthday party, I might as well grill the king salmon."

"I thought you were only going to serve us silvers," I said. "Weren't you saving the king for when we left?"

"Yeah," Heimo grumbled. "I was. But not anymore. It's your birthday."

THE MORNING PACE was slower than usual. There was work to do, but no one wanted to venture too far from the cabin in case Daniel arrived.

Aidan and I went to the spring to gather water for what would likely be the last time. It was nothing more than a small creek that ran into a pond encircled by frail, waterlogged black spruce trees.

In the morning and late afternoon, when the air was especially cold, ice fog settled over the pond, a blue-white haze. Frozen ice crystals; such a simple thing. But sometimes it dazzled us with its beauty.

By the time we returned Heimo had already left to explore a possible trapline just east of the river out across the tundra. So instead of joining him, I accompanied Edna and Aidan on their "bunny line."

They walked at a brisk pace, the two of them, side by side, a hundred yards in front of me. They cut east off the frozen river and followed a trail along a slough. I stopped at the river's edge. The ice was largely quiet, though I heard an occasional moan. From the woods, a raven called. It flew overhead and its wings made a sound like someone beating a rug with a broom. I heard a sound in the thick bushes like the scream of a woman. A lynx?

I felt as if I'd been given a simple but precious birthday gift: the sharp odor of spruce, the sound of water rushing beneath the creaking ice, the sight of Aidan squatting and tending to one of her snares while Edna instructed her, and, for one last time, the thin glow of the unseen sun on the southeastern horizon. Knowing how quickly the modern world overwhelms one, how easy it is to forget once I've immersed myself in my day-to-day life, I held on to the details and tried to imprint them on my memory.

I took one last glance upriver in the direction of Bear Mountain, which looked as if someone had painted its slopes with long, faded strokes of red. Then I turned and followed Edna and Aidan's path. They'd checked most of their snares and were now at the back edge of the slough. When I reached them, Aidan was setting the guide sticks that would lead the rabbit into her snare. Edna knelt beside her and gently moved one of the sticks closer to the noose.

By 4:00 p.m. Heimo and I had finished grilling the salmon

over an outdoor fire. We walked inside the cabin in time to see Edna pull a long strip of bubbling beaver tail from the cast-iron frying pan and lay it on a serving plate. Heimo peeled back the aluminum foil on the salmon. Aidan stood as close as she could just to inhale the aroma. Using his fork to slide the meat off the bone, Heimo gave each of us a large piece.

"Yukon River king," he said. "Best salmon in the world."

The chunk of salmon took up half of Aidan's plate. Edna cut off a sizable piece of beaver tail and set it on the other half. Aidan couldn't wait to devour the salmon, but she looked at the beaver tail uncertainly. She knew that even I—who will eat anything—felt ambivalent about it.

Aidan tried the beaver tail first, putting a small piece in her mouth. For a moment she looked as if she might gag. She had eaten everything put in front of her on this trip—fat, gristle, bone marrow, seal, caribou liver, kidney, and heart—but one tiny taste of beaver tail was enough for her.

Before the trip, I had described the taste to her as best I could: Imagine frying chicken in a cast-iron pan of Crisco. When done, set aside the chicken and forget about it. Then scoop up the drippings in the pan with a large spoon. Dump the contents of the spoon into a bowl of melted butter, whisk, and dig in. That's what beaver tail tastes like.

"Oh, my God," she said.

"What's the matter?" Heimo asked, smirking.

"It tastes like a, a—" Aidan was searching for the right word. "Like a bomb of fat."

Heimo and Edna burst out laughing. "I like that," Heimo said. "That's exactly what it is—a bomb of fat."

Aidan stuck her fork in her piece of beaver tail and looked at

Heimo and Edna as if to say, *No offense. I just can't eat this.* Heimo nodded, giving her the go-ahead. No offense taken. She gave it to me and then cut her salmon and put a large piece in her mouth.

"Now," she said, "I'm in heaven."

We finished our meal quickly, and Edna brought out the pie. "I used dried cranberries and a few blueberries, but I only had a little sugar left."

She set the largest piece on my plate. "You first," she said.

As I took a bite, Heimo cupped his ear.

"Plane," he said. Then he grabbed the handheld aircraft radio. "Daniel, is that you?"

"Roger that," I heard. "Tell Jim and Aidan to get their stuff. I don't want to be on the ground for more than fifteen minutes."

"Oh, shit," Heimo said. "We gotta move."

He ran out to start the snow machine and Aidan and I darted for the Arctic oven. We threw our gear into our backpacks and duffel bags and loaded the sled.

Down at the runway, Daniel was waiting. "Got everything?" he asked.

"Who knows?" I said.

He apologized. "This is the only weather window we had. Otherwise I wouldn't be able to get you until the end of the week. Four more days, at least."

We helped Daniel load our bags onto the plane and then helped him turn the plane into the wind for takeoff. Aidan gave Edna a long hug, but after three and a half weeks together, our good-byes seemed rushed and unfulfilling. As I climbed into the plane, Edna stuck a piece of aged seal meat in the pocket of my parka. Before we knew it, we were in the air. Daniel flew north and made a wide, slow turn over the river. Below I saw the soft light of the lantern coming from the cabin and Heimo and Edna winding their way through the woods on the snow machine.

As we flew south the night spread out bright and beautiful. A waxing moon seemed to fill the sky, spilling light over the Coleen River valley and over the hills and kettle lakes of the Yukon Flats. But a tailwind pushed us south at 140 knots, and soon I could see Fort Yukon and Circle to the south, Chalkyitsik to the southeast, and the small Native villages of Venetie and Birch Creek to the southwest. We crossed the Yukon River and Preacher Creek, and gained altitude over the Crazy Mountains. In the far distance, Fairbanks glittered.

PART III

>>>>>>>>>>>>>>>>>>>

CHAPTER 18

IT'S IN THE GENES

I T WAS SUNDAY NIGHT, JANUARY 5, 2014. We'd been home for just over three weeks when the phone rang at 10:00 p.m. The voice on the other end sounded distorted, with a far-away, almost computerized tone to it; I knew it was Heimo calling by satellite phone. The connection faded and I missed what he said.

"What? Come again."

"The. Wolves. Are. Howling," he said, enunciating every word. "I can hear 'em now. 'Bout half a mile downriver."

The connection grew clearer, and Heimo told me that on New Year's Day he'd shot a caribou. Two wolves had been feeding on the gut pile ever since.

"You and Aidan would love to hear them," he added. "Anyway, I gotta go. I'm standing outside and it's forty-one below."

The following morning I woke earlier than usual. In the back field, I heard the coyotes yip-yapping, sharp and high. I'd discovered their beds in the dense cattails of our pond. Perhaps they were on the move in the 4:00 a.m. darkness, dashing across the clover, running down a deer.

I turned on my computer and a headline in the day's *New York Times* caught my attention. ARCTIC COLD BLANKETS MIDWEST, FREEZING ROUTINES, it read. By sunrise I decided to see for myself what the fuss was all about. The thermometer outside our kitchen window said it was 21 below, so I dressed as if I were heading out on the trapline with Heimo. The air was thin and clear, and I spotted the bony knee of the moon poking through feathery clouds. Calhoun and I walked out back, where the prairie, covered in hoarfrost, looked like a field of ghosts. I stuck to the trail. As Calhoun plunged through the ice-lined grasses, I heard a high-pitched jingling that sounded like music. Near the end of the tree line, I saw that some of the branches of the leafless wild plum trees still held fruit that the girls were unable to get to on their ladders. In the still-frozen clover, whose leaves and stems crackled as he ran, I let Calhoun roam. For the first time I felt the full strength of the north wind. It had a raw, wild quality, as if blowing off Bear Mountain.

When I returned to the house, Willa greeted me at the door, dressed in her winter gear and ski boots, jubilant that school had been canceled. "Remember, Daddy," she reminded me. "Yesterday, you said that if I didn't have school, we could make a ski trail."

I'd forgotten about my promise. "It's really cold out there," I said, thinking that might deter her.

"Not too cold for me," Willa replied. Coming from any other kid, I might have my doubts. But not Willa. She's as warm-blooded as a woolly mammoth.

We skied east along the edge of the prairie field and then turned south past the marsh. Here, the wind was at our backs, pushing us across the snow. In the distance I could see the barbed wire hard-frosted and glittering.

Willa shouted to me, "Daddy, I feel like a kite."

When we circled back to the house fifteen minutes later, I asked, "We done?" Willa shook her head no. So I skied another lap with her. For the last six months, I'd devoted so much of my energy to Aidan that I worried Rachel and Willa had felt overlooked. All the reasons I had invested time in Aidan also held true for them.

It was almost 9:00 a.m. when we returned to the house. Aidan was sitting with her computer on her lap.

"It's colder here than in Fairbanks," she reported.

Rachel walked into the living room, still rubbing the sleep out of her eyes.

"I wanna ski today," she said.

"Really?" Aidan asked.

"Yeah, really," Rachel responded.

I, too, was taken aback by Rachel's determination. Rachel had always been our contrary child. When she was little, I would carry her in a backpack on our hikes. They were meant to be bracing interactions with Mother Nature, but she would often wail in my ears from beginning to end, unless she fell asleep. Later, when she was big enough to walk on her own, she would sometimes stop in the middle of the trail and refuse to go farther. My response was to try to break her will. "Let's keep going," I'd say to Elizabeth, who was uncomfortable with the idea. "She'll follow." But the thing about Rachel was, she wouldn't. She would stand her ground and not budge. Our experiment was short-lived because Rachel won. Worried about her, we'd walk back, and then she knew she had us. After consulting with some friends whose grown daughters are avid outdoorswomen, we switched to small monetary rewards. Money, it turned out, motivated Rachel; gradually she learned to enjoy our hikes.

"So what time do you want to go, Rachel?" I asked.

"Three thirty," she answered. "Before it gets dark."

"I'm in," Aidan interjected. "That'll give me time to work on the campaign."

The campaign, which Aidan had begun shortly after returning home, was to convince the U.S. Board on Geographic Names to legally designate the unnamed peak where Heimo and Edna had put the cross for their daughter Coleen as Coleen Ann Mountain.

During our winter visit, while Edna and Aidan stood at the foot of Guroy Mountain, Edna had told her a painful story. After Coleen's death, the Korths had asked the U.S. Board on Geographic Names, part of the U.S. Geological Survey, which is charged with "promulgating official geographic feature names with locative attributes," to name the mountain after their daughter. The puny, undistinguished peak meant nothing to anyone else, but to Edna and Heimo it was everything. The board had denied their request on the grounds that their daughter was of "no historical significance." Heimo and Edna were stung by the callousness. They had contacted Steve Cowper, then Alaska's governor, and Congressman Don Young, who had a cabin in Fort Yukon, asking for their help. Cooper and Young, in turn, contacted the board and urged it to reconsider. Heimo and Edna even started a petition, which they got hundreds of people to sign. But the board remained unmoved, and eventually Heimo and Edna gave up. To keep trying was like rubbing salt in a wound.

Edna had been staring off in the direction of Coleen's cross, knowing that, as much as she wanted to visit, the snow was too deep, and her back too sore for her to make the climb. As they walked away, Edna confessed to Aidan that one day she might approach the board again in the hope that its members would have a change of heart.

At noon, Rachel, Willa, and I ran Calhoun again in the back field. The wind was, if anything, blowing stronger than ever, but the girls resisted going back to the house until Calhoun's paws froze up. Only when he lay down in the snow whimpering and chewed at his icy pads did they agree it was time to turn in.

"Okay," I said, "who's going to make the fire in my office?" My office is housed in a small, gray outbuilding that used to be the farm's tack house.

Willa, who usually lights the woodstove before I take her to school in the morning, turned on a dime and broke for the tack house. Rachel was just behind her. Halfway to the building she tripped Willa, who fell, facefirst, into the hard snow. When she got up I could see the beginnings of a fat lip, in response to which she barreled into Rachel like a January wind. The two of them rolled in the snow like the little girls they still were. It was 20 below, but for all they cared it might as well have been above freezing.

When they'd had enough, Willa went to the house to inspect her lip and Rachel came into the tack house to build the fire. When it was drawing, she sat down on the couch and looked at the maps of Alaska I had spread out on the coffee table.

"Daddy, are you and Aidan going back to Alaska?" she asked.

"Maybe," I told her.

"Does Momma know?"

"Yeah, Rachel." I chuckled. "Momma knows."

Sometimes it takes me a while to learn from my mistakes, but in this case I didn't make the same mistake twice. Not long after we returned, I told Elizabeth that I'd hoped to take Aidan back to Alaska to do the river trip that we had forfeited when we went up to help Heimo build his cabin.

All Elizabeth said was "Give me some time to think about it," and then we dropped the subject. A few days later, she said with little fanfare, "It's not as if I'm surprised. I knew this was a possibility. And I'm not saying yes or no, but if you go you have to promise me one thing."

"What's that?" I asked.

"Just make sure you're ready," she said. "Before you and Aidan get on an Arctic river, I want you to promise me that the two of you will know exactly what you're doing. I don't want to lose either one of you." When I'd been researching rivers, before going out to help Heimo build the cabin, Elizabeth and I had discussed the various trips and the accompanying dangers. She knew enough about them to be concerned.

Rachel opened the door to the stove and moved the logs with the cast-iron poker. When the fire was blazing again, she announced that she was going to head back to the house. She opened the door to my office and then closed it. "So, Dad," she said, "what fun thing are we going to do when I'm fifteen?" Then she pointed to one of the masks on my wall. "How 'bout New Guinea?" She laughed as she left, but I knew she was serious. Rachel, too, had become an outdoor girl, and of all three of our daughters she was the one most interested in my trips to New Guinea. She'd made it known on numerous occasions that she was already looking forward to a daughter-father adventure. It seemed to me that Rachel envied the bond I had formed with Aidan and also wanted the opportunity to shine, to prove herself in the wilderness, as Aidan had. But it troubled me, too. What would I be capable of in five years?

At 3:00 p.m., Aidan came out. "Ready to ski?" she asked. She saw the maps spread out on the table. "Remember when we got these?"

It was our only day in Fairbanks after our winter trip. We were walking down University Avenue. At the bridge that crossed the Chena River, the walkway narrowed and cars and trucks sped by, just feet away. The cloud of exhaust that hung in the air nearly choked us. Our minds, and hearts, were still back on the frozen river, and we were lamenting our reintroduction to the modern world.

Aidan was missing Edna, their easy friendship, their daily trips on her trapline and, later, thawing out by the woodstove while re-counting the day's events. For me it was the little things: the smell of woodsmoke wafting up and down the river valley. After a long, cold day of trapping with Heimo, I always knew when the cabin was close. I could feel my body warm, responding to the scent. Aidan and I were both experiencing a kind of grieving. For me, the emotional reaction to being back in busy Fairbanks was about the realization that I may never have reason to return to the Coleen River, in winter or summer. It was as if I'd reached the last page of a beloved book, knowing that when I was done, I would pass it on to someone else, and would likely never open it again.

"C'mon, Aidan," I said. "I have an idea."

We hiked up to the university and entered the map store. It was warm and well lit. Our moods lifted as we lingered over 1:250,000-scale maps of the upper Coleen, the Sheenjek, and the Canning, following with our index fingers the river routes and contour lines, imagining rapid runs and weathered, wind-beaten mountains. After half an hour I realized I'd forgotten to ask for a map of the Hulahula.

"The Hulahula," I said again, enjoying the way the word rolled off my tongue.

"Yeah," Aidan said, "I like the way that sounds."

When the student behind the desk returned with the map, I opened it and we found the river's headwaters etched into the granite peaks between the Brooks Range and the Romanzof Mountains to the north.

"I can see it, Dad," Aidan said.

"See what?" I asked.

She folded up the map and put it into the pocket of her parka. "I can see you dreaming."

On the flight home, I was already writing and rewriting packing lists, checking off the names of bush pilots, and drawing up a budget. We had switched planes in Anchorage for the second leg of our flight, and everyone, including Aidan, aboard the plane, crowded with military families returning to the Lower 48 for the holidays, was asleep. I, however, was in full dream mode. With my headlamp on I scoured the maps we'd bought in Fairbanks, tracing, with my pencil, routes through the mountains and the courses of various Arctic rivers. But my mind, and my gaze, kept coming back to the Hulahula.

Aidan had come out to my office to see if I was ready to ski, but now she was immersed in the maps. Watching her, I knew that my mom had nailed it. That day on the phone after our summer trip, when she'd said that I'd passed my *fernweh* on to Aidan, I had felt hit hard by the truth. I had resisted making the connection, so much so that when she pointed it out, it blindsided me. But then it seemed so obvious. For me the grass always looked greener, the trout streams clearer, and the hills steeper someplace else. I'd spent much of my life feeling restless, but I'd always had the notion that one day I would find home and that feeling would end. I'd told myself that my return to Wisconsin was impelled by an irresistible homing instinct. Perhaps, though, it was a lie. Perhaps I'd come back to the only place that ever felt like home in the hope that I might recapture that sense of belonging. I'd built a chicken coop and tended our bees and seeded the prairie and cut and split wood to ground myself, to build a sort of firebreak, to put in the kind of sweat equity that would quiet the restive rumblings. And as much as I had come to love this little farm, where at the back edge of the land I could hear the whinnying of cranes and the hysterical night-time yipping of coyotes, sometimes I still felt ready to strike out for wilder country. There was so much to see, and I'd begun to realize that my time to see it was limited. Some people, like Heimo and Edna, and Wendell Berry, have a vision of where they should be in the world. I, unfortunately, did not. I was a middle-aged man, with a family that I loved, living in a place I was committed to, but sometimes I got itchy feet and dreamed of living in South Africa, Suriname, New Zealand, or on the shores of Lake Superior.

Aidan had begun dreaming big, too, not just of Alaska but of the infinite possibilities of living. It's what I'd hoped for when we first contemplated going north, that in addition to teaching her a variety of skills that would serve her well both in the wilderness and in life, Alaska would ignite her capacity for wonder, for imagining the largeness of life. But it was also somehow difficult for me to watch her studying the maps. Reality was staring me in the face: my daughter would soon pass me by. She would have countless adventures, most of which I would know only secondhand.

THROUGHOUT JANUARY AND February, a deep freeze settled over the upper Midwest. Despite the cold, we spent most of our weekends away from home at Aidan's and Rachel's cross-country ski races in northern Wisconsin and the Upper Peninsula of Michigan. During the week, Aidan was so bogged down with school that she had little time to pursue her campaign to rename the mountain. But what she had learned was discouraging.

In 1964, coinciding with the passage of the Wilderness Act, the U.S. Board on Geographic Names decreed that, "except in extraordinary circumstances, unnamed features in federal wilderness areas will remain that way." Aidan's hope was that the Korths' request fell under the realm of an "extraordinary circumstance." In late February, Aidan had begun drafting a letter about the Korths' time on the Coleen River, and Coleen's death, which she planned to use to persuade the board of the historical legitimacy of the Korths' claim. Together with *Grittygal,* a blog about her Alaska experiences, the campaign helped her believe that her life was about more than academics and sports. She knew, too, that Elizabeth had given her blessing, and we would be going back to the Alaskan Arctic for a third and final trip.

One day Elizabeth had come out to my office and noticed the maps and all my scribblings. "You say this is about Aidan, but you need this, too, don't you?" She said the words not as an accusation but with the kind of understanding that comes from being married to someone for almost twenty years. "You should go."

I sat down next to her, and together we looked over the maps. I showed her the high mountain country that I wanted to backpack and the various rivers that Aidan and I might paddle. When she left me to pick up Willa from school, she smiled. "Think you'll ever get it out of your system?"

Nominally, our trip would be a celebration of the fiftieth anniversary of the Wilderness Act, which created the legal definition of wilderness in the United States and would go on to protect 104 million acres. Aidan and I would backpack over the Brooks Range and paddle one of the Arctic's great rivers to the coast, a three- to four-week trip that would be the culmination of our Alaskan experience together. For me, at least, the journey had already taken on the feel of a calling, a last-chance opportunity for Aidan and me to see the Arctic together. I had the overwhelming feeling that to delay the trip would doom it. I knew that the following summer Aidan would have her sights set on college and writing her application essays. When she left for college, I knew there would be friends, or more likely an outdoorsy boyfriend, who might want to join her on an Alaskan adventure.

My body was certainly telling me that this would likely be it. Despite five operations, I was missing my ACL (anterior cruciate ligament) and most or all of the cartilage in both knees. Over the years, they'd grown arthritic and tender to the touch. After a winter training regimen of plyometrics, weights, cross-country skiing, and riding the stationary bike, I felt strong. But the question remained: could I haul a heavy pack across the Arctic? The truth was, I didn't know. I'd also had some lingering concerns about my atrial fibrillation (Afib), an irregular heartbeat, which had been corrected three years before with a cardiac ablation, a procedure that eliminates heart rhythm (arrhythmia) problems. Though I hadn't had one incident since the procedure, my cardiologist told me that at some point it could come back. And the last place I wanted that to happen was in the middle of the Arctic National Wildlife Refuge.

In early March, Aidan and I attended Canoecopia, the largest paddle-sports consumer event in the world, which Madison, Wisconsin, hosts every March. Julie Brown, a longtime National Outdoor Leadership School instructor, was about to begin her Canoecopia presentation on the 3 P's—peeing, pooping, and periods. Aidan and I walked into the room and there wasn't a chair left. Aidan managed to find a spot on the floor between two granola-looking twentysomethings, while I stood, just ten feet to Brown's right, the only man in the room. I felt like every eye was on me, as if I'd stumbled into a women's locker room and didn't have the good sense to leave. When the talk started, I was still squirming and looking for the door; between scribbling notes, Aidan would look up at me, nearly trembling with laughter. But as Brown settled in I realized that no one gave a damn about me; they were all here to learn something.

"A bandana is a girl's best friend," Brown said. She was talking about "wiping" after peeing, encouraging everyone in the audience but me to use a bandana to soak up the "drips and drops" and then to hang it on the outside of their pack. Urine carries low levels of bacteria, so a bandana actually works better than toilet paper or wipes, which have to be packed and burned.

Brown was funny, engaging, and so unself-consciously candid about everything from pooping positions to yeast infections and genital inspection that she put even me at ease. When she finished, the crowd stood and applauded. I closed my notebook and clapped, too.

Aidan and I were now on a mission to find a canoe for our trip. We'd already ruled out one-person, lightweight pack rafts, larger-oared rafts, and inflatable kayaks in favor of a backcountry canoe with a spray cover. Just outside the doors of the main hall, there was a map listing the exhibitors, including Pakboats, and their locations. Aidan took out her phone and went to the Pakboats website.

"Looks like the 170 might be the one," she said. "It's seventeen feet long, weighs fifty-six pounds, and can carry nine hundred and ten pounds. The website calls it a 'wilderness work horse.'" Then she went to Paddling.net and read snippets of reviews: "'Stable; tracks well; tough; handles well in whitewater; extremely dry' with the 'heavy duty' spray skirt; 'robust rubber lining,' but just in case, it says the 'skin is easy to patch.'"

Inside the hall, we made our way over to the Pakboats display. Alv Elvestad greeted us. The Norwegian-born Elvestad runs the company out of Enfield, New Hampshire.

He showed us the 170, and I tested the skin and inspected the gunwale rods, the cross-ribs, the air tubes that provide extra buoyancy, and the keel and chine rods. They were thick and shock-corded and, according to one of the reviews Aidan found, well built and durable. As I examined the canoe, Elvestad patiently answered my questions. Half an hour later, we exited the hall, convinced that we'd found our boat.

Though we were fairly certain we'd found the right canoe, we still hadn't settled on a river. We were drawn to the Hulahula, but I forced myself to keep making calls and sending emails, collecting information about other rivers. Yet every time I heard its name, I thought, *Yes, that's it; that's the one.*

CHAPTER 19

TRUST

I T WAS EARLY APRIL AND the pair of mating cranes, rust-colored and frisky—I could hear their croaky calls—had returned to the hay meadow. The air was damp and sweet with the smell of new grass. Blossoms puckered from our fruit trees. Spring was here to stay, and I knew that if Aidan and I were going to make our summer adventure a reality, we had lots to do. We had refined our gear list, and each day, during training hikes, I brushed up on my compass skills. And, as I walked, I went through the list of Arctic rivers in my head.

In the past few weeks, we'd narrowed down that list to three: the Canning, the Kongakut, and the Hulahula. For a solid week, Aidan and I debated the pros and cons of each river. Then we got a call from Burns.

Edward Burns Ellison, or Burns, as most of his friends called him, had been my classmate at the University of Colorado, Boulder. Already middle-aged when I met him, he had struck me as odd. Not odd in an unsettling way, more like interestingly eccentric. I figured he had a story to tell, and when we ended up eating chicken wings at a Boulder tavern after class one day, he didn't disappoint. Burns, as it turned out, was well traveled. He'd been to many places I hoped to see one day, including Ethiopia and much of South America. But the story that really grabbed me was one about his most recent adventure, a monthlong trek-paddle across the Brooks Range and down the Hulahula River to the Arctic Ocean. Burns and I grew to be the best of friends. After Elizabeth and I married, he became another member of the family, and Aidan's godfather. Over the years, I heard the story of his journey a number of times. And I never tired of it.

Burns was now eighty and suffering from periodic epileptic seizures and Parkinson's-like symptoms that had compromised his balance. There was a time when he half thought he might try to do the river portion of the trip with us. By the end of 2014, however, he realized the dream was unrealistic.

When he called, Aidan and I each picked up a phone. As he talked of his adventure, almost a "quarter of a century ago," I heard his voice shake with emotion. "Jimmy, Aidan," he said, his voice still trembling. "If you want my two cents, I'd vote for the Hulahula." He took a long breath. "I'd give my life to see it one more time."

That call sealed our decision. A week later, a package of notes and maps from my friend Bert—he and his wife, Janie, had accompanied Burns on his Arctic expedition—arrived, and our Pakboat canoe did, too. Aidan and I didn't waste any time. That night we assembled it. It took almost two hours, and as soon as we built it, we took it apart and assembled it again. It was tedious but necessary work. We wanted, when we got to the Hulahula, to know exactly what we were doing.

The next afternoon, Aidan and I made our maiden voyage in the canoe. We were paddling the nearby Baraboo River with our friend Dale. Dale is also our family physician and a master canoeist who has paddled many of Canada's most rugged rivers.

We'd chosen a lively five-mile section of the river. With the snowmelt, it was running harder than ever. We began by working on basic skills—pivots, sideslips, peeling out, ferrying, backpaddling, and eddy turns. Early on, it was apparent that Aidan and I needed practice. We were out of sync, and, worst of all, we argued and blamed each other. After one near dump, we settled into an eddy. Aidan looked thoroughly defeated. In the bow, she knelt slumped over with her paddle resting on the gunwales.

"Just takes practice," Dale said, pulling into the eddy.

Aidan harrumphed. About the last thing she wanted to do was spend another afternoon on the river with me. When we finally reached the pullout an hour later, both of us were relieved to be off the water. Our maiden voyage was a bust.

When we got home Elizabeth greeted us at the door, eager to hear how things had gone. Aidan brushed past her, barely managing a "Hi, Mom" before she walked upstairs and shut her bedroom door.

"It didn't go well," I told Elizabeth. "It was tense and Aidan told me I yelled at her too much."

"Well, did you?"

"I probably overdid it," I admitted.

"Probably?"

"Well, then, definitely."

Now Elizabeth was upset. "You need to go easy on her. You forget she's only fifteen."

"Yeah," I said guiltily. "I know."

It was eleven o'clock when I went up to bed and noticed that Aidan's light was still on. I knocked on her door.

"Studying?" I asked feebly.

She looked at me as if to say, *Whaddya think, Dad?* Then she answered, perfunctorily, "Yeah. History."

I sat down at the end of her bed, and she adjusted her feet to make room for me. "I'm sorry about today," I said.

She didn't respond right away. Instead, she wrote in her notebook. Then she laid down her pencil. "I was nervous today, Dad, and you made it worse."

"I know I did," I said. "I got frustrated."

"If that's the way it's going to be," she fired back, "I don't want to go to Alaska. I don't want to spend my summer listening to you scream at me."

Over the next week, we made it to the Baraboo River two more times. Aidan was becoming more comfortable on the water, and I was becoming more comfortable with her decisions. It wasn't easy; sometimes I had to bite my tongue. But it was a good lesson; I was learning to relinquish control. Still, it was clear we had work to do. Aidan and I had never canoed an ice-cold, glacier-fed Arctic river together, especially one like the Hulahula, whose rapids are classified as II, III, and III+, nothing, in other words, for inexperienced paddlers. The prospect of not being ready for that kept me up at night. When I slept, my dreams were edged with the sound of rushing water.

DESPITE OUR PROGRESS, the signs that time was slipping away from us were everywhere. Along the fence line, behind the house, the wild plums were budding out; Willa was counting down the days until summer vacation; and the garlic that Rachel and I had planted in early fall had sprouted. Each night, before going to bed, I studied the maps that Bert had sent. After sketching out a route, I penciled in X's at potential campsites.

During the course of our trip, we would cross all the ecoregions of the Arctic: the boreal forest, forest tundra, mountains, Arctic tundra, and coastal marine. Jack Turner, the writer and environmentalist, called a trip like ours—a three-and-a-half-week brush with wildness, one unmediated by park rangers or trail crews—an "endangered experience." Although the Arctic National Wildlife Refuge was created by forward-thinking men and women, man's influence there was almost nonexistent. There were no visitors' forms to fill out or backcountry fees to pay; no arrows to guide us along our route; nothing directing us to Gilbeau Pass; no warnings about the gorge's Class III+ rapids; and no tips on how to behave in bear country. In the refuge, travelers are on their own, free to enjoy the wild, to be inspired by it, to suffer, and, maybe, to die.

One of the final pieces in the logistical puzzle was reaching Robert Thompson to make arrangements for him to pick us up by boat once we arrived at the coast. Originally, my plan was to paddle from the mouth of the Hulahula River east to Kaktovik, Alaska, an Inupiat Eskimo village situated at the edge of Barter Island, a barrier island shaped like the skull of a musk ox, in the Arctic Ocean's Beaufort Sea. Other than Canada's Arctic Archipelago, Kaktovik is one of the northernmost points in North America. My intention was to stay inside the barrier islands, but people I'd talked with had warned me against it. Strong prevailing northeasterly winds often make paddling impossible there.

Thompson was a friend of a friend, a respected guide, registered with Fish and Wildlife, who had traveled thousands of miles across the Arctic. He lived in Kaktovik. When I reached him by phone, he said that the pickup would be pretty simple. "I'll get you on the west end of Arey Island," he told me. I immediately recognized the name from the maps Bert had sent me. "But you can't come all the way down the Hulahula," he continued. "Once you see the sand dunes and the hunting shack and the pingo—it looks like a small volcano—in the distance, you'll need to portage over to the Okpilak River and paddle that to the mouth. Then, it's a quarter mile crossing to Arey. It can be rough, though. And watch out for polar bears. You going to carry a sat phone and a shotgun?"

I assured him I'd have both.

"So how many of you will it be?" he asked.

"My daughter and me, and maybe two more," I replied. The two more were my buddy Dave Musgrave and Chris Jones, both longtime Alaskans. Dave and I had met on the Kongakut River in the Arctic in 2001. On my trips to Alaska following that summer adventure I had often stayed with him in Fairbanks. He had divorced, retired early from the University of Alaska, Fairbanks, remarried, and moved to just outside of Palmer, Alaska. Chris Jones was Dave's good friend, a former physical education teacher and fishing guide. On our way back to Wisconsin after our first trip, Aidan and I had spent a day with Dave and Chris climbing up to the Snowbird Glacier near Hatcher Pass in the Talkeetna Mountains. Both were in their early sixties, with the lean, fit physiques of athletes twenty years younger. Having retired, they spent their time climbing mountains, cycling, and cross-country skiing.

"If you don't mind me saying," Thompson offered, "numbers are good. I've been down that river. It can be dangerous, especially in a canoe. And you're bound to run into bears. You'll be safer with another person or two." He ended on an upbeat note. "Make sure you bring your fishing rods. There are some nice grayling holes just before and after the gorge. Once you get farther down, you should run into Arctic char. In August, they'll be coming up the river to spawn."

A day after talking with Robert, I got a message from Dave. "We're in," he said.

When I told Aidan about Dave and Chris, she was excited. I was, too. My hope was that she would learn from them, as she had learned from Heimo and Edna. Dave was definitely one of her admirers. He was also a Nordic ski coach who understood what made kids tick. Although we barely knew Chris, as a former middle school teacher, he certainly was able to build a rapport with teenagers. What's more, he, too, had a daughter.

IN EARLY JUNE, Aidan and I made a trip to northern Wisconsin's National Wild and Scenic Wolf River. For Aidan's birthday, her grandparents surprised her with a present that included a night's lodging at the Bear Paw resort and two days of white-water instruction. At a Class III rapid called Gilmore's Mistake, we were practicing a variety of river rescue techniques.

The water was cold and fast, and still high with spring runoff. As I tumbled by, I blew my whistle, man overboard. It was Aidan's job to rescue me. From the riverbank, she tossed the throw bag, with the safety rope, but didn't time her throw properly and missed me. I navigated the rapid and managed to swim into an eddy. As I exited the water, I saw her scowling.

"This is supposed to be fun," I told her as I walked by.

She shot me a look that didn't require interpretation.

I floated down again, and this time her throw was perfect. I looked back, watching her as the current ate up the slack and the rope tightened. She was sitting on her butt, leaning back with all her might, and digging her river shoes into the rock. She held tightly to the rope, and then, as I paddled for the slower water of the eddy, she pulled me in.

By 4:00 p.m., our class was over. We made arrangements with our instructor to meet early the following morning to test our skills on a challenging ten-mile section of the river.

When we met at 7:30, I saw that the instructor had brought along a partner, a teenage girl, Erin, who was one of the top competitive canoeists in the country. Once we got to the river, we made a plan: Tom and Erin would lead and demonstrate. We would follow. After an easy section of flatwater, the rapids began. We watched Tom and Erin dissect the river, back-paddling against the current and eddying out to give themselves time to scout and choose a line through the rapids. In the front of the boat, Aidan concentrated on Erin's strokes. I could see her imitating her, first a crossbow draw and then a pry, then a command to me, her belief in herself growing as she navigated a Class II+ stretch of white water.

Everything was going well. Erin had set a great example for Aidan. On land, she was sweet and unassuming, but as soon as she started paddling, she was fearless and focused.

We paddled into an eddy near the bank where Tom and Erin were waiting for us. We were about to enter a tough section of white water. Downriver, I could see a maze of rocks.

"Pick it apart," Tom said. "Take it slow."

Tom and Erin shoved off. We watched them carefully. One hundred yards down, they pulled into an eddy and, again, waited.

"Ready, Aidan?" I said.

As we peeled out into the river, turning our bow downstream, I could feel the power of the current. Aidan picked a nice line, and we navigated around a few rocks and then tried to slip by a large boulder. In the bow, Aidan made a last-second correction.

"No," I shouted, but by the time I tried to sweep the stern around the boulder, it was too late. We were perpendicular to the river and the middle of our canoe was caught, high-centered, on a boulder. I could see the aluminum midribs straining as the current pushed us against the rock. In the stern, with only a few inches of freeboard left, the river was about to pour in over the side of the canoe. I yelled for Aidan to lean into the rock, knowing that the only way to dislodge the boat was for me to get out. I slid into the cold water, and, holding on to the gunwale, made my way to the middle of the canoe. The current wanted to sweep me under the boat. I leaned forward and back, attempting to rock the canoe, and managed to pull the stern a few feet upstream.

"Push your bow off the rock when I tell you," I yelled to Aidan. Then, still holding the stern into the current, I scooched my butt onto another big rock, slid my legs into the canoe, and knelt as quickly as I could.

"Okay," I shouted to Aidan. She pushed her paddle against the rock. A second later, the current caught us, spun us, and pushed us backward downriver.

"Dad!" Aidan screamed.

"Pivot!" I yelled. "Pivot."

We turned the canoe around just as we hit another section of rapids. When we made it through, we saw Tom and Erin waiting along the riverbank. We pulled into the eddy and tied our boat off.

"Some tricky sections ahead," Tom said. Then he looked at me. "Jim, had you followed Aidan's lead, you would have made it past that boulder. You're doing the steering, but you have to react to her strokes. She's setting the course. You can't be dictating to her from the stern. You have to have faith in her."

The rest of the day went little better than the morning. Our three-hour trip home was a quiet one. We made small talk, but mostly we fretted. I knew what Aidan was thinking because I was thinking the same thing: were we ready for the Hulahula?

When we arrived home, I stopped at the entrance to our driveway. Willa and Rachel were on the tire swing, laughing like little girls at the county fair, and Elizabeth was working in the garden. The scene was so idyllic that for a moment I wondered why I was going to Alaska.

The girls shouted out a greeting from the swing, and Elizabeth walked over, rubbing her hands on her work jeans.

"So," she said. "How was it?"

"Rough," I answered.

"What does that mean?" she asked.

"Dad doesn't trust me," Aidan jumped in. And then I realized that I was wrong when I thought I knew what she was thinking in the car. She wasn't worried that we might not be ready for the Hulahula. She was upset that my lack of trust in her was ruining our paddling partnership. Because I was second-guessing her, I wasn't able to respond to her strokes.

"Again?" Elizabeth asked.

"Yes," Aidan continued. "Dad has control issues." She walked into the house.

Elizabeth gave me the same look she'd given me weeks earlier, after our first outing on the Baraboo River.

"Tandem canoeing isn't easy," I said, defending myself. "Anyone who has ever canoed with another person knows that. Most paddling partnerships don't work. That's why they call tandem canoes divorce boats."

Elizabeth wasn't buying my excuse. "Maybe so," she said. "But you have to make it work with Aidan. Don't forget your promise: if you're not ready, you're not going."

Over the next week, Aidan and I were able to make a few more runs down the Baraboo, which was still running above normal stage. We worked on our cadence, ran the rapids and caught the wave trains, then turned around and paddled or lined our canoe upstream and ran them again. I could feel us getting in sync and the boat responding. Aidan was becoming more confident about reading the river and choosing her strokes, and I was learning to be less controlling. But the trip that clinched it for us, the experience that convinced us we were ready for the Hulahula, was a family trip for Elizabeth's birthday on the famed Middle Fork of the Salmon River in central Idaho.

Friends of ours had secured a permit. When they invited us to join them, we were thrilled. Elizabeth had never expressed any interest in joining us in the Arctic, but she wanted to celebrate her fiftieth birthday on the river.

The Middle Fork is one of America's great river adventures and one of the original eight rivers designated in the National Wild and Scenic Rivers System in 1968. For ninety-six miles, it runs through the heart of the 2.5-million-acre Frank Church–River of No Return Wilderness, the second largest wilderness area in the Lower 48. Just days before we left, I learned that Frank Church, a senator from Idaho and a committed conservationist, was the floor sponsor of none other than the Wilderness Act. This gave the Idaho trip added significance for me: in a serendipitous convergence, my wife and the Wilderness Act were both turning fifty, and I was going to simultaneously celebrate two of the things that give my life meaning.

I also hoped the Middle Fork would be a training ground for Aidan and me. This was confirmed by day one, as we encountered not only big, rugged country but big water, too. Many of the rapids along the river's ninety-six miles are Class III and Class IV, especially at the lower end, where it dumps into the Main Fork of the Salmon. While Elizabeth, Rachel, and Willa chose to float the river in a raft with a guide, Aidan and I paddled inflatable kayaks, which are more stable and forgiving than regular hard-shell kayaks, and have almost nothing in common with a canoe, tandem or solo. But the experience taught us not to fear the water; we learned to tackle boulder gardens, wave trains, whirlpools, holes, drops and ledges, massive rapids, and long stretches of white water that demanded intense concentration. After seven days, Aidan was reading the river with a confidence that surpassed all my expectations. By the time we left Idaho, she believed in her ability to run the Hulahula. And so did I.

Elizabeth was now a believer, too. "Aidan came alive on the river, didn't she?" she said to me after we'd returned to Lodi. We were walking through the back field.

"Yes," I agreed. "She really did."

Then Elizabeth said, "Thank you for making the time to go to Idaho. That trip meant a lot to me."

"To me, too," I said. And it had. Being away in the Arctic had tested my relationship with Elizabeth. Oftentimes, even when I was home, large distances seemed to separate us, in part because my mind was in Alaska. I was always planning, preparing, imagining, and dreaming. I was restless. But in Idaho, my mind didn't wander.

CHAPTER 20

SAY GOOD-BYE TO SUMMER

IT WAS MID-JULY AND FAIRBANKS looked like Ireland from the air. In July and August, smoke jumpers are usually fighting fires all over the Alaska Interior, but now all I could see from the plane was a shimmering green. It had been a wet summer, the wettest in forty years.

Aidan was sitting next to me reading *Path of the Paddle: An Illustrated Guide to the Art of Canoeing*, which our friend Dale gave us before we left Wisconsin. We were relaxed now, but once we landed we had an assortment of pre-trip errands to run.

Four days later, on our last night in Fairbanks, we were at a friend of Dave's sorting through our food and splitting it into Ziploc bags. We'd been packing for an hour and still the food pile was astonishingly high. Could we possibly need this much? I participated with a secret dread: with my bad knees, was I up to hauling a seventy-pound backpack and a ten-pound shotgun across the

Arctic? Dave worried that the food we had would not be enough. We were told that we could rely on fish, but what scared us was the rain. The rivers would be high and no one could predict how that would affect the fishing. We took a vote and decided that we could rely on fish for three or four suppers, but Dave was clearly un-happy about it. It was our first small disagreement. I sensed there would be more.

It took us three hours to divide and pack the food into breakfast, lunch, and dinner bags, and by the time we were done, everyone was tired. Earlier in the day Aidan and I had left the campground where we'd been since arriving in Fairbanks and checked in to a local hotel because the forecast had called for two days of rain. Now we were eager to return to the room. Our plan was to wake early to pack our backpacks one more time.

Just as we were ready to leave, we decided that everyone, and especially Aidan, needed a bear spray instructional. We'd all heard about the bear attack on the Hulahula in 2005. Richard and Katherine Huffman, two seasoned backcountry travelers, were celebrating their sixteenth wedding anniversary by kayaking the river. Early one morning, just days after the summer solstice, a bear dragged them from their tent and killed them.

We positioned ourselves in the middle of a gravel road and tested the wind. There was not even the whiff of a breeze. Then we simulated a bear attack.

"Now," we yelled to Aidan, who drew her can and sent a stream of spray in the direction of the imaginary bear.

"Pump it," Chris told her. "You want to shoot in two-second bursts, shoot, pause, shoot, pause."

Aidan tried again. This time she got off two thirty-foot shots. The pepper cloud hung in the air, but then it began to drift our way. When had the wind come up? We backed down the gravel road, as if we were being pursued by a slow but determined enemy. At first we laughed at the absurdity of the situation, but, as if on cue, we started to cough and our throats burned. Then, we turned and ran.

We got halfway down the road, to where we could breathe more freely, and considered our options: we could bushwhack through the woods or return the way we'd come. Chris and I decided to dash back up the gravel road to the garage. I took a deep breath, covered my mouth with my handkerchief, and sprinted with Chris. Dave and Aidan followed. When we got to the driveway, we were all still rubbing our eyes and clearing our throats.

Back at the garage, we'd largely recovered and made arrangements to meet at 6:30 the following morning. Then we'd take the daily mail plane to Arctic Village, where we'd meet up with Kirk Sweetsir before heading by bush plane to Red Sheep Creek, the rough airstrip that lay at the southern boundary of the Arctic National Wildlife Refuge's Wilderness Area.

In the car, on the way back to the hotel, Aidan asked about the bear spray. "Seriously, Dad," she said. "What if I have to shoot at a grizzly upwind?"

I wasn't sure what to tell her. The unwelcome fact was that, although sprays can be propelled at high speeds, if a bear was coming from upwind, Aidan would have to let it get close—very close—before pulling the trigger.

She didn't like my silence. "I know what you're thinking, Dad. That sucks. Please tell me you'll always be nearby with the gun."

ON THE MORNING of July 24, Aidan and I woke at 5:00. Uncharacteristically, she seemed fully awake and got right to work.

Ten minutes later, she kicked at her backpack. "God," she said, "I'm sick of packing and unpacking and packing again. I thought I had a perfect system."

I laughed and told her to get used to it; backpacks are like the dryer that eats socks. You can pack with precision but still end up pulling out everything only to discover that you can't find the one thing you're after.

An hour later, Aidan and I were ready to go. We divided our gear into our backpacks and into the dry bags we'd use for the river portion of the trip. Then we went outside to check on the weather. It was overcast and cold and looked like it might rain again. As we were standing there, Heimo pulled up. Heimo and Edna were in town buying supplies before heading back out to the cabin on the Coleen. He'd called us the previous night to wish us luck, and now he and Rhonda, his elder daughter, had unexpectedly come to say good-bye.

Heimo wound down the window but stayed in his truck. "Too cold out there."

"How cold is it?" Aidan asked.

"When I got up this morning, it was forty-five."

Aidan looked deflated. She knew that summer temperatures in Fairbanks—and even above the Arctic Circle—could be in the high seventies or low eighties, but, since arriving in Alaska, we'd yet to see anything warmer than 58 degrees.

"Hey, I got an idea," Heimo said. "Let's check the NOAA weather report for the Brooks Range. Maybe you'll get some good news."

He called on his phone. When the recording began for Anaktuvuk Pass, an inland Eskimo village within the boundaries of the Gates of the Arctic National Park, he turned up the volume.

"It's not exactly where you'll be," he explained. "It's farther west, but the weather will probably be the same."

"Shh," Aidan said when the report for Thursday and Friday, July 24 and 25, began. We listened intently. "Cold, two to four inches of snow, and twenty-five-mile-per-hour winds."

"Shitty," Heimo said. The report got worse: more snow, more cold, and more wind. A low-pressure system from the Arctic coast, almost four hundred miles to the north, was moving through the middle of Alaska, bringing rain to Fairbanks and snow to the Brooks Range.

I grumbled. "That's one of the crappiest reports I've ever heard. Sounds like we're walking straight into winter."

When I looked up, Heimo and Rhonda were laughing tears. "Welcome to Alaska," Rhonda said, barely able to get the words out.

"Goooood luck," Heimo said, shaking my hand and then Aidan's through the open window. "Sorry," he said, "but I ain't gettin' out."

Then he rolled up the window, backed his truck away, and stopped. He wound down the window again, but only halfway.

He was still laughing. "Jimmer," he said. "You and Aidan might as well kiss summer good-bye."

CHAPTER 21

"IT'S A!?"

WE ARRIVED IN ARCTIC VILLAGE in the late morning. Dark clouds were moving down the Chandalar River valley, part of the low-pressure system from the Arctic coast, and in no time it was raining. When the storm passed, we heard the sound of a plane, and we all brightened. But it turned out to be not Kirk but instead another bush pilot transporting four biologists from the U.S. Fish and Wildlife Service in Fairbanks. They'd been out for two weeks and looked scruffy and tired, but happy. They warned us that the weather had been cold and wet and that the long-range forecast called for more of the same. We nodded knowingly.

Since we had what looked to be a brief window of good weather, I decided to test out my pack. Aidan helped me wrestle it onto my back. When I set off, my first reaction was one of shock—the pack was considerably heavier than the backpack I'd trained with at home, and I'd even left the shotgun behind. I walked for about a mile and then stopped to adjust the straps. An old, bowlegged Native man walked by in the opposite direction.

"Pack looks heavy," he said without slowing his pace.

I nodded and continued down the road toward the village, turning back when I saw the clouds building again up the river valley. When I returned, Aidan was studying her solar charger, trying to figure out how it worked and how to rig it to her backpack. Chris was reading and Dave was talking to one of the biologists, a friend from his Fairbanks days.

Aidan told me that she was going to test out her pack, too. Dave overheard. When Aidan disappeared to pee, he took the opportunity to place a large rock in her backpack. She returned, and Chris, playing along, said to her, "C'mon, Aidan, let's walk a little."

Dave winked at me and hoisted up her backpack while Aidan wriggled her arms into the shoulder straps. If she noticed the extra weight, she didn't say anything. Chris and Aidan walked to the end of the gravel airstrip and kept going. Twenty or so minutes later, they came back.

"How'd it go?" Dave asked, and, when nobody responded, he said to Aidan, "How'd your pack feel?"

"Good," Aidan replied. "It felt good. I felt strong."

I was laughing now because Aidan had deprived Dave of his joke. He helped her take off her backpack, and then he pulled out the rock and held it for Chris and me and the biologists to see.

"You didn't feel this?" he asked.

Aidan chuckled good-naturedly. "Nope," she said. "Not a thing."

"Plane!" Chris shouted.

We all turned upriver. Aidan was the first one to spot Kirk's white and blue Cessna 185 flying low beneath the clouds. We gathered our gear and walked out to the runway when he landed.

Kirk informed us that he could take only three of us and our backpacks at one time. We decided that Kirk would fly Aidan, Dave, and me into Red Sheep Creek, and then come back to get Chris. After that he'd fly back to Arctic Village one more time to pick up our folding canoes and extra supplies, which he'd transport to a place called Grasser's Strip, near the headwaters of the Hulahula River.

On the map our hike to Grasser's looked fairly straightforward. From Red Sheep Creek, we'd follow the broad valley of the East Fork of the Chandalar to the northeast. As the river made a hard turn to the east to its headwaters, we would cut north and then west in the direction of Gilbeau Pass, which would take us over the Continental Divide and the backbone of the Brooks Range, the northernmost mountains in North America. About ten miles west of the pass, we would bend north for Grasser's and the headwaters of the Hulahula.

It was a short flight to Red Sheep Creek. I watched the terrain below and thanked God that we'd had the good sense not to begin our hike farther south. Below I saw what looked like the Slough of Despond, muskeg, oxbow lakes, and swamp. As we neared Red Sheep, I was relieved to see the terrain changing. Mountains, tundra, and gravel bars began to replace bogs. But I'd walked across the tundra enough to know that looks can be deceiving, especially from the vantage point of a plane. We'd have a few days of slogging before the land dried out.

Kirk pulled the plane down low, and I felt Aidan's hand. It had become our ritual. I squeezed it three times: *I—love—you.* Kirk put the plane down easily. After helping drag out our backpacks, he said he wanted to show us something.

"You know what that is?" he asked, gesturing east at something in the tundra and willows.

I wasn't sure I knew what he was pointing at, but when he said it was a caribou fence, I was able to make it out. Gwich'in and Inupiat hunters had used the spruce-log fences for thousands of years before the introduction of the rifle. They built them, miles long, along the caribou migration routes, and when the animals came, they worked together to herd them into the fences and then into corrals, where they clubbed them. The caribou provided nearly everything they needed: food, clothing, bedding and shelter, fishhooks, and hide scrapers. But some years, the caribou failed to come, and then the people suffered.

Coming upon a caribou fence was a rare privilege. Though they are spread across the tussock meadows of the refuge, only someone who knew the landscape as well as Kirk would ever be able to spot them.

When Kirk took off, Aidan and I took another practice run with our backpacks, walking in the direction of the river.

"I can't believe it," Aidan said, looking north up the Chandalar. "It's all so big. There's just so much of it. It's a little scary to think about, isn't it, Dad? Something could happen to us and no one would know for weeks."

Aidan was right. Although human beings live more safely and comfortably than people ever have, to be in real wilderness is to understand that nature cares no more for us than it does for the wolf, or the golden eagle, or the shrew. Never had I understood this more than now.

When we returned to the airstrip, the fog had blown over and the sun broke out. We heard Kirk's plane returning with Chris. But because the fog had drifted south of us, we didn't see it until it was nearly overhead. Then, surrounded by pure blue sky and mountains dusted with white snow, Kirk's small plane was a thing of beauty. Colors in the Arctic have a brilliance I've never seen anywhere else.

Kirk made a pass, testing the wind. Then he came in again and put the plane down. When Chris got out he looked around and howled.

"Can you believe this," he said. "We're here."

We watched Kirk fly off and then we took a vote about whether to camp where we were or put a few miles between us and Red Sheep. There was little discussion. All of us were pumped up on adrenaline and eager to move.

As we walked, Dave pointed out yellow Arctic poppies and purple inky gentians. Despite their beauty, I was surprised by the lack of flowers. In 2001, on the Kongakut River, whole hillsides were in bloom. However, this summer had been a cold one, and perhaps the flowers had already gone to seed. The blueberry bushes, I noticed, had turned pale, and the leaves of the bearberry were tinged with red.

Initially, the walking was dry and easy. Despite my seventy-pound pack and the shotgun, I felt good, not exactly light-footed but not slow and clumsy, either. Aidan was fifty yards ahead, walking with Dave. I could tell by her stride that she felt strong and happy.

We walked for two miles at a fairly brisk pace, and then we came to muskeg. I was immersed in the physical joy of hiking and then suddenly my boots were wet and I was teetering from side to side. Now my backpack felt like what it was—an unwieldy burden.

We all stopped to assess the bog and plot a route through it or around it. For a moment, we contemplated walking down to the river, but we'd been moving away from it. There was a small ridge that followed the edge of a black spruce forest, where the ground was higher, but the woods, we all knew, meant bugs.

"Mosquitoes or water?" Aidan asked me.

I was thinking, and when I didn't respond, she trudged off. She'd never been good about making decisions—even in restaurants, she tortures herself, and us, with her indecision—but now she didn't bother to ask twice. She walked with certainty right through it.

Half an hour later, when we climbed out of the muskeg and reached the tree line, the mosquitoes were there to greet us. We followed the trees into a pretty meadow where a small stream, flanked by head-high willows, twisted its way through the grass. To me it looked like the perfect camping place—a windbreak and fresh water, dry wood for a fire if we needed one, and long lines of sight so that we could see grizzlies approaching. But we'd been walking for only three hours, and thanks to the bog, we hadn't even covered three miles. So I kept quiet about making camp. I didn't want the others to wonder if this was all I was capable of. At a pace of three miles a day, our food supply would run out before we reached Gilbeau Pass.

Just then I heard Dave say, "Looks like a nice spot to set up. What do you guys think?"

"Looks good to me," Aidan and Chris said in unison. Then Chris added, "No need to push it on our first day."

We set up a small cook site in a sandy area 150 yards downwind from our tents. While Chris and Aidan gathered wood, I got a small fire going, using cotton balls smeared in Vaseline as fire starter. Rachel and Willa had made up a large bag and given it to me as a going-away present.

At the campsite, Dave set up our bear fence. It was compact and added little weight to his pack. Although we all carried bear spray and I had the lone shotgun, the fence gave us added protection, especially at night while we slept. Battery-powered, it was designed to deliver ten thousand volts of electricity to a curious grizzly, a jolt that wouldn't kill one, but would be very unpleasant. No one was more delighted that we'd brought it along than Aidan. Though she was more comfortable with the idea of bears than she had been on our first two trips, the story of the husband and wife who had been killed by a grizzly on the Hulahula had stuck with her. Perhaps a bear fence would have saved them. What I didn't tell her was that there had been reports of bears learning to jump the fences.

THE NIGHT WAS a calm one, and the next morning we woke to winter. It was cold when we went to sleep and we all figured that we'd get a dusting in the mountains, but nobody had expected that the boughs of the spruce trees would be bent with snow or the socks we'd set out to wind-dry would be rock-hard and covered in tiny, white crystals. Aidan's water bottle, which she'd left out, was frozen solid.

It was too cold to linger over breakfast. We ate and then had a brief talk about how to make our way north. We decided to avoid the bog and head for the trees. But as soon as we entered the spruce forest, mosquitoes rose like smoke out of the sedges. They were so thick that Aidan and I put on our head nets.

As we continued walking, Aidan pointed to an area that looked as if an excavator had come through. "Dad," she said. "Is that what I think it is?"

"Well," I answered, "that depends. What do you think it is?"

"A bear digging?" It was more of a question than a statement, and there was a hopeful tone to it, as if she believed there was a chance that it was something else. But no such luck. A grizzly had, indeed, been tearing up the soil to get at the tasty roots that make up a large portion of its diet.

"Yup," I said. "We should be on alert."

When we finally got out of the thick spruce forest, we saw that the river had turned in our direction. We walked along the bank.

"Careful of those cutbanks," Chris warned. "They might collapse."

Half a mile upriver, we followed a wide and well-trodden bear trail. The walking was easy and we were happy to use it, until we came upon piles of dung, not steaming, but fresh enough to make us uncomfortable. I put a slug in the chamber of my shotgun and made sure that Aidan walked close behind me. She took her pepper spray from its holster and held it in her hand like a pistol.

When the trees ended and we came to a tundra opening near the river, we stopped for a lunch of tortillas and hummus. The breeze would keep away the mosquitoes, and if there was a bear in the vicinity, we'd likely be able to see it.

Now I could feel the wind, which had shifted to directly out of the north. I crawled between two large rocks for shelter. Aidan was still standing.

"What's up?" I asked her.

"I'm watching," she said. "For a grizzly. One could be tracking us. The breeze is right."

Chris was sitting against a boulder. He had his binoculars out and was looking downriver. Maybe he, too, was watching. Aidan was correct; the wind was right, and grizzlies have a sense of smell seven times stronger than a bloodhound's.

We ate and rested, and by the time we were ready to walk again, the sun was gone, and a damp fog had settled over the valley. We leaned into the wind and sleet and picked up our pace, as if we might walk through the low-hanging clouds and emerge on the other side, where we'd be greeted by a midsummer sun and the scent of Labrador tea rising off the tundra.

An hour into the hike we were spread out. Dave was out front, Chris and Aidan were in the middle, walking and talking, and I was pulling up the rear, plodding doggedly. Aidan was ambivalent about walking with me. She liked to stay nearby because I was carrying the shotgun, but part of her was like a filly eager to run. She wanted to be out front, leading the group to the Gilbeau Pass turnoff.

As I came down into a little gully choked with hip-high willows, my foot caught and I tumbled into the tangle of branches. My head was on the downhill side, and, because of the weight of my backpack, I couldn't push myself up. I considered yelling out, but the ignominy of calling for help kept me quiet. I managed to pivot my body, so I was lying on my belly, facing uphill. Pulling on the willows, I got to one knee. Now I was cursing the topography, and feeling guilty for hating it.

Suddenly, someone shouted, "Bear!"

Still trapped in the gully, I couldn't see anything. I tried running through the willows and nearly tripped again. When I finally got to the top, I was panicking. Where was Aidan?

"Aidan!" I screamed. Every paternal instinct I've ever had was in overdrive. Then I saw Chris and Aidan, and Dave, about thirty yards in front of them. That night, Aidan would tell me that she wanted to run back to me, but was too frightened to move.

"Bear!" Dave yelled again. I heard the tension in his voice. He was looking back as if he had just realized that the person carrying the group's shotgun was too far away to be of any use.

I was moving as fast as I could, while carrying a ten-pound shotgun and a seventy-pound pack. Meanwhile, I was scanning the tundra. *Where's the bear?*

I caught sight of a large, brown mass in the willows to our right and slowed to a purposeful walk. The last thing I wanted to do was provoke a grizzly by running. My eyes were fixed on it, and the adrenaline was pounding through my body. I kept walking, but never let my eyes stray from the bear. When I was nearly abreast of Dave, I saw two horns emerge from the grizzly's head. *Horns?* I asked myself.

Then I heard Dave again, this time relief. "Ahh, it's a musk ox."

We'd stumbled upon a musk ox, an animal resembling a bison, but without its aggressive temperament. When the fear subsided and my mind was no longer fastened on the image of a grizzly charging us, I wondered: what was a musk ox doing all alone, and what was it doing here? Although some males are solitary in summer, musk oxen are usually found in "social groups" or small herds. And they're usually on the coastal plain, not on the Chandalar River south of the Brooks Range.

We walked as close as we could without spooking him. He was browsing, throwing his head back and forth, simultaneously ripping tender, protein-rich leaves from their branches and warding off mosquitoes. He was the size of a very large barren lands grizzly. His shaggy coat—Inupiat Eskimos call musk ox *omingmak,* "the bearded one"—hung on his six-hundred-pound frame.

Aidan was riveted. I stood next to her without saying a word. Finally, she said, "He looks prehistoric, doesn't he? I feel like we're in a time warp."

Three more hours of hiking, and we came to a creek, spilling out of the mountains to the west. It was running surprisingly fast, much faster than the other creeks we'd crossed. The question was whether to camp on the near bank and cross in the morning, or cross it now and begin our hike the next morning in dry boots. Chris and Dave wanted to get to the other side. Aidan was cold and preferred staying put. I was tired and my knees ached, so I, too, suggested staying where we were. But after more discussion we agreed that if we found something that looked doable, we'd give it a shot.

Chris and Dave went upriver to scout, while Aidan and I scouted downriver. Every step was so painful, I wanted to lie down. But then we saw bear tracks, and, again, I felt the adrenaline. Aidan, however, was so cold that she barely flinched.

"I'm freezing," she said, and then she pointed to a thin layer of pancake ice not far from the tracks.

When we returned upriver, Dave said that he and Chris had found a spot where we could cross. It was fast, but not too deep. "Chris and I can go first," he offered.

I saw Aidan examining the river. If she had to ford a creek against her will, she was going to do it her way. When Dave and Chris reached the middle of the stream, I could see just how strong the current was. But they got across, and then Dave shouted, "You guys can do it."

Aidan was already thirty feet downstream. "I'm going here, Dad," she yelled back.

"Wait for me," I told her.

She waded in, and I walked in ten feet downstream from her. If she fell and got caught in the current, I might be able to grab her as she tumbled by. She reached the middle of the creek, stumbled, and regained her balance.

"Slow," I told her. "Don't rush it." It was an easy thing to say, but when the water that is pressing against your legs is fed by snowmelt from the mountains, the impulse is to get to the other side as quickly as possible.

When Aidan reached the far bank, Chris grasped her by the elbow and pulled her out of the water. Then it was my turn. I handed Chris my gun and reached for Dave. He grabbed my elbow and I took hold of his. He tried to pull me up, but, weighing only 150 pounds, he started to slide down the bank and wisely let go.

"Forget it," I said. "Let me try it."

Using my trekking poles, I tried to propel myself forward, but my knees were shot. I missed the lip of the bank and fell chest-first onto the rocks. I hit with a thud, and for a moment I couldn't breathe. Then, I struggled to my knees, wheezing.

Chris and Dave were both tugging at me now.

"Screw it," I growled. "You'll never get me up." My hardheadedness kicked in and I threw my poles onto the bank. I got down on my hands and knees and dragged myself up using rocks and willow trunks. When I finally made it to flat ground, I felt as if I'd climbed Everest.

Though I was panting and sweating, I didn't rest long. It was sleeting and Aidan was shivering again.

Splitting up, we looked around for a place to camp and eventually chose a spot behind a small copse of willows. Aidan and I set up our tent quickly and then wrestled with the rain fly, which strained to escape in the wind. The finished tent pulled and bucked at its guy lines.

"I know I should help with firewood and the water and the cook tent, Dad," Aidan said. "But I'm so cold."

"I understand," I said. It was only our second day and already both Aidan and I had come up against our limits. "Now, get in the tent, and change into dry clothes," I told her. "Your only job is to get warm."

CHAPTER 22

BE STILL MY HEART

T HE WIND WAS STILL HOWLING when I woke early the next morning. Instead of venturing over to the creek to start the WhisperLite and boil water for coffee and oatmeal, I lay in my bag writing in my trail diary. I scribbled for thirty minutes and then closed my eyes. By the time I wandered out of the tent, Aidan, Chris, and Dave were sitting around a small fire, scraping the bottoms of their oatmeal bowls. Aidan took one look at me and informed me that my beauty sleep had backfired. After yesterday, I was happy to hear her laugh again.

While Chris and Aidan did the dishes, Dave and I looked at the maps, trying to situate ourselves in the Arctic's vastness. We agreed that by the end of the day we should be close to the mouth of the broad valley that led to Gilbeau Pass. The Chandalar River is shaped like a bent arm, traveling north and then turning to the northeast. At what would be the elbow bone, we needed to head north-northwest for the pass.

As we were packing up, the sun made a brief appearance. Aidan, ready to go, took a seat against a rock and faced east. The feeling of the sun was something to be savored.

We began walking before the clouds gathered. The country had opened up and we had long views in every direction, so my worries about suddenly coming upon a bear were no longer as pressing. If there was a grizzly rummaging through the valley, we'd likely have ample warning. Aidan seemed less concerned as well. She was hiking out front, setting a blistering pace. Occasionally, she looked back to make sure I wasn't eating too much of her dust.

We'd been hiking for four hours when we stopped for lunch along the river near a small cutbank that emptied into a deepish hole. It was the first place we'd seen that even had the possibility of holding fish. Elsewhere, the river was too fast and too shallow.

While Aidan optimistically began to build a small cook fire, Chris, Dave, and I prepared to fish. Dave was ready before any of the rest of us and walked up the bank. I put together Aidan's three-piece pack rod first. By the time I snapped on a small spinner, she had the fire going, so I let her fish while I built my fly rod and chose a fly. As I was tying on a scud, I heard Dave downriver.

"Yippee," he yelled. "A grayling."

A few minutes later, I heard Aidan holler. "Got one."

The fish were small, but it was a start. I knew that Dave, still worried about our food supplies, would be relieved. Chris and I cleaned and cut up the fish. I ate the roe from mine while Aidan readied a small pan of cooking oil and black pepper for frying and Dave tried his luck farther downstream. He quickly returned, lured by the smell. A catch of two grayling wouldn't fill our bellies, but the sound of frying fish was a morale booster.

Twenty minutes later, when we hit the trail again, Chris and

Dave were playing their favorite game. One hummed a few bars of a song and the other tried to guess the tune. From Aidan's perspective, the two were hopelessly mired in yesteryear. When I joined in it was a real old-timers' hour.

After an hour of stupid fun we put our heads down and tried to pound out a few more miles. By four in the afternoon, I'd burned through my second, third, and fourth winds and was ready to lie down belly-up, like a worn-out fish. The only thing that kept me going was the thought of camp.

Aidan noticed me straggling and walked back to me.

"Can I take something, Dad?"

"No," I said.

"Don't be proud," she scolded me. "You're hurting. I can tell."

I didn't say anything.

"C'mon, Dad," she urged. "We have to help each other. You took care of me yesterday when I was so cold."

Reluctantly, I agreed to relinquish my sleeping bag. We crammed it into the top of her backpack and then we walked together in silence. Although I'd only given up three to four pounds, the difference was palpable, and Aidan wasn't fazed by the extra weight.

An hour north, when we hit a matted stretch of willows, I pulled my shotgun from my pack, and I carried it at the ready, as I would when hunting grouse or pheasants.

"Hey, bear. Hey, bear," the four of us shouted every few seconds.

The willow bar was a long one. When we left it behind and, again, entered open country, we were grateful.

"What about trying to find a place to camp?" Chris asked. "I don't know about you, but I'm tired."

Aidan and I both agreed, and though Dave had a bit of energy left he was amenable. We picked a spot on a gravel bar. Aidan and Dave collected wood and built a fire, while Chris and I, fishing rods in hand, scouted the river. I didn't see anything that resembled grayling habitat, but I fished anyway, every rock and eddy I could find. I would have fished longer—there were still a few rocks and eddies I hadn't tried—but I was extremely tired. My legs felt heavy and unresponsive, and since lunch, I'd been plagued by indigestion. Earlier, I'd popped two Rolaids, but they hadn't helped. The burning continued.

As I followed Chris back to the campsite, my heart skipped a beat. I stopped and breathed deeply and felt it skip another beat and then another. *Shit,* I thought. *Shit. This can't be happening. Not now.*

I'd been episode-free for so long I'd almost forgotten that I'd ever had atrial fibrillation (Afib). But, quickly, the warning signs come back to me. *Relax,* I told myself. *You need to relax.* I took a deep breath and coughed and then felt for my pulse. In the past, a hard cough would sometimes jar my heart back into a regular, or sinus, rhythm. But it was still rapid and irregular: *boom-boom, boom-boom-boom, b-boom.*

Calm down, I told myself again. *You've been here before.*

It was 2006, and I was trekking with a small team that included Dave across New Guinea's Papuan Peninsula, trying to retrace a World War II trail through remote and rugged terrain, when my heart began to fibrillate. I was in the midst of the jungle, far from anything resembling help, and I was frightened. I knew that if my heart didn't go back into sinus rhythm, the chances of my making it out weren't good. Eventually my heart converted and I made it to the peninsula's north coast.

Now, instead of going back to the campsite, I returned to the river. The last thing I wanted was to worry anybody, especially Aidan. I cast noncommittally into the rushing water and tried to remember some of the deep muscle relaxation techniques I'd learned when I was first diagnosed with Afib. Ten minutes later, my heart was still beating wildly. By the time I'd returned to the fire, just three hundred yards from the river, I was out of breath.

"Anything?" Chris asked.

"Nah," I answered, as calmly as I could.

Twenty feet away, Dave and Aidan were going through the food, trying to figure out if we had enough. I walked over and helped them sort meals. In the end, we figured that if we reduced our portions we would have six more days to make it to the river. It was enough, if nothing went wrong. Dave delivered the news to Chris, who clearly wasn't happy about hiking hard on short rations. In the meantime, my mind was racing through my list of options in the event that my heart continued to fibrillate. None of them were good.

The first would be for the four of us to stay put, and wait and hope that my heart went back into sinus rhythm. As a precaution, one I'd never expected to use, I'd brought along a prescription of metoprolol, a beta-blocker used to control heart rates. I could pop a fifty-milligram tablet and hope like hell that it kicked my heart into rhythm. If not, I'd have to hope that the baby aspirin I take every day would keep my blood thin enough to prevent a stroke.

The problem with this plan was that, for every day we sat, we'd be eating food that we'd need on the trail. I'd brought along bird shot, just in case we got low on food, but we'd yet to see any ducks or ptarmigan. I also had a leghold trap that Heimo had given me, in case of a food emergency, so that I could try to trap ground squirrels or marmots. I'd seen holes along the way, too many of them. Each burrow has an assortment of entrances, which allow the animals to escape predators, and I only had one trap. Putting it near the right hole would be a matter of luck.

The second option might have been the worst one of all. We could distribute some of the weight from my pack, if Dave and Chris were willing, and press on. The problem with this plan was that my resting pulse, normally 54, was vacillating between 85 and 110 beats per minute. I knew that as soon as we started to hike, particularly if we were climbing, my heart rate would spike and likely go into tachycardia, an abnormally rapid beat that is usually accompanied by dizziness and shortness of breath—two symptoms that would definitely put me in danger when scrambling over boulders in the high country. If I chose to press on, I would be fully committed until we reached the Hulahula. Once we left the broad Chandalar River corridor, it would be impossible for anything but a helicopter to get me out.

The third option, and perhaps the most practical, was to divide the food and for Aidan and me to make our way back to Red Sheep Creek, the nearest landing strip. It would be heartbreaking for Aidan to forfeit the hike that she had been anticipating, fearing, and dreaming about for so long. But if we could make it to Red Sheep, I could use the sat phone to call Kirk. If he was dropping supplies off at Grasser's anyway, there would be a chance that we could catch a ride with him. That way, if I felt better, we could at least enjoy the two-week river portion of our adventure. However, at that point, I'd have to seriously consider the wisdom of heading back out. I knew that the river was nothing I wanted to tackle if I wasn't feeling 100 percent.

My worry about the plan of hiking back to Red Sheep was that, in my condition, it was a four- to five-day tromp, at best. Could I burden Aidan with the responsibility of taking care of me? What if things got really bad? What if I had a stroke or a heart attack? Afib can trigger both because a heart that doesn't beat regularly allows blood clots to form in its upper chambers. These clots can break off and travel to the brain, the heart, other organs, or anywhere else that blood flows. And what if, God forbid, I died on Aidan? She would be on her own in one of the wildest, most remote places in the Northern Hemisphere.

Aidan and I set up the tent and then I walked slowly up the ridge to get a bit more firewood, seizing the chance to clear my head. I looked up and down the beautiful Chandalar River. Two miles to the north I could see the valley that led to Gilbeau Pass. I grabbed a small armful of wood and made my way back down to the campsite. The round trip was more than I could take. My heart was rushing, beating so hard it felt ready to leap from my chest, and my legs felt like deadweights.

When supper was ready, I ate quickly and retired to the tent to take some metoprolol. With my jackknife, I cut the tablet into two pieces and took one. Then I lay back on my sleeping bag, hoping that if I could calm my nerves the medicine would stand a better chance of working. When Aidan came in, she saw my pill bottle lying on my sleeping bag.

"You okay?" she asked.

I didn't want to alarm her, so I lied.

"Fine. Just tired and my knees ache."

"That's not the ibuprofen bottle," she said keenly.

When I didn't answer, she pressed the issue.

"What is it for, Dad?"

I paused, wondering whether or not I should lie again.

"It's for my heart," I said.

"What?" she asked, raising her voice. *"Your heart?"*

"Shh," I told her.

"Why?" she asked again.

"Please."

And then I filled her in. She knew I'd once had problems with atrial fibrillation, but over the years she, too, had forgotten all about it. She asked smart questions, inquired about our options, and then suggested that we wait until the morning to make a decision, preferably after we'd consulted with Dave and Chris. Her own inclination was to walk with me back to Red Sheep Creek.

"How would you feel if we had to turn back?" I asked.

"Disappointed," she said. "Very. But if you haven't had a problem for almost three years, I'm hoping you'll be better by tomorrow."

Then, after taking everything in like a rational adult, she asked, "What do you think, Dad? What are the chances of your heart getting better?"

I laughed. "I don't know, Sweetie. At this point, I can only hope."

I held her face between my hands and gave her a kiss on the forehead. She looked like a sixteen-year-old girl who was trying to be brave.

IT WAS MIDNIGHT. Outside, a fog had settled into the valley, and the sun hung low in the north. The mountains looked like spirits drifting through a gray sky. In the distance I could hear the clamor of the Chandalar.

I found a low spot in the bear fence, straddled it, then swung my second leg over and kept walking. I sat in the sand at the river's edge, remembering a line from the William Stafford poem "Ask Me": "What the river says, that is what I say."

Like Stafford, I was drawn to the water to wait. Floating somewhere among the mountains on a swirling wind was a raven. He called and then called again.

I wondered if there was a bear across the river roaming one of the deep and rocky draws. Could he feel that winter was coming, that the willows would soon drop their leaves? Or was that movement, near the granite wall, just below the snow line, two wolves feeding on what remained of a young caribou? I could picture their drooping tongues and bulging bellies scraping across the rocks. Would they move south and find the lone musk ox? Having eaten their fill, would they lope away uninterested, or would they slash at his thick coat and lunge for his flanks and nose? Would they sever his muscles and rip open his belly and feed on him even before he was dead?

Up ahead, I could see the Chandalar's big bend. So close. I'd imagined it time and again sitting at home on the screened-in porch, studying my maps, while outside the humidity sat low over the land. I'd memorized some of the map's details, the swamps and willow bars. I'd even given names to a number of the unclaimed creeks and summits.

Having been at the river for over an hour, I was chilled. I took one last look to the north. A quick check of my pulse confirmed that its rhythm was still erratic. I walked back to the tent, relieved myself far from the electric fence, and then stepped over the wire. I wondered dimly if a grizzly would have such an easy time gaining entry.

I crawled into the tent and my sleeping bag and washed down

the other half of the metoprolol tablet with water. Perhaps if I combined the river's healing with modern medicine, I would wake in the morning and my heart rate would be steady and strong. Perhaps, then, I might still walk along the bony back of the continent.

M R . G R I Z

WHEN I WOKE I NOTICED it immediately: my heart was beating steadily and my body felt calm. It had been years, but I remembered the sensation, the relief I felt when my heart returned to sinus rhythm. I waited eagerly for Aidan to stir so I could give her the good news. Outside I heard someone milling around.

Dave was disabling the bear fence; when he saw me, he asked how I was feeling.

"You looked a little rough yesterday," he added.

"Yeah," I agreed. "Long day." The night before I'd made the decision that if my heart had converted back to a normal rhythm, I wouldn't mention anything about my troubles. Part of me felt that it would be irresponsible not to discuss my Afib with Dave and Chris, but I'd convinced myself that I'd keep quiet to spare them. Dave's concerns about our food supply weighed heavily on him. But the truth was that pride probably played a far greater role in my decision than I cared to admit.

"Walking on the gravel bars must be hard on your knees," he said.

"And how 'bout you?" I asked. "How are your feet?"

"A little sore," he replied.

We walked to the cooking area. I spotted fresh wolf tracks in the mudflats, and Dave showed me grizzly prints that were just as fresh.

"Man, he was close," he said.

I didn't tell him about my late-night wanderings, but the thought that there was a bear so close to camp made my hair stand on end. Back at the cook site, Dave boiled water and made a pot of coffee in Chris's portable French press.

"Want a cup?"

I shook my head. Normally I am a prodigious coffee drinker, but this morning I couldn't risk the caffeine, because it's an Afib trigger. I did need something to wake me up, though, so I walked down to the river. I cupped water in my hands and rubbed it over my face. I was tempted to dunk my head in the river, but then remembered that anything sudden, especially ice-cold water, could also throw me out of sinus rhythm. When I returned to the eating area, Aidan was sitting next to Dave.

She looked at me without saying anything. Her eyes asked if I was okay. I nodded and smiled and watched her brighten. The sun was out, if only temporarily, and I asked her if she wanted to go for a short walk.

When we were out of earshot, she wrapped her arms around me. "Dad," she said. "You're better. I was so worried about you. I had nightmares. I dreamed that we walked back to Red Sheep Creek, but no one could pick us up. We were fishing and hunting to feed ourselves. Then, eventually, we had to walk to Arctic Village, through the swamps."

"Oh, God," I said. "That *would* kill me."

"But you're better," she said again. Then she asked me if I planned to say anything to Chris and Dave and added that she thought I should.

I told her I didn't think I would. If she disapproved of my decision, she let it go, not wanting to diminish the joy of my recovery.

I reminded her that I wasn't out of the woods yet. "I might need your help today," I said. "I'm not going to be strong."

"I don't care," she exclaimed. "I'll do anything to help. We can even switch packs. I'm so happy I could run up those mountains with a hundred pounds."

"Easy, girl," I cautioned her. I reminded her that the worst-case scenario I'd described to her—getting caught in the mountains where rescue by bush plane was impossible—was still something that worried me.

When we returned to the campsite, Chris and Dave were packing up. Chris admitted he had a "hikeover" from pushing it too hard the day before, but they were getting ready to go.

"We thought it might be nice to walk in the sun for once," Dave said.

An hour later, when we stopped at a feeder creek that looked like it might hold fish, I saw that Aidan looked tired. She was carrying a fifty-pound pack and toting an additional eight to ten pounds from mine. Adjusting to the weight increase would take her at least a day, but my hope was, by that time, I'd be feeling strong enough to resume carrying my full weight.

I helped her swing off her pack and lay it on a gravel bar.

"You okay?" I asked.

She was massaging one of her shoulders.

"I didn't think it would matter, but it does," she admitted. "But, more important, how do you feel?"

"Okay," I said.

I had been awake for much of the night, and for at least eight of those hours my heart rate had been running fifty beats per minute faster than normal. I was tired, but my heart rate was strong and consistent.

Instead of resting, all of us fished at different points along the creek. I caught two grayling barely bigger than my index finger. Dave, Chris, and Aidan were equally unlucky—so much for the Chandalar River valley serving up any bountiful meals of fish.

We pulled on our backpacks and turned north-northwest into the drainage that would take us to Gilbeau Pass. The short rest had been good for me. My legs felt stronger. Aidan, too, looked like she'd found her gear. She was out front with Chris, cruising. Dave was in the middle, walking a bit gingerly on his sore feet. I was about a hundred yards behind, leery of pushing too hard.

We walked the willow bars as far as we could, following the game trails that smelled of caribou hair and poop. In some places, the bushes looked as if they'd been mowed down by a megaherd of South Dakota bison. The pregnant cows had blazed a series of straight-line thoroughfares, their broad hooves beating down the lichens and churning up the mud and sand. By the looks of their tracks, they were moving north, stopping only to check the wind, driven by the need to reach the coastal plain. There, having made one of the longest migrations of any land animal on earth—they migrate between four hundred and fifteen hundred miles from their winter range—they would calve, and their newborns would feed on the plain's nutrient-rich grasses.

We shouted, whistled, and whooped like cowboys on a cattle drive. A grizzly, or any other animal enamored of solitude, more than likely wanted nothing to do with us. After an hour of wading through the willows, we came upon open tundra. The sun was burning through the mist. Elsewhere, it's easy to forget the beauty of the sun, the way the body and brain respond to its warmth and the movement of light. But there in the gray gloam of the Arctic, under the influence of a monthlong low-pressure system, it was a gift to be celebrated.

We lay down on the tundra and let the sun fill us up. Even Aidan was happy to break. She usually detested what she called our "old-man pit stops," when Chris, Dave, and I reclined on the tundra and took an afternoon "power" nap; instead of resting, she got chilled waiting for us to wake. She would have much preferred that we keep hiking and have an extra half hour at camp. But not today.

I was awakened by my own snoring. Dave and Chris were still asleep. Aidan was sitting next to me writing in her diary.

"Did you snooze?" I asked.

"Nah," she said. "I was just writing about the sun, how nice it is. Now I know how Heimo and Edna feel in January when they see it again. Someday I'd like to be with them to see the sun return."

I told her that I remembered it well, how Heimo danced and then chased his shadow like a boy running after a butterfly.

When Dave and Chris woke we set out again, hiking along the edge of a cold, clear stream that tumbled down from Gilbeau Pass. The sun lit up the valley. I should probably have been considering whether, given my condition, it was imprudent to press farther on into the mountains, but I'd forgotten my reservations. All I wanted was more beauty.

Unfortunately, we didn't walk for long. Clouds were building in the mountains, and we decided to look for a place to bed down. We found one on a sandbar and set up camp hastily. Working fast, we tied down the tarp extra tight, took out the middle, support pole, and huddled under the thin nylon, feeling small and vulnerable. Just minutes after we finished, the wind swooped down from the high country into the valley, faster than a spooked caribou, and the rain beat down like falling stones. But the squall passed as quickly as it came.

"That's the way it works, Aidan," Dave said. "The winds come up the valley in the morning and down in the evening. Convection makes the warm air rise up, and at night, it's reversed. The cool air comes down off the mountains."

Aidan nodded.

"That's your science lesson for today," Dave said over his shoulder as he walked to the willows to relieve himself.

The air was still and quiet, and soon the sun returned. When it did, Dave and Chris decided to walk up the valley and reconnoiter while Aidan and I used the opportunity to dry out our sweaty hiking shirts and our boots and socks, which smelled of marsh and peat. Then we sat in the sand and stretched our knotted leg and back muscles. When we spotted Chris and Dave coming back, we decided to do what they'd done, hike upstream and see if we could get a glimpse of the terrain we were going to face tomorrow.

Without my backpack, I felt light, unburdened, and happy to be alive.

"I feel like running," I told Aidan without breaking a smile. "Wanna race?"

"C'mon, Dad. You're kidding, right?" she said. "I beat you when I turned nine. Remember? It was on that sandbar on the Wisconsin River? Mom was the judge. Did you let me win?"

"Heck, no," I answered her. "That's why Momma and I were laughing so hard: because I was trying to win with all my might."

Aidan giggled good-naturedly. It's a sound I've always loved.

We climbed as high as Dave and Chris had, and then we went farther up. Ahead, the slope was covered in scree, rounded and sharp-pointed rocks of all sizes. It looked impassable. Down by the stream, it didn't look much better. The mountain walls were steep and tight.

"Which way do you think we should go tomorrow?" Aidan asked.

I hesitated. "I don't know. You can see where the canyon bends. It's hard to tell what it might look like up there. We could scout it now, but it would take us a while."

"I'll go, if you think we need to," Aidan said. "But maybe we should skip it. We're already a ways from camp. Tomorrow, I think we should walk the creek as far up as we can."

"I think so, too," I agreed. "We can always climb up and out before we overcommit."

We hadn't had a stretch of sun like this since we began our hike at Red Sheep Creek, so we took our time getting to camp. When we made it back, Chris broke out a chocolate bar. He gave us all a chunk and then raised his piece in the air to salute the weather.

"What do you say we treat ourselves to the blueberry crisp to-night?" Dave said, feeling festive.

The sun and warm weather—it might have been fifty degrees—and the prospect of crossing Gilbeau Pass tomorrow had brought out the best in all of us.

After a supper of freeze-dried Mountain House stew, Dave divided the blueberry crisp. We all eyed our portions like ravens circling a kill. And Dave was precise. Five spoonfuls for each of us. No one dove in. We all employed the same strategy: savor it.

Aidan took a small bite and closed her eyes. "It's so good."

"This stuff ain't bad," Dave chimed in. "In fact, it's . . ." He paused and then he shouted, "Deeelicious!"

We all licked our bowls clean, trying to get every morsel of sweetness. When I picked up the dishes to take them down to the water to wash, Dave reached for his bowl.

"One last lick," he said, stuffing his face back inside.

After supper and dishes, Dave and Chris went for another walk, and Aidan and I sat in the sun on the sandbar and looked at our maps. What I saw, or didn't see, amazed me every time—an unnamed landscape.

Gilbeau Pass was one of the only features labeled on the map. As the crow flies, it looked to be about three miles away. In those three miles, we'd gain sixteen hundred feet in elevation. Aidan and I plotted a route that followed the creek for the first mile. When it narrowed, we'd have to climb out and hike the ridges. That, we could see, would be an up-and-down affair. We'd have to climb in and out of drainages, and scramble over talus slopes littered with rocks.

By the time Chris and Dave returned from their evening saunter, Aidan and I had already retired to the tent. She was writing. I heard her pencil scratching fast across the pages of her diary.

"What in the world are you writing about so feverishly?" I asked.

"Stuff," she said. "Just stuff."

I left it at that and turned over. Outside I could hear Dave and Chris whispering and, in the background, the sound of the stream tumbling over rocks.

Aidan's pencil stopped. "I'm writing about being happy," she said. "Being tired, and miserable sometimes, but happy."

I WOKE EARLY again and walked down to the cook site and made coffee. By the looks of things, everyone was going to need a pick-me-up. The sun had disappeared, displaced again by a cold, blankety fog. For Aidan I made hot chocolate, with a small spoonful of Chris's whey protein. It was her special indulgence, what got her out of the tent in the morning. Chris's and Dave's was strong coffee. Mine was, too, but once again I decided to forgo the caffeine.

I'd been thinking about something Aidan said the night before. She'd been talking about experiences that strip life down to its bare essentials, simplifying what for most of us is a demanding and complicated existence into basic needs. On an adventure like this, we evolve. Two days in, our minds and bodies rebel against the drudgery and hardship. Then, at some point, we get used to it; we become honed and hardened. And then there's an ultimate level, reached only when we begin to want, and even crave, the experience, regardless of how demanding it is.

Aidan was somewhere between levels I and II. The fear she'd felt before the trip was gone. She realized that she would not have to fend off grizzlies storming out of every thicket, or worry constantly that we would turn up the wrong drainage and lose our way. Her fears had been replaced by a vague sense of insecurity. That, too, would diminish, was diminishing, as she became more comfortable with the experience. On our two prior trips, to Heimo and Edna's, I'd seen her change before my eyes. She hadn't suddenly transformed, but each day she had grown mentally and physically stronger without even realizing it was happening.

For me, any emptiness I'd felt when Kirk dropped us at Red Sheep Creek was gone, replaced by wonder. I was still concerned about my heart, and my knees throbbed throughout the day and night, but mostly I was awestruck by the wildness, happy to be hiking with two friends whom I liked and trusted, but mostly grateful to have Aidan with me and to see her challenged, infuriated, and inspired by the raw reality of our adventure.

When Dave walked up, I was deep in thought.

"Shit," he said, looking up the valley.

"Huh?" I answer absentmindedly.

"I said, What happened to the sun? Remember when we met on the Kongakut? We had nothing but sun."

"For three weeks, it was seventy-five degrees," I said, coming back to reality. "And on July fifth, we woke up to four inches of snow."

"Effin Arctic," Dave added. "Next time, we're biking through Mexico."

IT WAS EIGHT o'clock when we hit the trail. We tried to follow the stream, but the canyon walls closed up faster than the maps indicated they would.

"Better get out while we can," Chris said, leading us up a steep bank.

The incline was so sharp that I almost tumbled backward. Earlier, Aidan had told me that her hamstring was sore, so I insisted that I carry my full pack. Now, I was scrambling up the high bank on all fours. When I got to my feet again, my legs felt heavy and rubbery. I was puzzled. With my bout of Afib two days behind me, I'd expected to feel stronger. Instead, I felt depleted.

The mountain slope was a maze of granite, shale, and marble rocks that were big enough to obliterate a car. Despite their size, each had somehow found its angle of repose. I couldn't say the same for my equilibrium. Even with my trekking poles, I stumbled and banged my knees and shins. Standing above me, after seeing me take an especially hard fall, Aidan screamed, "Daaad!" Seeing me struggle to my feet, she threw off her backpack and hurried over to me.

"Are you okay?" she asked.

"My balance is for shit," I said, disgusted. "I don't know what's wrong with me."

"Let me take some weight," she offered.

"No," I growled.

"Please," she said.

"No," I said again. There was something about my tone that made her back away.

"Dad," she said, warily, "are you okay?"

I didn't respond. I left her standing there. When I reached her backpack, I stopped. She followed close behind me. I watched her bend down, grabbing a shoulder strap. She tried to swing her pack onto her back and failed. On her second attempt, I lifted her pack while she swung.

"Sorry," I said, as she tightened her waist belt buckle. "I'm having a hard time."

She studied me, as if she was trying to figure out if I was hiding something from her. Then she looked at my pack and cinched up the shotgun.

"I know you are," she said.

We walked together in silence, with her just a few steps in back of me. The hiking was easier now that we were on a stretch of open tundra. Even better, Dave—whom we called Davy Crockett, as he usually led the way—had found a caribou trail. During the warm summers, when the bugs plague them, caribou often seek out these windswept mountainsides.

"Do you mind if I walk ahead, Dad?" Aidan asked. Whatever I'd done to persuade her that I was okay had worked.

"Not a bit," I told her. "Thanks for looking out for the old man."

For the next hour I dug down deep, shifting into a primitive mental gear that allowed me to keep moving forward. I noticed little aside from the barrenness of the mountains. The green was gone and now there was nothing but dark, striated peaks and river-size fields of rock speckled with quartz and feldspar.

After more than a half day of arduous hiking, we reached Gilbeau Pass and the small lake that marked the Continental Divide. On one side, all waters flow, eventually, to the Yukon River and, on the other, to the Arctic Ocean. For at least seven thousand years the coastal Inupiat Eskimos and inland Gwich'in had used this same route to hunt, fight, and, mostly, to trade. The coastal region near Barter Island was the epicenter of the trading activity. Inupiat traders would come from the Colville River delta, far to the west, and from the Mackenzie River delta, far to the east in Canada. Meanwhile, Gwich'in traders would come north from Arctic Village with wolverine furs and white spruce pitch (which the Inupiats used for infections and coughs), often using Gilbeau Pass and the Hulahula River drainage. In summer they made the 150-mile trip on foot and in winter by dogsled. They often used dogs to carry supplies in caribou-skin packs. Once they reached the coast, the Gwich'in would trade for knives and tobacco, and, later, rifles and ammunition. Perhaps, as they came through Gilbeau Pass, they drank from this small lake or stopped to watch a peregrine falcon soaring on waves of wind.

"We're here," Aidan said, walking back to me, all smiles. "Can you believe it?"

We scaled a ridge to the north of the tarn. The landscape, laid bare by wind, was starker than anything we'd seen. We descended and then stopped to slap tired high fives and to take pictures. But it was cold and gusty, so we moved on quickly.

The satisfaction of making Gilbeau Pass infused Aidan with energy. She kicked in the afterburners and was out front, hiking fast. Part of me enjoyed the picture of my daughter blazing the trail, filled with joy, but another part didn't like to see her so far ahead. Short of whistling, I had no way of getting her attention. I certainly couldn't catch her. For me, crossing the Continental Divide didn't mean that the hiking got easier. The thing about bad knees is that going down is often harder than going up.

Sometimes I even lost sight of her, which made me extra anxious. Earlier in the day, Aidan had told me that she was no longer afraid of hiking alone. Although I was proud of her newfound confidence, I reminded her that it is important always to be watchful in bear country.

We were walking into a valley through a series of draws, crotches, and cracks, always surrounded by mastodon-size boulders. I came up out of one and was relieved to discover flat ground and a caribou trail. Then I looked down and felt like I'd been struck by lightning. In front of me lay a pile of steaming grizzly dung. I threw off my backpack and pulled out my shotgun. I scanned the rocks for Aidan, and, catching sight of her red windbreaker, I shouted to her, but she didn't hear me. Then I whistled as loudly as I could. She whipped her head around and I signaled desperately for her to come back.

"What's up, Dad?" she asked, as she got close.

"Bear shit back there," I said. "And it's fresh."

She ripped her pepper spray from her holster like a Wild West gunslinger. I could tell that she was frightened, but there was also something else, something new and different. It dawned on me: she was electrified by the possibility of seeing a grizzly at close range.

Seconds later we heard a shout. "Bear!"

We walked in the direction of the yell as fast as our heavy packs allowed. From the sound of the voice, the urgency, I knew the bear was near. We came around a rock ledge to see Dave and Chris pointing at a large, honey-haired grizzly bounding up the side of a mountain steeper than an otter slide.

"He was right here when we came around the corner," Dave said. "He looked at us for a moment and then he ran."

Aidan was beaming. "A grizzly!"

We watched the bear, marveling at his athleticism. He was now walking up a 60-degree slope of scree and snow. If we were to try it, we would tumble down like loose rocks, but the bear climbed straight up and then moved laterally across the mountain. Because he was going in the same direction we were, we kept an eye on him for the next half mile. But then he came to a large drainage, turned south, and disappeared.

"See ya, Mr. Griz," Aidan said. "Thanks for the visit."

On the south side of the stream that flowed west-northwest out of Gilbeau Pass, the mountains blocked out the sky, but on the north side they fell away, and we discovered a long meadow of alpine tundra with well-trodden caribou trails. Aidan was again out front, chewing up territory with her long strides. When I saw her stop and sit down, I thought her hamstring was bothering her again. But then she yelled, "Look." She'd found a caribou antler shed and had it propped up on top of her head.

"Hold that pose," Chris shouted, hustling over to her.

Chris took the photo and showed me: Aidan, with a head of horns, is smiling ear to ear.

We walked another three miles until all of us—except Aidan—were utterly spent. "I'm done," Dave said as the icy wind grew icier. We took temporary refuge behind a huge boulder.

We pressed our bodies against the rock to escape the wind and discussed where we would camp for the night. We could put our tents on the leeward side of the rock, but where would we cook? There were no rocks downwind that we could cook behind. And where would we get our water? We'd have to hoof it a quarter mile down to the stream, fill up our water bags, and tote them back.

"How 'bout down there?" Chris said, pointing to a promising-looking area along the riverbank.

We wrestled on our backpacks and headed down to see. We were happy to discover that the site offered water and some protection from the wind. We decided to forgo putting up our cooking tarp and ate a quick supper, just something to fill our bellies, among some rocks. It was something I wished we'd done more often: keep it simple and skip the tarp, since setting it up was always something of an ordeal, especially in the cold and the wind.

I washed up in the creek, and, by the time I climbed into the tent, Aidan was almost asleep.

"I'm not writing in my diary tonight, Dad," she said. "It's too cold. But tell me about what happened when we saw the bear. I want to remember."

I lay buried in my sleeping bag with my fleece hat pulled low over my ears and recited the details of our grizzly encounter. When I reached the part where we rounded the corner and saw it run, Aidan was asleep. Outside, the wind barreled out of the cold mountains, moaning.

CHAPTER 24

WHERE THE WOLVES SING

NOBODY WANTED TO GET OUT of bed, least of all Aidan. Her water bottle was frozen again, and there was a sheen of frost on the rain fly. I left the tent and disabled the bear fence.

"What's it like out there, Dad?" Aidan asked. "And please tell me it's sunny."

"Sun's out," I said.

"Really?" she asked. "Are you telling me the truth?"

"Nope," I said. "Just responding as ordered."

"Okay, then," she persisted. "What's it really like?"

"Crappy," I told her. "Sleeting and gray."

Dave came out of the tent bundled up as if he was heading off on a polar expedition. While I filtered water he made the morning oatmeal.

"Not much left," he said when I joined him at the rocks. "We're getting low."

By the time it was done, Chris and Aidan had joined us. Aidan, wearing every stitch of clothing she'd brought, looked as if she was ready to hit the trapline with Edna. For the last five days, we'd tried to keep our eating clothes separate from our sleeping and hiking clothes so the bears didn't think we smelled like dinner, a precaution we'd always observed in the Lower 48 when backpacking in black bear country. When the temperatures are in the sixties, seventies, and eighties, that's doable. But here, because of the cold, it was just not possible.

We broke camp quickly and settled into a pace that everybody seemed happy with. Dave was out front, followed by Chris and Aidan. I was close enough behind them to eavesdrop on their conversation. As I listened I surveyed the scenery. The sky hung low and heavy, and the brooding, gray-black mountains crowded the valley.

In the early afternoon, the pass bent north and the landscape once again opened up, and with it my heart did, too. For much of the morning, I was plodding, grimly, eyes to the ground, breathing like a man tugging on a rope. But I'd found a rhythm. Instead of dreading the miles we had ahead of us, I embraced the experience, the sharp and massive mountains, the wind scything through the now spacious valley, the reappearance of the sun, the benevolence of its light.

We took a break to rest our feet and chew on some nuts and chocolate. While sitting there, I saw something dash up a hill about three-quarters of a mile up the valley. I watched for more movement, wondering if perhaps I'd seen a wolverine. Then I noticed it again, a flash of color. I asked Chris for his binoculars and glassed the valley.

"It looks like a dog down there," I said.

"Couldn't be," Dave replied. "Maybe a wolf?"

I went on looking, but saw only mottled, windblown tundra.

As we continued hiking, I kept my eyes fastened on the hill. I spotted something that looked like a person. *Impossible,* I thought. I'd heard of people hallucinating on the coastal plain, because of the way light moves across the flat, unbroken landscape. But not in the mountains. Then I heard a dog bark and saw another person. As we approached, I realized we'd stumbled into a small group of backpackers—four people and two dogs. It took me a moment to integrate them into the scene. Five hundred or so people raft the North Slope's remote rivers every summer, but few bother to traverse these mountains to get to their put-in points. Most just fly in via bush plane to places like Grasser's Strip.

After regarding each other warily on our approach, Dave and the group leader, a veterinarian from Fairbanks, began chatting. Soon they realized they knew each other and had a bunch of friends in common. The other three guys, who were lying on the tundra looking exhausted, nodded hello and we nodded back. They, too, were headed for Grasser's and the Hulahula. After five minutes or so, we moved on.

By late afternoon, as we started to scan the landscape for a suitable campsite, I knew the Hulahula River valley was close. We had been able to see the broad mountains that lined the river's path from a distance; the way I really knew we were close was the smell. Elizabeth once told me that smell is the most enduring sense because it goes straight to the brain. As I hiked, I searched for a word to describe it, but nothing seemed to fit. I wondered if the Gwich'in or the Inupiat had one. It occurred to me that as people moved farther away from nature, and their experiences in the outdoor world became fewer, it would be harder to describe the smell of a river, or the color of the tundra, or the sound the wind makes as it sweeps through a valley.

We found a campsite and worked fast. After the tents were up, Aidan built a fire while Chris and Dave prepared supper. Meanwhile, I took the leghold trap that Heimo had given me and put it near the hole of a ground squirrel. I set the "dog" on the trigger and covered the pan of the trap with dirt and sand. I cut off a green branch from a dwarf willow and used it to rake the area, and then I peed around the trap and the hole. Rabbits, I know, love salt, and I'd heard about trappers pissing near their snares for bait. If the trick worked on a ground squirrel and I managed to trap one, I'd gut it and skin it and we'd have pure protein for breakfast.

When I finished, supper was almost ready. Without looking at my watch I would have had no idea what time it was, 6:00 p.m., 10:00, or midnight. Twenty-four hours of light reveals time for what it is—an invention. Only my tired body had some sense of the hour.

All night our tent rattled in the gusts. I woke early again, crawled out, and checked the trap. Nothing. Then I sat on the tundra and enjoyed the solitude, wondering how many people had ever had the opportunity to sit here in the muted glow of the early-morning sun. I grew tired, went back into the tent to sleep some more, and woke two hours later. I checked my trap again—nothing—and then sat with Dave and sipped coffee. It was surprising how little we'd talked since Arctic Village. During the day he was usually out in front being Davy Crockett, and at night, the cold and wind often cut short our conversations.

While talking, we boiled the last of our oatmeal, and then I woke Aidan. Chris was already doing a plyometrics workout on the tundra. When it was time to eat, the sun was out, and for the first time we lingered over breakfast and talked about the Hula-hula. It was the word on everyone's mind, and lips, because if all went well we'd reach its headwaters after one more day of hiking.

While we broke camp, Aidan gave me a history lesson on the origins of the river's name. The river, she said, had no known Inupiat name. Hulahula was assumed to be Hawaiian, meaning "the dance." One possible historical explanation is that natives from a hunting party out of Herschel Island, off the coast of Canada's Yukon Territories, saw and killed caribou along the river and celebrated their good fortune with a dance. How, and why, they chose a Hawaiian word to name the river remains a mystery. Another story is that homesick whalers from the Hawaiian Islands named it the Hulahula because of the way the river moves here and there like the hips of a dancer.

By 8:00 a.m., we were on the move. Making and breaking camp was now second nature. We worked together like a well-oiled machine.

As we walked, the sun flooded the broadening valley. Up ahead lay the Romanzof Mountains of the Brooks Range, with their rugged escarpments and disappearing glaciers. The Romanzofs, named by the British explorer Sir John Franklin, cover an area sixty-five miles long, between the Hulahula River on their western border and Kongakut River on the east, and twenty miles wide, between the high mountains of the Continental Divide and the northern foothills of the coastal plain. Made of shale, sandstone, volcanic rocks, and limestone, abundant with fossilized coral, the Romanzofs rise as steeply as any mountains in the world.

After consulting our maps we agreed that Grasser's Strip, and our canoes and supplies, was probably a day and a half away and was on the west—river left—side of the Hulahula. That meant we'd need to cross Itkillik Creek. It didn't look like much on the maps, but when Kirk dropped us off at Red Sheep he had encouraged us to be careful because it was likely running high after so much rain. In any case I was confident we could make the crossing. We had ropes, and I had a small emergency life jacket for Aidan, which she could inflate if the water looked intimidating.

As we walked along the hills bordering the east bank of the creek, we decided to cross as soon as we could. We kept a close eye on the river. There were long stretches of rapids, but an hour down from our campsite, we found a slower, though deeper, section to ford. The water rose to our waists and the current tugged at our legs, but by midmorning we were on the west side of the Itkillik and bound for the Hulahula's headwaters.

By early afternoon, after a brief lunch break and power nap, we came upon a well-situated ridge, from which we could see our destination. For the next few minutes Aidan and I stood filled with gratitude and awe. If I'd had the knees for it, I would have walked back a mile or two to re-create the experience of cresting the ridge, and that moment, so vivid, when I looked north into the broad and green valley of the Hulahula. I would do it again and again.

When we reached the river, we sat back to take in the scenery. Chris glassed the mountains to the north and spotted a herd of Dall sheep, maybe two dozen of them. The Brooks Range is home to thirty thousand Dall sheep, with the headwaters of the Hulahula having one of the highest concentrations. They are altitude-loving animals. Most live year-round in the snow shadow of big, wind-scoured mountains, where it's easier for them to forage among the exposed grasses.

Chris gave the binoculars to Aidan and walked down to the river. While she was watching the sheep, he signaled to us. When we reached him, he was beaming like a panner who has just found a knuckle-size nugget of gold.

"There," he said. "Look."

He pointed to the sand at a large, and fresh, wolf track. I'd seen a lot of wolf prints, but never anything so big or perfectly formed. The track was as wide as his boot.

Back at the campsite, we built a fire and fed it for a few hours. Although everyone was tired—we'd pushed hard to get to this point because of concerns about running out of food—we all stayed up later than usual, enjoying the clear skies, the bounty of light, and the rumble of the river.

The following morning I was half asleep when Dave and Chris shouted. I hurried out of the tent, wondering if I should grab my shotgun, and saw Dave pointing to the hills above the river. I stopped and then I heard it—howling. There were wolves and they were calling to each other.

"Get up, Aidan, get up," I said, standing at the tent's entrance.

"Huh, huh?" Aidan replied.

"Get out here," I said. "Hurry."

When Aidan exited the tent, she was still mostly asleep.

"C'mon," I told her. "Wolves."

As we walked in the direction of Dave, she came to.

"I hear 'em, Dad," she said. "It sounds like they're singing in harmony."

I stopped walking and listened. She was right. They weren't howling the same note. It was as if they were deliberately harmonizing. They say that wolves howl to assemble the pack, to communicate over large distances, to locate each other, or to sound an alarm. They had certainly caught our scent, seen us, and heard us, and they may have been warning each other of our presence in a valley that had been entirely theirs. But to me the wolves sounded . . . happy.

When we reached Dave, he handed us the binoculars.

"Three wolves," he said.

Aidan looked first, but I could see them without the field glasses. One wolf, a white one, laid his head back and howled. Another stopped to answer.

We watched and listened to them as long as they would allow us. Then the wolves moved on, climbing into the crags.

CHAPTER 25

AT THE HEADWATERS

WE FOLLOWED THE HULAHULA NORTH, warmed by a suffusion of sunlight. Not far down from our campsite, I nearly stepped in a pile of bear crap. It was fresh and full of kinnikinnick berries. It was a timely warning. We had a long section of willows ahead of us. I uncinched my shotgun from my pack. Then we all began to shout, "Hey, bear, hey, bear."

We walked the willows for a mile and then realized that we had a clear, three-mile shot of open tundra to Grasser's. As we followed the river, I studied it. I knew Aidan was doing the same. For months we'd imagined how it would be, and now, we were here. The river was fast and dotted with rocks. As we moved farther north, however, the current slowed as the river spread its muscular girth across the valley.

"What do you think, Dad?" Aidan asked at a point where the river narrowed and the rapids grew large.

She was looking for a line downstream. "Don't worry," I said. "We'll make it."

As I said this, I recalled what my contact at the U.S. Fish and Wildlife Service in Fairbanks had told me about the river.

"The Hulahula is bony," she said. "Lots of obstacles—boulder gardens, wave trains, and hydraulics. It's hard to say how you'll fare in a canoe. I did it in a pack raft. Just be really careful."

We arrived at Grasser's by noon and were happy to see that nothing had disturbed our folding canoes or our bear barrels packed with food. Although we had much to do, first we celebrated. Chris opened a bear barrel and pulled out a bottle of whiskey. He twisted off the top and passed it around. I drank, Dave drank, and then he passed it to Aidan, who looked at me as if to ask, *What should I do?*

"It's up to you," I said. "You earned it."

Aidan put the bottle to her lips cautiously. Then she said, "What the heck?" and took a swig. Afterward, she tossed her head back and forth.

"Awful," she said, and handed it to Chris. Chris took a long pull and the bottle made another round.

"To the miles behind us," Dave toasted.

"Command your horses and gather your forces," I said.

"To the wolves," Aidan said, taking a much smaller sip.

"To the miles ahead," Chris announced.

Aidan stepped away from the drinking circle as the bottle made a third round. Chris took it back to the bear barrel before we decided to go on a bender, and I joined Aidan by the river.

"I can't believe it," she said. "All that walking and trudging, but now that we're here it seems like it happened so fast."

"A metaphor for life," I said. "One day you're your age and then you're my age, and you wonder what the hell happened."

"But we sure did pack a lot of life into the past week," she added. "That's what I love about traveling."

I told her how, shortly after we married, when Elizabeth and I were hiking through New Zealand, New Guinea, Indonesia, Malaysia, and Thailand, we'd call her parents or mine to say that we were safe. We had hundreds of things to tell, but we kept the conversations short. When we'd ask what was going on at home, we'd usually hear the same answer, *Oh, not much. Just the usual.*

The father of a good friend used to say that "life is maintenance." Before becoming a husband and father myself, I dismissed the thought as resignation. No longer. Middle age, landownership, nineteen years of marriage, and three daughters have all taught me that never-ending maintenance is an inescapable reality.

"Dad?" Aidan asked. "How do you really live each day?"

I'd tried two strategies in my life: one was to travel and to keep moving. I liked the feeling of motion and the sense of wonder and discovery that accompanied it. But then I ran into the perpetual wanderers, people who had spent a half decade or more on the hippie highway, and I knew their life was not for me. More recently, I'd tried to become what Wallace Stegner called a "sticker." Stegner divided Americans into two categories: boomers and stickers. The difference is about commitment. Boomers are the perpetual wanderers looking for something they often never find. Stickers are "those who settle, and love the life they have made and the place they have made it in." My dad is a sticker. His dad was not. He was a charming, educated, ne'er-do-well Tennesseean who was never happy where he was. He left the family when my dad was five and reappeared only once every few years after that. In response, my dad built his life around family and home. He loved to travel, but if he, too, had a wanderlust, he never spoke of it. He seemed content to stay put.

"I don't know," I told her. "I've never been able to find the answer." Just then, she pointed to a bird, a peregrine falcon floating among the mountains. For the moment just being where we were seemed enough.

A while later, we left the river to assemble our canoe. We opened the bag, emptied it, and organized the pieces: the skin of the canoe, the gunwale rods and terminators, the keel rod and the chine rods, which run longitudinally along the bottom of the canoe, the cross-ribs, and the seat support rods. I noticed Aidan looking at all the various parts, and I knew she was glad that we had taken the time when we were home to build the canoe.

It took us only an hour to put the canoe together and put on the spray skirt. In the meantime, the wind had built. The sun was still out and shining as if it were a warm summer day, but when we finished, our hands stung from the cold.

Aidan went to the tent to take a nap while I repacked my backpack and dry bag. It was a tedious, time-consuming job, positioning everything for easy access. When I crawled into the tent, I saw that Aidan was still asleep. Normally, I wouldn't wake her, but I knew how long it would take her to arrange her dry bag. I am orderly, but she's a perfectionist. She would fold and roll all her clothes and then tie them with string.

It took Aidan two hours to sort through and rearrange her backpack and dry bag. Then we took everything over to the canoe to see how it would fit. That's when I noticed that we'd forgotten to use the plastic ties on the canoe joints, where the cross-ribs join the keel rod and the chine rods. On flatwater it wouldn't be a problem, but on a powerful river like the Hulahula, these joints needed to be strong and tight. Where were those ties? Having unpacked everything that Kirk had flown in, I realized that they could be in one of only four places: either my dry bag or backpack or Aidan's. I could see Aidan's look of consternation. The last thing she wanted to do was unpack everything.

I volunteered to go first, and when I had finished and failed to find the ties, I told her it was her turn.

"They're not in there," she responded. "I know it."

"Doesn't matter what you *think* you know," I said. "We need 'em, and you're going to have to look for them."

She heard the impatience in my voice, and she bridled.

"They're not in there," she said again. "I packed it perfectly and they're not in there."

"You gotta look," I told her.

"Nope," she answered.

Now I was angry. "Quit acting like a damn spoiled brat," I yelled. "You sound like a five-year-old. If you don't look, I will. And I won't be neat about it."

Chris and Dave, having been listening, moved away. Aidan and I had gotten along well on the trip. If they'd been waiting for a father-daughter altercation, we were giving them one now.

When Aidan didn't answer, I said, "All right, goddammit," and I grabbed her dry bag. I unclipped the sides, unrolled it, and was about to turn it upside down and dump everything out, when she yelled, "Stop!

"All right," she conceded. "You don't have to be a bully. I'll look. But I won't find anything."

I walked away without responding and sat downstream. Gradually I calmed down. The mountains came out, their dark gray forms silhouetted against a sky of clear, blue air. In the crevasses that divided them, long, green tongues of vegetation crept down toward the greener valley. The river, fed by a glacier melting under the intense afternoon sun, was running harder than ever. There had been times when I questioned why I'd come back to the Arctic, but right now, despite the brutishly cold wind and my disagreement with Aidan, was not one of them.

Barry Lopez called the history of Arctic exploration "a legacy of desire." Men came for gold, furs, whales, dominion over trade routes, favor from the gods, national pride, personal glory, oil and gas. The Arctic was the landscape upon which they imposed the extravagance of their dreams. My dreams for this trip were not monetary and had nothing to do with self-aggrandizement, but one does not come to a place like this to work, plod, argue, shiver, sweat, and suffer without the hope of some reward. To say otherwise would be untruthful. I want. Perhaps more than I care to admit. I want an indelible bond with my daughter. I want her to remember this trip for the rest of her life. I want her to remember me after I am gone. I want Awe. I want to feel alive. I want Aidan to be filled with life and wonder.

Aidan whistled from upriver. She was standing along the bank, holding something in her hand. I walked toward her, slowly. When I got close, I saw the ties.

"I found 'em," she said. "They were at the bottom of my dry bag rolled up in a shirt."

"Good," I said. "I'm just glad they're here." We went over to the boat and used the ties to tighten the joints. Neither of us said a word.

At suppertime, Chris pulled out the bottle of whiskey again and Dave unearthed another Mountain House dessert. It was clear that they felt festive. I, too, felt like celebrating. There were times when I'd doubted I would make it this far. My bout of Afib had scared me, and its aftereffects had slowed me down, but I felt strong again and ready to take on whatever the river could dish out. Aidan, on the other hand, was still acting prickly, and kept her distance. She built a small cook fire, going about her business quietly. Elizabeth says Aidan has inherited a number of traits from me, most good, a few bad. One of the worst? A reluctance to admit when she is wrong.

When the fire had good coals, Aidan put on a kettle of water. I asked Dave if he could watch it while Aidan and I took a short walk. Aidan heard me and looked up as if it were the last thing in the world she wanted to do.

"C'mon," I said. "We'll be back by the time the water boils."

When we were out of earshot, I apologized to her. "I'm sorry if I came down hard on you. I'm glad you found the ties."

I'd barely gotten the last word out when she said, "You embarrassed me, Dad. You treated me like I was a child in front of Chris and Dave."

What I wanted to say was that I'd treated her like a child because she'd acted like one, but I kept my mouth shut.

"You can't do that," she said angrily. "I saw the way you looked at me when you noticed that we didn't have the ties. It was like, 'Oh, I, James Campbell, couldn't possibly have misplaced them. I'll look through my stuff, but I know it must have been my ditsy daughter.'"

I was taken aback by her interpretation of the incident. In the last year, Aidan had become hypersensitive to criticism and perceived criticism. Being critical, however, was far from what I'd intended, from what I was feeling. All I cared about was finding the ties. But could I have been sending out signals that I knew I was not to blame? That the responsibility lay in her lap?

She continued. "You have to believe in me, Dad. I'm going to make mistakes. I'm going to misplace things and read the river wrong and use the wrong stroke, but you have to believe in me."

I was surprised to hear her mention belief. That old word rearing its head again. Didn't she know that I trusted her, that if I didn't, we wouldn't be here in this remote and dangerous place?

"I do believe in you," I told her. "More than you know."

"I want you to prove it, Dad," she said. "Otherwise, they're empty words." I could tell she wanted to say more, but instead she just shook her head.

When I saw her resignation, I knew I could not defend or explain myself. I simply nodded toward the fire.

"C'mon, Cap," I said. "Let's go eat."

CHAPTER 26

A BONY RIVER INDEED

I WOKE VAGUELY AWARE OF SOMETHING weighing on my mind. I walked fifty feet from our tent to the canoe. Only then did I notice the weather. The air was crisp and clear, and for the time being the wind was down. I inspected the canoe, testing the tightness of the ties and the spray cover. At home I had put Aidan in charge of learning how to put on the cover, which would keep the inside of the boat and our gear dry. She'd watched YouTube videos and then, when she still had questions, she'd called the Pakboat company and talked with someone there about how to do it. After that, she'd practiced putting the cover on and taking it off. The preparation had worked. The skirt felt watertight.

Walking downriver, I studied the current. There was an Arctic tern searching for food among the rocks. Every winter the tiny tern chases the sun to the Antarctic, making the incredible journey back to the Arctic in time for the summer nesting season. In the process, it flies 44,000 miles. The tern seemed oblivious to my presence. Perhaps she had felt the cold or noticed the diminution of light and knew that soon she would need to find the strength to make the longest migration of any animal on earth.

About a hundred yards from our put-in, a row of large rocks spanned the river. I looked for a line and spotted one near the left bank. It was not a difficult read, but if we missed the chute we could end up in trouble.

As I watched the river, I tried to figure out what had caused me to sleep so fitfully. And then it occurred to me: today was the last chance I'd have to get out by bush plane until the coast. All the doubts, misgivings, and ambivalences that I thought I'd left behind suddenly came back, burying my optimism of the previous day. On the map, the distance that separated us from the Beaufort Sea looked like a fairly straight shot, but I knew the map's simplicity was deceptive. Those hundred-plus river miles would be hard. They would require every bit of skill, strength, and resolve we had.

Once I located the cause of my distress, the questions multiplied fast: Was I up to the task? Was my bout with Afib an isolated incident, or was it a warning of what might come? Was I endangering Aidan for a dream? Did we have the skills to take on the river? Canoeing a big, rock-ridden river—especially an ice-cold one, fed by high-altitude glaciers—is a physically and mentally demanding undertaking. At the end of each day, we would be exhausted. And that was the best-case scenario.

BY LATE MORNING our canoes were packed, and we were ready to shove off. We were loaded down, so much so that I was worried about the canoe's responsiveness. Aidan and I wandered over to separate bushes to relieve ourselves before we got going. On the way back, she whispered to me, "Dad, I'm scared."

"I know you are," I said. "So am I. But we'll get it."

Back at the boat, we pushed the bow upstream. While we settled in, Dave and Chris held the gunwales and steadied the canoe.

"You guys ready?" Dave asked.

"Yup," Aidan shouted. "Let's go."

They gave us a push, and Aidan and I peeled off into the current and let the boat pivot our bow downstream. It was the first time we'd experienced the strength of the river. Though I'd mentally prepared for this moment for months, its raw power caught me by surprise.

I saw the rocks in front of us, but I kept quiet. This was Aidan's show. As our bowman, she had the job of reading the river and picking out our line. It was her chance to build the confidence she'd need for the next two and a half weeks. As the current pushed us, I grew anxious waiting. *C'mon, Aidan. Hurry up. Figure out where we're going. Let's make it through this first rapid,* I thought. Just as I was about to yell out a command, she drew the canoe left, and I knew she saw it; we glided through the chute as if drawn by a magnet.

"Nice work," I shouted over the sound of the river.

"Thanks," Aidan shouted back, and I could hear it in her voice—the relief, the emerging confidence, the thrill of meeting her fears head-on.

We pulled into an eddy to escape the current and waited for Chris and Dave. They chose a different course through the rocks. When I saw their canoe nearly turn broadside, I loosened my spray skirt and prepared to jump out and toss them the throw bag with the safety rope. But, somehow, they made it through.

The river picked up speed and tumbled over rocks for another quarter mile or so, and then it broadened and flattened out into shallow, braided channels. Aidan and I hugged the cutbank on the river's left side, where there seemed to be enough water and current to carry us forward. Chris and Dave again chose another route. Just fifteen minutes into our paddle, and we'd already separated.

Gradually the channel we'd chosen became nothing more than a trickle. We got out, and for much of the next hour we pushed and pulled the heavy boat. We were sweaty and tired when we came upon a large, open sandbar.

"How 'bout some lunch?" Aidan said.

We dragged the canoe up onto the sand and sat down. Aidan took out two granola bars and a bag of nuts from her day pack. The sun was bright and warm, so I slipped off my sweaty splash jacket, turned it inside out, and laid it over the stones.

"Nice job through those rocks," I told her again.

"It was weird," she said. "I was watching them when we peeled out, and I was nervous. But then, as we got close, it all became clear. I felt calm, and I knew that I was choosing the right line." She paused and stuffed a handful of nuts in her mouth. "I love this, Dad," she said.

We sat awhile longer and then walked east across the sandbar to look for Chris and Dave. We'd gone two hundred yards when Aidan looked downstream and saw them. Dave was waving his paddle back and forth. If he were on the river, it would be the signal for Emergency, but now he was just trying to get our attention. Getting separated was a good lesson. For the next week to ten days, the Hulahula would narrow, but once we got to the flat coastal plain, it would spread out again into multiple channels, divided by enough distance that it would be impossible to spot each other. There, it would be important for us to stick together.

We pushed the canoe off the sandbar and found a channel with just enough water in it to carry us downriver. When we reached Chris and Dave, we confirmed that our first stop would be at East Patuk Creek, where the big peaks of the Romanzof Mountains begin. Dave and Chris, in particular, wanted to linger on this section of the Hulahula and spend their afternoons hiking in the mountains.

When we reached East Patuk Creek, Aidan was disappointed. "I was just having fun," she said as we finished an invigorating section of rapids and slid the canoe into an eddy just south of the creek's mouth. "I wanna keep going."

The humdrum of setting up camp was an emotional letdown after the rapids run. But we had found a pretty campsite with a clear view of the snow-covered heights of the Brooks Range to the south. Across the river was a four-thousand-foot mountain and behind us was a fifty-four-hundred-foot peak, rising up from the green floor of the river valley. Behind that was the eighty-one hundred-foot Okpilak Glacier, which fed the Okpilak River, which we would need to paddle near the end of our trip in order to get to Arey Island.

After we got situated, Dave and Chris took their canoe across the river, hoping to do some climbing. Aidan and I elected to stay behind. Aidan planned to write in her diary, and I wanted to inspect, and perhaps patch, a small abrasion on the Pakboat's PVC skin.

When Dave and Chris returned in the late afternoon, I was fishing and Aidan had the water boiling for supper. After a rudimentary but delicious meal—why does basic food taste so good in the outdoors?—we settled in under the screen tent that Dave had brought for the river portion of our trip and played Rummy 500. As at Heimo and Edna's, a nightly card game was something Aidan would come to look forward to.

By the time we quit, there was little light. Clouds had slid down from the mountains and lay low and heavy over the valley. Still, the evening was warm, and for the first time I fell asleep with my bag unzipped, wearing nothing more than a fleece pullover and long johns. When I woke hours later, however, I was shivering. I scrambled for my clothes, climbed into my bag, and pulled it up over my head. Outside a wind had kicked up, and it blew rain at our tent. It hit so hard, it sounded like hail.

Morning came too soon, and a miserable one it was—cold and wet. We'd gone from summer to winter in a matter of twelve hours. Fresh snow covered the mountain across the river. We all huddled around the small table in the screen cook tent, sipping coffee or hot chocolate and discussing whether or not we should push on. The river had come way up overnight and now looked like a different body of water—as muddy and brown as the Mississippi. We decided to stay put for one more day.

Aidan, it turned out, was relieved. I'd assumed that she was looking forward to another day of paddling, but she told me she had gotten chilled during the night and woke up feeling achy. When Dave and Chris told us they were going to climb the mountain behind us, Aidan encouraged me to go, assuring me that she would be fine alone. But I decided to remain at camp with her, and we spent the morning in the cook tent talking, she wrapped in her sleeping bag. She wanted to hear about my past. She wanted to find out what I was like before I married and had a family: What was I like in college—was I a student, an athlete, a partier? Did I have a girlfriend? Did I ever love someone other than Mom? Did I always know I wanted a family? What would I be doing if I didn't have children? We'd often talked about my past, on the way home from a track meet or a cross-country skiing race. But, on those occasions, I'd told her only enough to satisfy her curiosity. Here, she insisted on the uncensored story—the good and the bad—and, for the most part, I was honest with her about the things I'd done well and what I regretted.

It was noon when she finally tired of getting to know her dad and went to lie down in the tent. While she slept, I walked downriver to get some idea of what the Hulahula had in store for us. The rain had fizzled out, and the fog was beginning to lift, but the cold felt as if it would stick, and the river continued to rise. When I returned to our campsite, I saw the branch that Chris had stuck in the sand to measure how much the river had come up. It was completely submerged and the small gravel bar onto which we'd dragged our canoes the previous day was no longer visible. Fortunately we'd had the good sense to drag them four feet higher up onto the bank.

When I returned, I decided to take a nap, too. Instead of disturbing Aidan, I went to the cook tent, sat on a bear barrel, and put my head on the portable table. I woke, sensing something. When I stepped outside the tent, I realized what it was. The sun was back.

By early afternoon, Aidan was awake and feeling better. We toyed with the idea of going on a short hike, but chose instead to canoe downriver and test out the rapids. We'd have the advantage of paddling an empty boat. When we climbed into the canoe, I could tell that she was anxious.

"Remember yesterday," I told her. "Don't forget that feeling."

The first rapid we took was a little rough. We bumped a boulder and slid over another. When the river slowed, Aidan turned. "Sorry, Dad. That was bad."

"Don't worry," I told her. "The boat is designed to do that."

Aidan had no problem navigating a short rock garden and a small, unbroken section of waves. This time, when she turned, the smile was back.

After three-quarters of a mile, we pulled out and took turns lining the boat back up. It was our punishment for a fun ride down. When we reached the campsite, we agreed to run the river again.

The following day, our third on the river, we were treated to a bluebird morning. We woke early, spent three hours eating breakfast, breaking camp, and loading the canoes, and got under way, hoping to put in some miles before the afternoon wind raced through the valley.

Initially, the river went easy on us. We made it through Class II and II+ runs without a hitch. Then we entered a small, tight canyon. We back-paddled and picked our line. At the first turn, I could see that the current would drive us toward the rock wall and just before impact would shoot us out into the middle of the river. If we quit on it early, the wave would likely turn us.

"Ready?" I asked Aidan. "Don't bail early," I warned her. "Take it right up to the wall."

"Ready," she said.

The current seized us quicker than I'd expected. My first instinct was to steer out of it, but I tried to remain calm. In the bow, Aidan was stroking hard. The wall was coming at her. All I could see was her on a collision course with twenty feet of rock. If somehow we misjudged the current and we hit, Aidan would be badly hurt. I had to do everything in my power to trust the river and not draw us away too soon. Aidan missed the wall by inches, and the stern of the canoe scraped it ever so slightly. Seconds later, we were thirty feet downriver in a pool that was as calm as bathwater.

Behind us, I heard Dave, or Chris, shout, "Woooweee!"

Then they paddled by us. "Man, that was a close one," Chris said.

Ten minutes later, we came round a bend and everyone stopped paddling.

"Christ," Dave said.

The section of river ahead of us was the definition of a boulder garden. It was a maze of large rocks and tricky drop-offs with a huge amount of water flowing through it. Canoeists call it heavy water, and it was nothing to be trifled with.

"We gotta scout this," I told Aidan.

We pulled out on a gravel bar just upstream of the garden. We studied the river as best we could, but no one was satisfied.

"Dad," Aidan said. "Let's canoe over there and walk up and see how it looks."

"Good idea," I said. I saw that Dave and Chris had done the same and were already paddling to the left bank.

We pulled our canoes into a small gravel-bar eddy and walked up and down the bank, watching the river. After forty-five minutes, we decided to try to line the boats downstream rather than paddle. The problem, as we soon discovered, was that the banks were thick with alders and our lines kept getting caught in the branches. Then we got into the cold water and tried to walk the canoes down along the edge of the cutbank. Soon the water was waist-high, so we abandoned that plan, too.

After a brief discussion, we decided that our only alternative was to walk the boats back upstream, get in where the current wasn't too fast, paddle out to the middle of the river, and attempt to pick the best line we could.

"I'm nervous, Dad," Aidan admitted. "I'm not sure I want to do this."

Dave overheard. "We'll go first."

From the gravel bar, we watched Dave and Chris paddle out to the middle of the river. Then they spotted some sort of line. They power-stroked at a 45-degree angle for the left bank. They banged into a few rocks, and I worried they'd go over. But somehow, some way, they made it through the garden. It was not a thing of beauty, but they were safe. About two hundred yards downriver, they tied off their canoe. Then they walked about halfway back and climbed onto a boulder. I could see that Chris had a throw bag in his hand. Dave held his paddle straight up and down in front of him—*Come ahead.*

"Ready, Aidan?" I asked.

"No," she replied. "But what choice do I have?"

We paddled into the current and let it swing our bow downstream. As we approached the boulder garden, Aidan chose a line and yelled, "Left, left, left!"

I did a sweep stroke and turned the bow to the left, and then I pried the stern to the left, too.

Seconds later, I heard her again. "Right, fast, right," and saw her perform a crossbow draw, pulling the bow to the right just inside an angry-looking rock.

Now she was screaming again: "Left, left!"

Again, I swept her bow to the left. For a moment, there was a lull. We'd evaded a dozen large rocks and were halfway through the maze. "Beautiful," I shouted. "Great work."

Aidan responded by crying out, "Hard left. Left, left, left!"

I tried to turn the canoe, but there was just not enough room. We broached up against a rock. We hit hard and the powerful current wrapped us around it.

"What should I do?" Aidan yelled over the roar of the river.

"Just keep calm," I said. "Don't panic."

In the stern, I paddled as hard as I could, but the canoe wouldn't budge. I considered getting out and tugging on the bowline, but the current was too strong. It would knock me off my feet and wash me away, and Aidan would be alone, terrified, and helpless.

"The canoe feels like it's going to break," Aidan shouted. "We gotta do something."

I looked at the straining aluminum midribs and couldn't believe they hadn't snapped. The full force of the river was pushing the canoe against the rock. If the midribs did break, the canoe would lose its tension and the current would wash over the top of the skin and spray cover and drive the boat to the bottom of the river. If Aidan managed to get out of her spray skirt, the current would hurl her downriver through the rocks. She would smash into one rock and then another, and another. Although her PFD (life jacket) would keep her head above water, it would feel as if she were drowning. The waves and rapids would wash over her and she would gasp for air. The chance of rescuing her would be next to nothing. Even if Chris succeeded in throwing her the safety line, and she miraculously managed to grab on to it, she would need all her strength to hold the rope and Dave would need even greater strength to pull her against the rush of the river. If he managed to get her out of the water, she would likely be badly hurt. Perhaps she would have broken a leg or an arm in a collision with a boulder. At that point, we'd be confronted by a whole new set of problems.

All these images raced through my head as I tried to dislodge the canoe. "Just stay where you are," I shouted to Aidan. "I'm going to climb out and onto the rock."

I loosened my spray skirt and slithered out of the boat. When I did, Aidan screamed. The canoe pitched forward and water rolled across the top of the polyurethane-coated cover. I got to the rock and pushed down on the stern to raise the bow as high as I could, simultaneously shoving the canoe forward. It moved, slightly. I shoved again and it inched farther forward. Trying a third time, I pushed it with all my might. It bucked forward, and somehow I managed to slide through the skirt and into my seat before the river took off with the boat.

"Paddle!" I yelled to Aidan.

In the stern, I was digging with all my strength; in the bow, Aidan was stroking for the left bank. It was no use; we lacked the speed we needed to avoid the rocks. I saw a large one up ahead and knew there was nothing we could do to avoid it. "Shit!" I screamed at the top of my lungs. "Shiiiiitttt."

We hit the rock broadside and the boat's nose plunged into a whirlpool. If not for the spray cover, we would have been swamped. Once again the current pressed us tight against the rock. I tried to push us off.

In the bow, Aidan was screaming. "Water's coming in."

I had to work fast. If I wasn't able to move the canoe, the nose would plunge into the whirlpool and the downward force of the current would drive Aidan to the bottom of the river and hold her there.

I climbed onto the rock, and then I leaned back against it and threw my body forward with as much force as I could.

"It moved," Aidan shouted.

I pushed a second, a third, a fourth, and a fifth time. On my sixth shove, the boat rocked forward and I grabbed the gunwales and held it against the current. Standing on the ledge, I got a leg in the canoe. Then I swung my other one in. When the canoe took off, the bow dove and then came back up.

Aidan was again stroking for the left bank. We paddled around a number of rocks and then pulled the canoe just upstream of Dave and Chris's boat. Chris was there to grab our bowline and pull the boat to safety. After he tied us off, we crawled up the bank, where I lay back in the dirt, completely spent.

Aidan seemed to be in shock. She sat rocking back and forth, her legs pulled tight against her chest.

Minutes later, Dave walked up. "Jesus, that was close." Then he sat down next to Aidan. "You okay?" Aidan looked like she was about to cry.

Dave and Chris went downriver to scout. When they were gone, Aidan said, "I can't do this, Dad. I'm too scared."

When I didn't respond, she kept talking. "All I could think of out there was that I was going to drown."

I got up and sat next to her and put my arm around her. What I didn't need to tell her was that we had no options; we had eighty miles of river ahead of us. But I, too, was scared. Just three days into the river portion of our trip and already I had doubts about whether we had the skills to canoe the Hulahula.

I sat there holding her until Dave and Chris returned. "Wish I could say it's over," Dave informed us. "What's up ahead isn't any better."

Aidan looked at me. I could see how frightened she was.

"I think we can line it, though," Dave continued. "It won't be easy. There's a big drop-off about fifty yards down. We wouldn't make it if we tried to paddle it."

Ten minutes later, I was hip-deep in the water, clinging to the gunwales at the back end of the canoe, trying to guide the boat over and around large rocks. Aidan tugged on the bowline as she walked a thin game trail that weaved through the alders. Occasionally, when the trees got tight and matted, she, too, climbed into the river. It took us thirty minutes to get to the drop-off. Chris was along the bank studying it. He pointed to a succession of rocks that formed a kind of stairstep down the ledge.

"That looks like our best bet," he said.

Aidan and I waded into the river and stuck as close to the bank as we could. She grabbed the bowline and I took the stern line and slowly we released the canoe into the current.

"Keep that line tight," I told her. Meanwhile, I leaned back on my line with all my weight. By the time the boat got to the stairstep, my hands were already cramping.

"Easy," I shouted to Aidan.

I had barely gotten the word out when I slipped on a moss-covered rock and fell hard on top of two other rocks. I was lying on my belly, moaning and clinging to the rope, knowing that if I lost my grip the canoe would likely go off the ledge sideways and dump. Our gear was lashed down, and the canoe had flotation tubes built into it and a spray cover stretched across the top, but if it turned over, the river would toss it like driftwood downstream. We wouldn't be able to recover it until the current slowed. By that time, who knew what condition the boat or our gear would be in? Our gear would likely be wet, and then our first job would be to dry everything out. Hypothermia is a constant threat when canoeing in the Arctic; we needed warm, dry clothes above all.

"Hold on, Dad," Aidan shouted. "Don't let go."

I managed to get to my knees and then to my feet.

"Pull," Aidan screamed. "Pull the line in."

I yanked at the line, but I couldn't overcome the force of the current, which had turned the canoe at a 45-degree angle to the path of the river. Chris jumped into the water and helped me rein in the stern, tug-of-war style.

With the boat tracking again, I took a minute to regain my strength and then Aidan and I eased it toward the drop-off.

"Ready?" I shouted.

The bow went over the ledge, buoyed up, and was followed by the rest of the boat. In another boat, the fall might have done damage to the canoe. But the Pakcanoe and its flexible hull had lived up to Alv Elvestad's promise.

At the gravel bar fifty yards down from the drop-off, all four of us sat in the sand. We'd just spent the last hour waist-deep in ice-cold water, so we knew we couldn't sit for long.

"I'm beat," Dave said.

"Me, too," I agreed. "Let's call it quits."

"Right there with you," Chris said.

As we went over to our canoes, Aidan remained sitting. I walked back to her. "You okay?"

"I don't ever want to have another day like today," she said. "I'm tired and cold, and I can't stop shaking."

"Dave and Chris just left to scout for a campsite," I told her. "I'm sure they'll find one close."

By the time we got to our canoe, I saw Dave one hundred yards downriver, waving his paddle. "See 'em," I said. "We'll be there in no time."

When we pulled up, Dave helped me drag the canoe onto a sandbar. "It's not the prettiest," he said, "but this hill should help break the wind."

"I don't care how pretty it is," Aidan said. "I just want to get warm, go to sleep, and forget that today ever happened."

We unpacked the canoe and set up the cook tent. Just as we

finished, a dense fog rolled up the valley and stopped no more than fifty yards downriver. It was so thick it obscured everything around it.

While I put up our sleeping tent, Aidan sat on a large rock, wrapped in her sleeping bag, and watched the mountains and hills disappear. Soon the river was gone, too. But we could hear its roar.

CHAPTER 27

PADDLE AND PRAY

THE MORNING WAS GRAY, WET, and cold, and Aidan was out of sorts. She'd slept poorly, dreaming all night of overturned canoes and savage bears. But what really had her upset was her hair, which was matted and plaited like dreadlocks. It seemed ridiculous to me that of all the things we had to worry about, she had chosen to focus on her hair. She insisted that she'd never be able to get out the snarls and tangles and would have to have it cut when we got to Fairbanks. She accused me of being insensitive for not showing the proper concern. When I told her that she'd look beautiful even with short hair, I merely added fuel to the fire.

After our near disaster yesterday, we'd made the decision to stay off the river and use the day to recover. We also hoped to get in a hike to the Esetuk Glacier, which feeds Esetuk Creek, which enters the river at the beginning of the gorge. If we could make it to the glacier, we'd have spectacular views of Mount Michelson and Tugak Peak, two of the Romanzofs' highest mountains.

After breakfast, we paddled across the river, pulled our canoes onto the tundra, and walked up a draw formed by a small stream called Kolotuk Creek. The night's mist hung low over the valley, but up ahead I could see the faint rays of the sun. Despite our ordeal yesterday I felt fairly strong, especially without the dead-weight of my pack. As we climbed higher, the sun struggled to escape the clouds.

We broke for lunch and I used Chris's binoculars to study the stretch of river that had given us such a beating yesterday. It looked big and brutal. It was no wonder we'd had such a hard time of it. Most of the people I'd talked with had done the river in big oared rafts, the safest way to experience the Hulahula. Doing it in a canoe offered a more challenging, and invigorating, experience. But it was a gamble, and now, looking down on the white water, I had to wonder if I'd been foolish in taking that gamble.

Our rest was not a long one. We were all eager to get a glimpse of the glacier—with the Arctic's climate changing more dramati-cally than in other areas of the world, the glacier, and others like it in the Romanzofs, would likely disappear in this century—and none of us knew how long it would take to get there.

We kept climbing higher. After all the false summits, Aidan joked that we were like the bear that went over the mountain. "What did he see?" she asked as we crested yet another ridge. "More mountains. Always more mountains."

Aidan and I looked at our 1:63, 360-scale map of Mount Michelson, and Dave checked his GPS. It was late in the after-noon, and just as it seemed we should be getting close, a pea-soup fog moved in. Aidan and I kept walking, following a compass course. We made it to the top of one more ridge, but couldn't see more than fifty feet in front of us. So we briefly discussed our options: to keep going, despite the fog; to sit tight and wait to see if it lifted; or to head back to camp. Since we'd already been hiking for five hours, and still had the return trip in front of us, we decided to turn back.

Two hours later, we made it down to the river. A damp, bitterly cold wind that felt as if it was coming right off the polar ice pack whipped up the valley.

IT WAS 6:30 a.m. on our fifth day on the river, and we were already breaking camp. We wanted to get moving as soon as possible, so that we could make it to the mouth of Esetuk Creek before the winds kicked up. They came in like clockwork, beginning at noon and building throughout the day.

Three hours later, our canoe was packed, the gear was lashed down, and we were ready to go.

"All set?" I asked Aidan.

"Ready," she said.

After we made it through a tricky section of rapids, Aidan turned to me. "I needed that," she said. "They were a challenge, but not scary bad."

"You did great," I said. "And you're shouting out your commands now; that helps me. It gives me more time to move the canoe."

What I chose not to say to her was that two days ago, in the rock garden, her voice had been shrill and panicky, and her commands had come too late for me to respond. With a heavy load, the canoe was not a marvel of maneuverability.

By early afternoon, we were just above Esetuk Creek. We'd pulled out onto a gravel bar to scout an intimidating set of rapids. It had been a good morning—we'd spotted a golden eagle and sheep in the mountains and canoed past a large field of overflow ice, called *aufeis*. We didn't want to spoil it by being rash.

"Man," Chris said, looking at a long section of white water, followed by a fifty-yard wave train with four-foot crests. "That's some big water."

We contemplated lining it, but after scouting the banks, we determined that our only option was to run it. One side of the river was all cliff; the other was thick with alders.

When we got into the canoe, Aidan said, "I'm scared again, Dad. I'm not sure if I can do it."

Her mind might have hesitated, but her body didn't. She did what she'd grown accustomed to. She climbed through the spray skirt, knelt on the pads, and braced her feet against the foot pegs that I had jury-rigged for her. She was ready to go.

When we shoved off, I was once again surprised by the torque of the river. I wanted to be able to pick our way through the white water, but the current was just too strong.

"Here it comes," I shouted to Aidan.

We made it through the rocks without incident, but then we hit the wave train. I heard something that sounded like a war whoop and realized that it was Aidan. It was a cry of exhilaration and terror.

We made it through the first wave train and had only half a minute to prepare for the next one. "Paddle left," Aidan yelled. And then she called out the individual rocks, rounded behemoths that would roll us if we did more than bump them.

If the last wave train was big, this one was even bigger. Aidan hit it first and was buried by water. The only way I knew she was still in the boat was by a glimpse of her blue paddling jacket. Although I wanted to enter it straight, I had trouble bringing the stern around. A wave pounded me and I could feel the canoe wanting to roll.

Aidan felt it, too. "Dad," she screamed out. "We're going over."

I did a high brace, slapping the water with my paddle and dragging it back to me. I managed to right the boat just in time for a succession of waves. When the last one spat us out, I could see the canyon wall dead in front of us. Aidan did a crossbow draw, moving her bow to the right away from the wall, and I drew the stern even harder to the right. Then, suddenly, it was over. The water calmed and I saw Chris on the riverbank waving his arms.

"Eddy out, eddy out," he was yelling with some urgency.

When I looked downriver, I saw why. Esetuk Creek spilled in from the right, and just past that, the quiet patch ended in a jumble of rocks. With no time to pick a line, we wouldn't stand a chance.

When we turned the canoe into a calm eddy, I was shaking, and not from the cold. Aidan was still kneeling in the bow.

"How are you?" I asked.

"Happy," she said, out of breath. "Happy it's over."

TWO HOURS LATER, after setting up camp, we went scouting again, walking the ridge along the Hulahula's eastern edge. The landscape had changed. To the west was Kikiktat Mountain. It was massive, though at 5,095 feet, not particularly tall. To the east, the high peaks of the Romanzofs had given way to a topography that reminded me of South Dakota's Badlands. There were hoodoos, pinnacles, chimneys, and multilayered rock faces.

Below was the dreaded gorge that the dozen or so people I had talked with before the trip had warned me about. From above, the river looked like an angry, twisting serpent. It was hemmed in by a narrow canyon and jam-packed with big rapids. We were all thinking the same thing as we looked down: *You gotta be fucking kidding me.*

We walked downriver a mile and a half or so and then realized that if we hoped to make it out without a major disaster, we needed to scout the rapids at close range, from the banks. We walked the tangled banks for two hours and returned to camp in dark moods, tired and thoroughly intimidated.

Gluttons for punishment, Chris and I tried fishing—Robert Thompson and someone at Fish and Wildlife had told me that we might find grayling or char near Esetuk Creek. But the water was still running high, and after fighting the faster current for days, the fish were unlikely to expend the energy needed to feed. We returned empty-handed and discovered that Dave was again concerned about our food supply.

"I don't know who told you this river had fish," he said. "We sure haven't found any," and then he informed us that we might be able to make it to Arey Island on what we had, but if our pickup was delayed by bad weather—the coast is known for fog and high winds—we could be in trouble. I joked with him that I'd brought more stored fat to the Arctic than either he or Chris, so I'd be willing to eat less. The joke didn't go over well.

The history of the Arctic is rife with stories of starvation. Early explorers (many of them English) of the Alaskan and Canadian Arctic traveled "heavy" on well-funded expeditions, often made with large-capacity vessels, hundreds of sailors, and thousands of tins of food. However, when the ships met with disaster, and the men were forced to travel overland, they realized that the North is a hungry land, punctuated by periods of feast amid longer periods of scarcity. To ward off hunger and scurvy, the Native inhabitants ate what the land gave them—raw fish, the organs of mammals. The explorers treated them with scorn, but when they began to starve, they, too, ate anything the land offered, boiled or raw—bearded and ringed seals, walrus, willow leaves, fireweed and bluebell shoots, birds' eggs, tubers, and seaweed. As they grew hungrier and more desperate, they boiled moss and caribou hooves and ate them, too. Then they ate their boots and the larvae of warble flies and sucked on the putrid bones of dead animals. Still, many of them died. To those who survived and went on to tell their grisly tales, the Arctic was the "land God gave to Cain."

The shame of it was that the campsite we'd chosen was probably our prettiest one yet. Our cook tent was down among some willows near the creek, while our sleeping tents were on a flat, green rise that looked up the river valley to the glacier-ringed peaks of the Brooks Range.

That night, after supper, I spent some time sorting through my shotgun shells. I had slugs and buckshot for bears, and I had ten No. 4 steel-shot shells, which I'd brought along for emergencies like the one we might be up against. If need be, I was confident I could shoot ducks on the coastal plain. I could ground-swat them at the edge of a tundra pond or shoot them in the air. I'd been hunting ducks successfully since I was a kid. I knew Bert had had to do it on his Hulahula trip, and I had no doubt that if things got dire, I could do the same.

That night when I went to bed, the sun was out, but there was a November wind blowing through the valley. I had on every stitch of clothing I owned, and still I could feel the cold's sting. My worry was less about our food situation than about the weather. If it was cold here in the canyon, what would it be like on the wide-open coastal plain or on wind-blasted Arey Island?

I crawled into the tent, and Aidan, wearing her heaviest gloves, was still scratching notes in her journal.

"I'm writing about the summer that never was," she said with a laugh.

I was happy to hear the lilt in her voice. Here, I thought, is the breath of fresh air, in all her youthful resilience, that my mother had talked about. There was no trace of the fear that she'd felt just two days before. It would be so easy for Aidan to be beaten down by the river and the cold. But she seemed to understand intuitively that to give in to pessimism or moodiness or self-pity would be to invite the kind of lingering, negative emotions that had no place on a trip like this.

She wrote a bit more and then she put down her notebook. "Do you miss home, Dad?" she asked. Without waiting for an answer, she said, "When I get older, I want to have a home, but I want to go all over the world. I think that's the thing about traveling. It's good to know you have a home. Sometimes I feel a kind of longing. Sometimes I think about walking in the back field or swimming in the creek with you and Mom and Rachel and Willa." She paused. "I have a complicated relationship with home, I think, maybe like you did when you were my age—loving Wisconsin deep down, but wanting to get away and experience the world."

She stopped, as if waiting for me to respond. Apart from loving her candor, I didn't know what to say. Before the trip, I'd envisioned talking along the trail or while we canoed. In reality, there had been little time for talk. There was always work: the repetition of setting up camp, breaking camp, loading the canoe, unloading it. And the river had given us little time for relaxation. We were always confronting one obstacle or another.

"Remember," Aidan said, sitting up in her sleeping bag, "how you used to put on snowshoes and pull me on the sled through the marsh? And how every April, we'd canoe Spring Creek, when the cranes came back? And how when we went hiking, Mom would sometimes bring a small picnic in her backpack? How we'd sit on the hill and gather hickory nuts? My favorite, though, was hunting for crawdads in the creek. Remember how Rachel, Willa, and I would dare each other to catch them by hand? How sometimes we'd have to sit in the grass and pick off leeches and Willa would cry about the 'bloodsuckers'?"

Her words were a kind of incantation. If ever there is a moment in a father's life when his heart feels as if it will burst with joy and gratitude, this was it: when his child is talking about her life with such fondness.

Aidan closed up her notebook, stuck her pen in its spiral binding, and wriggled deep into her sleeping bag. "Dad," she said. "Do you think we'll ever do this again? Do you think maybe we'll come back to Alaska again together?"

I laughed, knowing all too well the parallel universes we would inhabit once she left home and how seldom the two would cross. Aidan and I were moving in different directions: she was embracing the fullness of life and I was struggling to come to terms with its opposite.

"If you think you'll want me along," I said.

"Dad," she said, as if I'd just uttered something ridiculous, "I'll always want you along."

CHAPTER 28

GRIT AND THE GORGE

WE ALL WOKE EARLY AGAIN. I walked to the river, hoping to get a glimpse of the valley ahead, but the low-slung sky offered no views beyond the first set of rapids. At the cook tent, Dave was preparing an extralarge kettle of oatmeal with an extralarge helping of nuts, cranberries, and cocoa butter. Despite his fears about our food supply running low, everyone knew how exhausting the day would be and how much we'd need the extra calories.

Tension on a trip like this comes with the territory—even among friends—but everybody's fuse seemed a few seconds shorter than usual. "Let's get a move on," I barked at Aidan, who was meticulously packing her backpack. When I offered Dave a hand taking down his tent, he grunted a barely audible "No." The previous evening I had tried to help him set it up in a fierce wind, but my help had turned into a hindrance, and eventually he put up the tent on his own.

By 8:30 a.m. we'd already broken camp and paddled across the river, away from the mouth of Esetuk Creek. We were scouting again. The rapid we would encounter just fifteen yards downriver was a large one, followed, almost immediately, by a hairpin turn and another big set of rapids. Aidan spotted a nice line and we elected to run it.

Aidan and I paddled upstream against the current, hugging the rock wall to river left. Thirty yards up, we turned the bow slightly in to the current, leaned downstream, and peeled out, letting the river do the work. Now we were looking right at the rapid.

"Let's go," Aidan called.

The next thing I knew she was surrounded by water. I couldn't see her, but I heard her yelling, "Left, left. Hard." I knew that we were through the first rapid and bearing down on the wall and the hairpin turn.

I heard her again. "Harder, Dad. Harder."

I saw two boulders looming up out of the water, followed by a five-foot drop-off and a large wave curling back upstream. How could we have missed it when we were scouting? Adrenaline shot through me. Aidan pulled the bow to the left and I tried to pry the stern in the same direction, but it was slow to respond. The rocks bumped my right gunwale and I saw the bow bounce toward the ledge. Aidan missed it, just barely, but now she was on a collision course with the huge wave. She was screaming, but all I heard was the river and the echo of her voice. If she couldn't get the bow over, the wave would capsize us. When she caught its edge, and it kicked her sideways, I knew she'd be okay. But I had less than a second to do the same. Again, I jammed my paddle into the water and tried to crank the stern away from the ledge. I missed it, but the outside of the wave caught the back of the canoe. I could feel it about to dump us when I slammed the face of the blade against the water on my left side. The next few seconds passed in a blur, but when we exited the wave, we were still upright.

The rapid dumped us out into a calm section of water, and we dragged the canoe onto a sandbar. "We gotta bail, but first grab the throw bag," I told Aidan. "Here come Chris and Dave."

Though they'd had an easier time of the rapid than we, Chris and Dave had also taken on a lot of water and needed to bail. They pulled their canoe onto the sandbar next to ours.

"Where did that come from?" Dave asked. "None of us saw it."

We emptied the water out of our canoes and walked downriver to see what the Hulahula had in store for us. The canyon walls tightened and the river made an abrupt turn to the right. From that point on, our only option was to run the huge rapids blind or line the boat down the willow-choked bank on the right side of the river.

We waded into the numbingly cold water and pulled the boat downriver. Our progress was impeded by moss-covered rocks. We slipped and fell, banging our shins, knees, elbows, and hands.

Just when we thought things couldn't get harder, they did. The rapids got bigger and the rock walls closed in. So much water was pushing through the narrow canyon that Aidan could barely hold on to the bowline. In the stern, I'd choked up on the rope to control the canoe and was leaning back on it with all my weight. Too much slack and the current would turn the canoe broadside and capsize it.

It was almost noon when I saw Chris and Dave walking back to us. They'd tied off their boat downstream and had come to help. Aidan's head was down and she was plodding forward.

"Stop, Aidan," I yelled.

"What?" she growled.

"It's Chris and Dave," I said. "They can spell you for a bit."

Aidan pried her cramping hands off the rope and Chris took over as we entered a part of the river with the largest rapids we'd seen yet. The last fifty yards of rapid run was excruciating. My shins were battered from falling and my arms and leg muscles ached from holding the stern line and restraining the canoe. At one point, I allowed too much slack to build in the line and the boat took off. I leaned back and waited for the jolt as it tightened. When it did, it felt like my shoulders were going to pop out of their sockets.

When we were finally through, Chris tied off the bow and Aidan the stern, while I lay back on the rocks, panting. It took minutes for me to make it to a sitting position.

"For my next trip," I announced, inspecting a gash on my shin, "I'm going to the beach."

"Don't worry," Dave interjected. "You'll be on one in about fifty miles. It's called the Beaufort Sea Beach and we'll have it all to ourselves. Us and the polar bears."

We spent another grueling two hours lining the boats and then arrived at a section of rapids we decided to run. Under different circumstances we probably would have elected to line them, but fatigue had made us less careful.

Chris and Dave went first. We watched their boat lean hard to the right downriver and thought for sure they were going over, but somehow they pulled out of it. Aidan looked at me as if to say, *Okay, Dad. It's our turn now.*

"I got the line, Dad. You ready?" she said with the kind of confidence that took me aback. Just days before, she wouldn't have asserted herself. Now, it was Aidan, though exhausted, bruised, and bloodied, making sure I was ready.

"All right," I said. "Let's go."

The current grabbed us with a ferocity we'd yet to experience. It threw us at the rapids. For fifty yards, we were enveloped by water. Half a minute later, it spat us out into an area so calm that for a moment I wondered if we were on the same river.

"Way to go, Aidan," Dave hooted.

For the next quarter mile we had an easy flatwater paddle and I used the opportunity to relax. But Aidan watched the river like a raven.

"Relax and enjoy the scenery," I told her.

"Relax and enjoy the scenery," I heard her mutter. The Hula-hula was too full of surprises for her to let down her guard.

"Anybody hungry?" Dave shouted across the water.

"Starving," Aidan said.

We tied off on the left bank and lay back on a large rock, eating pilot bread and peanut butter. A snack never tasted so good. The only problem was the mosquitoes. It had been so cold we'd had few encounters with them, but five minutes into our meal they emerged from the bushes in droves.

"Paradise lost," I said to Aidan, getting up from the rock. Chris and Dave had already fled the mosquitoes and were downstream on a ridge, inspecting the river.

"How does it look?" I asked, when we caught up to them.

"The walls are tight," Dave said, "and there doesn't appear to be a place to pull out, so once you start, you're pretty much committed."

"The Hula Effin' Hula," Chris said. "It just keeps coming."

"We're goin' now," Dave announced. "See you below the canyon."

Chris and Dave were already a hundred yards ahead of us when we shoved off. We navigated the first stretch of Class III rapids and then came to a place where the river made a dramatic turn to the left. We tried to back-paddle to get some sense of what lay ahead, but the current was too strong.

We came hard at the wall, and for a second or two the current held us there. I could smell the deep, musky scent of wet rock and moss. My inclination was to get away from the wall as soon as possible, but we let the water do the work. If we'd learned anything since we started a week ago, it was that sometimes we had to surrender to the river. The current threw us violently back into the rapids, and Aidan chose a line in a split second. There was no yelling now, only intense concentration. And then it was over. The gorge was behind us.

Aidan flashed me a smile. She raised her paddle and swung it back and forth. "Victory!"

Up ahead was a wide-open country of long, molded green mountains. One hundred yards down from the end of the gorge, we spotted Chris and Dave. They'd found a campsite along the left bank of the river, between Kikiktat Mountain and a 2,250-foot-high glacial moraine that went by the name of Kingak Hill.

When we made it to shore, Chris had the bottle of whiskey waiting. He walked up to us and handed it to me.

"To the gorge," I said.

I took a long swig and then another. I gave it back to Chris, and he had one, too.

"Gimme that thing," Aidan said. She took a gulp and grimaced. "To the Hula Effin' Hula." Then she coughed, cleared her throat, and spat. "Yuck."

Chris took one more slug and pocketed the bottle.

We set up camp, and Aidan got out the cards. We played

Rummy 500 and passed the whiskey around. After two good swigs, I started to feel it. Dave handed it to me one more time, but I abstained. "I wanna be able to find my way back to the tent," I said.

"Suit yourself," he replied. "Means more for me and Chris."

After an hour of cards and supper, Aidan, Dave, and I walked back to our tents. One of Aidan's favorite times was when, at the end of a trying day, she could crawl into her sleeping bag and write in her journal or read a book. I was helping Dave put up the bear fence when we heard Chris shout.

"Bear!"

Dave picked up his bear spray, Aidan rushed out of the tent with hers, and I grabbed my shotgun. We all ran for the cook tent.

When we got close, we heard Chris again: "Grizzly comin'."

As the bear approached, we realized it was not just one grizzly but three—a honey-colored sow and two cubs, one black and the other blond. We stood together and talked to the bears in calm but loud voices.

"Howdy, bear," we said. "Just passin' through your country."

If the grizzlies smelled us, or heard, or saw us, they didn't show it. I'd read that grizzly bears are the masters of studied indifference. They know exactly where you are, but pretend not to.

When they were fifty yards away, they came to an abrupt stop and the sow stood on her hind legs and sniffed at the air.

"Man," Chris said. "She's big, really big."

Slowly, she got down on all fours. "Go on, girl, go on," I said aloud. The last thing I wanted to do was pull the trigger. If she ran at us I'd be forced to make a two-second decision about whether she was bluff-charging or coming for real. I knew that, if it was the real thing, I would orphan the two cubs, but I would shoot as fast as I could to defend my own.

But the momma grizzly and her two cubs turned. They shuffled away and lumbered up to the top of a low bench just west of our campsite. They disappeared until curiosity got the best of the two cubs and they wandered back to the edge of the ridge and watched us. Then, suddenly, they bolted.

After they did, we decided that we needed to investigate. We didn't want the sow and two cubs wandering into the camp when we were asleep. We walked up to the top of the ridge and surveyed the tundra.

"Where'd they go?" Aidan asked.

We hiked west for an eighth of a mile, and then we split up. Aidan and I went north and Chris and Dave went south. When we met back at the cook tent, everybody was wondering the same thing: *Where could they have gone so fast?*

Having no way to find out more, Aidan and I said good night to Chris and Dave and then headed for our tent. While Aidan crawled inside to organize our sleeping bags, I glanced back toward the ridge, and for a moment thought I saw the cubs still watching us.

CHAPTER 29

HYPOTHERMIA

I T WAS COLD AND MISTY again, and everyone was moving slowly and stiffly after our trials in the gorge the previous day. We broke camp in a grim silence that all but erased yesterday afternoon's good cheer.

Dave and Chris were ready to go well before Aidan and I, so we made plans to meet at the mouth of Old Woman Creek, two miles downriver, where they would stop to fish. Inupiat families from Kaktovik make the fifty-mile trip in late spring and early fall to fish for Arctic grayling and char at the springs and to hunt caribou.

As we were lashing down the gear in our canoe, Aidan pointed above the ridge at a large golden eagle with a wingspan seemingly as big as a Piper Cub plane. It was soaring, hunting perhaps, and I wondered if it had spotted caribou on the tundra behind the ridge. Golden eagles kill more caribou calves than either wolves or bear.

Having made some last-minute adjustments to the spray cover, we were ready to go. Suddenly, we heard a snort. We whipped around, thinking the same thing: the sow and her cubs had returned. But no; it was a bull caribou with a huge head of antlers and a mane that had already turned white for winter. Neither Aidan nor I moved, and the caribou didn't see us. The wind was at his back, out of the west, so he didn't scent us either. He walked toward the riverbank snorting some more and coughing, and then he stopped. When he looked at us, just thirty feet away, I saw his nostrils flare. Turning, he ran back in that effortless, straight-backed, high-kneed carriage that reminded me of the way Michael Johnson, the Olympic gold medalist, used to run.

We pushed the canoe into the current and were immediately confronted by a long set of rapids. The river made tight twists and turns all the way down to Old Woman Creek. But the biggest problem was the fog. It was so heavy that it was difficult to see the rocks, boulders, and river walls. It was hard even to see where the water ended and the land began.

At Old Woman Creek, Chris and Dave had already packed up their rods. I didn't need to ask.

By early afternoon we were ready to call it a day. The gorge had worn us out physically and mentally and we needed time to recuperate. When the sun returned, and the sky was a flawless blue-gray in every direction, we found a place to camp near a bend in the river, just down from a long stretch of willows that would serve as a windbreak. After unpacking our canoes and setting up the cook tent, we decided to take advantage of the sun to dry out everything—our HydroSkin tops and bottoms and Aidan's wet suit, our sleeping bags and tents. Soon our campsite looked like a gypsy fair, every bush and branch draped with clothes and gear.

When we were finished, Aidan fished while I did some overdue maintenance on my WhisperLite stove. Dave and Chris took a hike to the east in the direction of a long, broad terminal moraine that rose dramatically out of the flat tundra. To the west of our campsite lay the Sadlerochit River and Mountains. In Inupiat, *sadlerochit* means "area outside of the mountains." The mountains top out at around forty-five hundred feet and run west to the Canning River and the border of the refuge. Unlike the eroding Brooks Range, they are young mountains that are still rising.

When and Chris and Dave returned, they were excited. They'd climbed to the top of the moraine and could see the coastal plain stretching, floorboard flat, all the way north to the Beaufort Sea.

WE BROKE CAMP hurriedly the next day, our eighth on the river. It was too cold and bleak to dawdle. It was misting again, the wind coming directly out of the north, off the ice. Winter was on its way.

We navigated a few more rapid runs, and then the Hulahula quieted down. For a mile or so there were periods when Aidan and I didn't even put our paddles in the water. We lay them across the gunwales and took in as much of the changing scenery as the mist and fog would allow.

We crossed the imaginary boundary that divides the refuge's Wilderness Area from the infamous 1002 (referred to as ten-oh-two) Area, which extends approximately one hundred miles from the Canning and Staines Rivers on the west to the Aichilik River on the east and sixteen to thirty-four miles inland from the coastline of the Beaufort Sea to the foothills of the Brooks Range. The decision to put the 1.5-million-acre chunk of Arctic coastal plain in a special category was preserved in Section 1002 of the Alaska

National Interest Lands Conservation Act (ANILCA). Before the land was protected into perpetuity, or developed for its predicted oil reserves, ANILCA stipulated that studies needed to be done—a comprehensive inventory of fish and wildlife resources, an analysis of the potential impacts of oil and gas exploration and development on these resources, and an assessment of the area's projected oil and gas reserves. Today, thirty-five years later, the 1002 is still in limbo. Although the oil companies already have offshore and onshore drilling rights to 90 percent of the Arctic coastline, the debate over whether to drill or not to drill in the 1002 continues. President Obama has indicated that he'd like to end the debate by extending wilderness status to the coastal plain, a decision that would be fought by the state of Alaska and Alaska's Senator Lisa Murkowski, who chairs the Senate Energy and Natural Resources Committee.

Having lulled us into a sense of complacency, the Hulahula picked up speed, curving and thrashing through rock gardens and small gorges, making good on its name. When we reached an especially long section of rapids, we pulled our canoe onto a gravel bar to confer. We studied the river and picked out a line. We tried to keep our distance from Chris and Dave's boat ahead, but the current was pushing us. When their boat got hung up in the middle of the river and started to turn sideways, our line through the rapids disappeared. We drew the boat right to avoid colliding with them. Instead, we pounded into some rocks. The bow stopped dead and the current swung the stern downriver. I saw more rocks and braced myself. Bam!

The next thing I knew, I was submerged in four feet of rushing, bitterly cold river water. When my life jacket popped me up, the paddle was still in my hand. I panicked. *Aidan! Where's Aidan?*

For a moment I thought I spotted her orange life jacket in the rapids downriver. I struggled to my feet, and the current knocked me down and rolled me over rocks for another twenty feet. I got to my feet again and, using the paddle to balance myself, was able to make it into a small eddy. I looked downstream. Nothing. Then I looked upstream and spotted the canoe with Aidan still in it. She was screaming. Then I heard three blasts from her emergency whistle.

Dave and Chris had witnessed none of this. They had dislodged their canoe from the rocks, and, by the time I was thrown from the boat, they had already rounded the bend ahead.

I ran up the gravel-bar bank and then waded into the river, and three feet of rushing water. Again, the current took out my feet and carried me downriver. I managed to swim to an eddy. I crawled up the gravel bar and again ran upriver to Aidan.

When I finally made it to her, I could see the canoe was tipped to the side, taking on water. Aidan was desperately holding on, one hand on a gunwale and the other on a rock, fighting a current that wanted to drag her out of the boat and wash her away. I tried to move the canoe, but it had taken on so much water I couldn't budge it.

"Hold on," I yelled to Aidan. I grabbed the bailer and stuck it through the hole in the spray cover. Standing in the hip-deep water, I bailed frantically. Then I stuck my paddle under the spray cover and used both hands to right the canoe.

"Push off on the rock," I yelled to Aidan.

While she pushed, I pulled up on the gunwales. It worked. When the canoe was riding flat in the water, I grasped the stern line, clung to the gunwales with the line in my hand, and yanked the boat toward me. After it moved, I knew that when I yanked again the bow would whip downstream. I pulled a second time, and as soon as the bow was free, the current grabbed it.

The canoe was now parallel to the current and I was clinging to the stern line, using all the strength I had to hold the boat and get close enough to it to crawl in. If I lost it, the river would spin the boat and sling it downstream. Alone in the bow, Aidan would have little control and would likely capsize in the next set of rapids.

Somehow I managed to throw my body onto the canoe and wriggle into my seat. Aidan had already located an eddy and was paddling for it. When we reached the calm pool, she jumped out of the canoe and pulled it onto the sand.

"You're soaked," she said. "We should build a fire."

"Let's get the water out of the boat first," I said. "And then let's get downriver. If Dave and Chris heard your whistle, they'll be worried."

When we finished bailing and dumping the water out of the canoe, we got in again.

"This is stupid, Dad," Aidan said. "You need to get warm."

Ignoring her, I pushed the canoe into the current. A quarter mile downriver we rounded a bend and saw Chris and Dave walking along the bank toward us. Aidan gave them another blast to let them know we'd had trouble. When we saw their canoe pulled up on a gravel bar, we pulled into the eddy and waited for them to walk back. In the meantime, I eyed the gravel bar. I didn't see any wood, so there was no chance of making a fire. I pulled out one of Bert's maps. I knew that Burns, Bert, and Janie had had a similar accident on this stretch of river and that they'd taken refuge for two days in a shack the people of Kaktovik kept for fishing and hunting. I judged the shack to be ten to twelve miles farther downriver. Robert Thompson, too, had mentioned there would be Native shacks downriver of Old Woman Creek, which we should use if we got in trouble.

"You guys okay?" Chris asked, as he and Dave got close. "What happened?"

After we filled them in on the details, Chris looked around.

"No wood here," he said. "Let's get in the canoes and look downriver."

I seconded the idea. I could feel the cold creeping in. I needed to start paddling.

The river was as lively as ever, and as long as we could avoid mishaps, I was thankful for it. The paddling didn't exactly keep me warm, but it did keep me from freezing. By early afternoon, it was misting hard.

"I'm worried about you, Dad," Aidan said. "We should stop."

About an hour later, when we stopped for a quick lunch, I was shivering badly. We chose a long, upraised willow bar, and I sat against a clump of willows to get out of the wind. Aidan sat next to me with her arm wrapped around my back. But there was no avoiding the wind. It tore through the trees. When I couldn't stand it anymore, I skipped back and forth across fifty yards of sand. Then I did jumping jacks. When I felt less cold, I sat down again.

Chris walked over and stood in front of me. "You okay?" he asked. "Don't be a hero."

"I just gotta move," I said.

Dave overheard. "Okay, let's get back in the boats, then."

The wind was now coming out of the northeast and was stronger than ever. It bullied our canoe. I shook even when I paddled. I knew that I was getting hypothermic, losing not only heat from my skin but also core heat. As we moved downriver, I scanned the banks, but each time I spotted a pile of driftwood, I decided to press on, hoping that soon the shack would appear on the horizon. But I had to wonder: *Was the cold getting the best of me? Was hypothermia clouding my judgment? Could it trigger another episode of Afib? Would the shack still be there?* Bert, Burns, and Janie had rafted the river over two decades ago.

When the river slowed, Aidan turned. "Be smart, Dad."

I had Bert's map out again. My hands were shaking, my feet were cold, and my neck and shoulder muscles were tight and sore—all signs of hypothermia. But if Bert's marks were correct, I figured the shack was about three to four miles down on the river's right side.

Aidan heard me fold the map. "Why are you always looking at that map?"

When I told her, she grew angry. "Dad," she scolded me. "That was so long ago. The shack probably isn't there anymore. Is that what you've been waiting for? I thought you were smarter than that. You're going to get hypothermia."

"Keep paddling," I said.

Aidan growled. "You accuse me of being pigheaded. But now you're being pigheaded and dumb. This is serious."

Half an hour later, on a large sandspit that temporarily divided the river in two, I saw a collection of wood, enough for a bonfire. I felt weak and sluggish. I had almost given up hope of finding the shack and was about to announce my intention to build a fire when Dave yelled, "Look. What's that?"

On the horizon, I saw something that appeared to be a roof, and then, as we got closer, I realized it was the shack. It looked like an old, abandoned homestead on the cold North Dakota prairie.

"Dad!" Aidan saw it, too. "There it is!"

I could hear the relief in her voice.

When we pulled into a side channel, we realized that there were two plywood shacks, a large one and a smaller one. Both sat on a hill, separated from the river by a patch of soggy lowland. We tied off our boats.

"This is the place," I said, hopefully.

Dave looked at me. "What?"

I filled him and Chris in on Bert's story. As I told them, I realized that my mind was moving slowly. I was searching for basic words.

The second and smaller of the shacks looked almost like a work shed. Outside, huge Conibear traps hung on the west-facing wall. I stepped inside the small, enclosed porch. It was cluttered with junk—old oilcans and drums, coffee cans, tools, shovels, and rusty leghold traps. Farther inside, the shack was completely dark because the windows were boarded up. Dave found a hammer and used the claw to take off the boards. Now, it was light enough that we could see without our headlamps. There was a table, bunk beds with mattresses, a queen-size sleeping platform with a dirty mattress, a kitchen counter with a washtub, cupboards with pots, pans, and silverware, and, just as Bert had told me, an oil-burning stove. There were also marmot or ground squirrel droppings all over the floor.

Aidan found some writing on the wall from other paddlers who had used the shack. "Let's stay," she said, disregarding the poop.

Dave seemed reluctant; I couldn't figure out what was bothering him about holing up for one night, but it seemed to be an issue of propriety. This was someone else's cabin, not ours. But he knew, as I did, that keeping backwoods cabins unlocked is a venerable—though disappearing—Alaskan tradition. Weary travelers had always been welcome. When he discovered a Coleman lantern, a stove, and some food that looked as if they'd been left behind by rafters, whatever misgivings he had disappeared. He and Chris lit the oil stove, and it started to pump out heat. Then he smiled. "Looks like we're spending the night."

By then I was shaking almost uncontrollably. Aidan saw. "Stay here," she said. "I'll get our stuff from the canoe."

When she returned, the cabin was warming, and we unpacked our dry bags to see how our gear had fared when water poured into the canoe. We were overjoyed to discover that much of our stuff was still dry, or merely damp. Dave hadn't been as lucky. He and Chris had taken on water on a number of occasions, and upon examining his dry bag he realized that he had a small hole in the seam at the bottom. When he pulled out his clothes, they were wet.

Ten minutes later, our clothes were draped over every hook and hanger in the shack, and the gear I was wearing when I went in the water was already steaming.

"Nap time," Dave said, now prepared to take full advantage of our accommodations.

Aidan and I laid our sleeping bags on the double mattress. I crawled into my bag and was out in seconds.

When I woke, the shack was warm and Dave had the Coleman camp stove fired up. Having found some Spam and hot sauce, he was making a meal fit for wilderness royalty.

"This will warm your belly," he said.

Chris and Aidan were already sitting at the table waiting to dig in. Chris was sipping coffee and Aidan hot chocolate.

"Can I get you a cup?" Chris asked.

My head had felt as if enveloped by an Arctic fog when I woke, but a cup of strong, black coffee brought me back among the sentient.

Dave's meal was just what the doctor ordered. We all wolfed it down.

"Cards, Aidan, or are you off cards now?" Dave said, teasing.

Aidan pulled the cards from her dry bag. They were damp, but we played with them anyway—two solid hours of Rummy 500. We were warm, well fed, and happy, but we knew we had another big day ahead of us. We were about twenty miles from the coast and eighteen miles from where we'd have to cross over to the Okpilak, and none of us had any idea how difficult the portage would be.

CHAPTER 30

THE WAY DISTANCE GOES

AFTER BREAKFAST, WE REPACKED OUR dry bags, dumped the dishwater and honey bucket, shut down the oil-burning stove, reboarded the windows, and said good-bye to our Hulahula oasis. No one was more grateful for it than I. We carried everything we'd brought up the previous afternoon back to the canoes and shoved off under blue skies. Yesterday's distress was a distant memory.

The thing about paddling through the immense flatness of the coastal plain is that you begin to doubt your senses, sight especially. For the first time in my life, I felt what the early ocean explorers must have felt when they feared they would drop off the edge of the earth. The river seemed to be going uphill and then it appeared to end abruptly in nothingness.

The coastal plain distorts your depth perception, too. Things look bigger and closer than they are. Two caribou trotted along the riverbank, keeping pace with our canoe. I'd seen lots of caribou, but these two, a bull and a cow, looked as large as moose. When they dove into the river, it appeared as if they were jumping into our canoe, and I flinched. In reality, they were fifty yards downstream. By the time we reached the point where they'd entered the water, they were already on the far bank, running alongside us again.

They say the coastal plain lacks spectacle, but what struck me was the distance. It seemed to go on forever—an unending green without a hill or a tree in sight. The lushness of the tundra is deceiving; that plants can even survive here is just short of miraculous. They must contend with extreme cold, a growing season less than two months long, fierce winds, lack of precipitation, and fragile soil, which, because of the permafrost, is as thin as a caribou hide. When the ground is disturbed on the coastal plain, it takes decades to recover, a fact the oil companies that want to drill here like to ignore.

The closer we got to the coast, the more birds there were. There were jaegers, terns, harriers, and gulls. The air was filled with the sounds of other birds: the coarse calls of tundra swans and the high-pitched cackling of snow geese. There were birds hidden in the grasses that I could not see but could hear. If Heimo were with us, he would have been able to identify all of them. Like the caribou, the gulls followed us as we floated downriver.

The river was becoming increasingly braided, so choosing the channel with the most water was the key to making progress. We tried to hug the cutbanks, where the water was the deepest. Now, when we chose wrong, we often ended up having to drag the heavy canoes. It was exhausting work, and, as grateful as I was to have escaped the rapids without a major disaster, a part of me missed the thrill of running them.

By midafternoon we realized that we were too far west. Standing on a gravel bar elevated a few feet above the river, we looked east and spotted the channel we'd missed. It took us the better part of an hour to get there. When we reached it, we tied off our canoes on some hip-high willows and then we walked the riverbank. I knew now that the portage was close. I saw the volcano-like pingo jutting from the tundra, the hunting shack and the sand dunes that Bert had marked on his map. Dave, who had the coordinates in his GPS, was more exact.

"Another half mile," he said.

We got back into our canoes and continued paddling. Dave watched his GPS the whole time, convinced the coordinates were wrong. Again, we tied off the canoes and sloshed through the wet tundra.

"This can't be it," he said.

Having just returned from reconnoitering, I knew he was right. I had turned back after getting bogged down in the water and quicksand-like mud one too many times. "Farther down," I said.

We paddled downriver and Dave spotted a small slough to river right. Chris noticed a tiny sand beach, maybe ten feet long.

"Looks like it to me," Chris said.

Aidan and I pulled the canoe onto the sand, and I climbed up the bank. The dunes that Bert had said to use as a landmark for the portage to the Okpilak River were directly east of us. We left the canoes and searched for a route across the tundra, which was dotted with small, rounded frost heaves.

"What do you think?" Aidan asked.

"Seems like the place," I said. "According to Bert's map, we're dead-on."

"Look, Dad," Aidan said. She was pointing south at a collection of small thaw lakes and ponds. "There have to be ducks."

Aidan and I walked in the direction of one of the ponds. The closer we got, the more water there was. It was like sloshing through rice paddies. Even from a distance we could hear the chuckling din of ducks. They let us get surprisingly close. Then, suddenly, they all rose—pintails, old-squaw and eider ducks, goldeneyes, canvasbacks, wigeon, and red-breasted mergansers. I could hear the slap of feet across the surface of the water. The sky was dense with ducks. If, later, we were in dire need of meat, I could flush the ducks again, close my eyes, aim my shotgun at the sky, and pull the trigger. Like shooting fish in a barrel. We'd have food enough for a number of meals.

Back at the sandbar, Chris and Dave were already unloading their canoe.

"You'd think they could put a small sign up that says, 'Portage Here,' instead of letting us guess," Chris said with a laugh. He got a chuckle from all of us. We knew he was kidding; there are few people who love wilderness more than Chris.

Carrying all our gear across three hundred yards of tundra, and then dragging our canoe into a stiff headwind, was no easy task. When we finished we sat back on the soft dunes and rested. Unfortunately, they lay in an east-west direction and offered little protection from the wind.

After ten minutes all of us were cold. Chris and Dave went off for one of their customary rambles, while Aidan and I scouted the river. The Okpilak couldn't have been more different from the Hulahula. It looked like the Platte River of Nebraska, choked with dirt and mud, a mile wide and an inch deep. I looked across the river at the east channel. According to the people at Fish and Wildlife in Fairbanks, that's where we needed to be. It was the one that emptied into Arey Lagoon.

When I was ready to go back to camp, I could see Aidan was concentrating on the tundra.

"What are you looking at so intently?" I asked.

"I think I see a polar bear," she said.

"Where?"

When she pointed, I stood as close to her as I could and looked down the length of her arm to her index finger, as I would a gun barrel. I saw a flash of something white.

"Let's keep an eye on it," I said.

Instead of heading back, I decided to walk the bank farther upriver. Aidan followed close at my heels. When I stopped, she bumped into me.

"What's going on?" I asked.

She was still staring off into the distance. "I'm watching the polar bear," she said.

Again, I looked down the length of her arm.

"Let's go back to camp, Dad," she said. "I don't want to be out here."

I hadn't even considered that we were in polar bear country, despite the warnings. Robert Thompson had told me to watch for polar bears as we got closer to the coast, and the folks at Fish and Wildlife had said the same. In summer, when the pack ice breaks up, they come inland.

Ursus maritimus, the sea bear, is a tireless traveler. Barrenlands grizzly bears range far and wide in search of food, but compared to polar bears, they stick to their neighborhoods. Barry Lopez writes that, in northwest Greenland, the native people call the polar bear *pisutooq,* "the great wanderer." These bears can swim a hundred miles without resting and regularly walk twenty miles per day. They are also tireless hunters. In late fall and winter, while grizzlies hibernate, polar bears roam the sea ice in search of food. Although they prefer a diet of seal, in summer they will come fifty miles inland to dine on sun-fattened crowberries and blueberries—and perhaps, too, the occasional paddler. They are top predators, and, unlike grizzlies, they don't fear people.

"Dad," Aidan said again. "Please. Let's get back to camp."

"Okay, okay," I agreed. "But I don't think that's a bear."

Before our first trip to Heimo's, Aidan had had bear nightmares on almost a nightly basis, but since she had grown so comfortable hiking in grizzly territory I'd forgotten about her early obsession. The polar bear was a new object of an old fear.

We walked back to camp, and I picked up my shotgun.

"Where are you going?" Aidan asked.

"Back to the river," I told her, "to check out that white thing you saw."

"I want to come with you," she said, jumping up.

I got a quarter of a mile downriver and stood atop a five-foot dune that qualified as relief on the coastal plain. I looked south. Again, I saw the white that Aidan was referring to. But it hadn't moved.

"It has to be a patch of ice, or maybe snow geese or swans sitting on a pond," I told her.

"I hope so," she replied.

As we walked back to camp, she said, "Dad, I was excited to see a grizzly, but I don't think I want to see a polar bear."

"Slow down," I said. "If a polar bear is close, you have to act exactly like you did when you saw the grizzlies."

When Chris and Dave came back, we wrestled to set up our cook tent, only to realize that the wind was blowing so furiously that the tent stakes would never hold it. There were no willows or rocks to help anchor it, either. So we pulled the canoes over, turned them upside down, and tied off the tent to the thwarts.

We ate a quick supper of Mountain House stew and then broke open one of our last two chocolate bars. Though Aidan had enough packs of cocoa to last her another week, I could tell she was in mourning. If there was one thing that would cause her to miss civilization, it was not dirty clothes or the absence of a shower or not being able to pick up her phone and text her friends; it was a lack of chocolate.

Aidan was savoring her last piece when Dave saw something to the west, in the direction of the Hulahula. Aidan took an immediate interest. I knew what she was thinking: *I told you I saw a bear.* But it wasn't a bear; Chris confirmed that with his field glasses. It was a small group, making the portage.

When they got near, Dave took Chris's binoculars. "It's Cort, my vet friend, and his rafters," he said.

When the group made it to the dunes, Dave went over to talk. A few minutes later, he returned.

"They're going to Arey Island, too," he said.

"Should we give them a hand?" I asked.

"Naw, Cort says they have enough bodies."

It took them an hour or two to haul their gear across the slough. When they finished they looked beat, but by early evening they, too, had their tents and their cooking operation set up.

We were sitting in our cook tent playing cards when one of the rafters came by. He said that Cort wanted to invite us for supper. Then he mentioned that Cort was a great cook and was making gumbo and fried onions and potatoes.

"Those rafters got it made," Chris said. "Now that's the way to travel."

We picked up our bowls and spoons, and Dave led the way. "Don't be meek," he warned us. "I know enough about Cort to know that if he didn't want to invite us, he wouldn't."

When we arrived in camp, everyone was friendly and welcoming.

"C'mon," Cort said. "Fill up."

Aidan and I sat down together with heaping bowls. We'd barely taken our first bite when Cort, a bear of a man, summoned us. "There's lots more here. Don't be shy about coming back."

Within a minute I was halfway through my bowl, and now I was hungrier than I'd been at any point on the trip. It was as if my appetite, which had been lying dormant, had somehow been triggered. Aidan elbowed me when she was done, as if to say, *You first*. We went back, and Cort ladled spoon after spoon into our bowls. We returned a third time, and then, trying to exercise a modicum of self-restraint, we stopped. When everyone was done Cort dug out one of his coolers, pulled out bags of chocolates and candies, and passed them around. Aidan's eyes lit up.

"Dad," she said. "Can you believe it? Chocolate." Then she lay back against the sand dune with half a bar. "This is happiness," she said.

We lingered among the rafters, talking, laughing, and telling stories. I felt like one of the early trappers of the Shining Mountains who had come out of the woods to attend a rendezvous. Aidan gravitated to Cort's wife, Connie, a friendly woman who had joined Cort on rafting trips that had taken them across Arctic Alaska and the world. When fatigue finally got the best of us, we thanked everyone for their generosity and ambled back to camp, content.

At our tent, Aidan said, "I don't know how Heimo and Edna do it, being away from people for so long. I didn't realize how much I missed being with others, especially another female." She paused, and then she laughed. "No offense, Dad, but I'm tired of you guys."

CHAPTER 31

GOOD-BYE, ALASKA

BY 7:00 A.M. WE WERE lugging our gear through the deep sand to the Okpilak, where we loaded our canoes and lined them upriver. Even along the bank, the water was often so shallow that Aidan and I had to get in and push the canoe to keep it moving. Up ahead, Dave and Chris had started to paddle across the river. We watched them, hoping to follow, but halfway across they ran aground. We picked a different route.

When we finally made it to the Okpilak's east bank, we had a clear picture of what was in front of us—a day of dragging. The previous night someone had speculated that the full moon might have some effect on the water levels in the Okpilak. Whatever the reason (was the Okpilak Glacier, which feeds the river, shrinking?), the fact was that in most places, regardless of which channel we chose, the river was nothing more than a trickle.

By the time we stopped for a midday break, we were thoroughly disheartened. There had been times when I'd thought that our trip was nothing more than drudgery, but I never thought this last section would try my will. Although we'd been pulling and pushing the canoe for hours, the mouth of the Okpilak seemed as far away as ever.

It was cold and the wind was icy, and Aidan was eager to keep moving, so we left Dave and Chris sitting on the tundra alongside the river. Forty yards downstream, we ran into a large sandbar.

"Ugh!" I moaned.

We spent the next two hours dragging. Gradually, as the day progressed and the tide came in, the river began to fill up, but it never reached the point where we could paddle. There was just enough water to drag the canoe without constantly bottoming out. Late in the afternoon, Aidan saw Arey Island in the distance. Arey is a narrow, treeless, seven-mile-long sand and gravel spit that separates the Beaufort Lagoon from the Beaufort Sea. At 70 degrees north latitude, it was the last piece of land separating us from the North Pole.

An hour later, we made it to the mouth of the Okpilak and were ready to rejoice. We'd been dreaming of Arey Island, of not having to break and make camp every day, of relaxing and reading a book while we waited for Robert Thompson to get us. Then we saw it up close. Before we got to the island, we realized, we'd have to unpack the canoe, move it and our gear over a quarter mile of sand, repack the canoe, and then paddle two hundred yards across a whitecapped lagoon.

Now Aidan was doing the grumbling. "So close," she said.

By the time we'd toted all our gear to the lagoon, arranged it in the canoe, and lashed it down, Chris and Dave and Cort's rafting crew had arrived. We helped Chris and Dave transport their gear and gave the others a hand as well. Then we returned to our canoe and plotted our route to the island. Wind roiled the water of the lagoon. I knew what Aidan was thinking: *We've come this far and now this!*

"Current's moving fast," I said. "The last thing we want is to miss the island and end up in the open ocean."

I waded out into the lagoon with a paddle to test the current and realized that, like the Okpilak River, it was shallow. So I kept walking, checking the bottom, hoping it wouldn't suddenly turn into loose sand and mud and slide out from under me. When I got halfway, the water was at my hips, so I turned back.

Together Aidan and I pulled the canoe sixty yards into the lagoon before getting in and paddling northeast at a right angle to the wind and waves. I could tell my comment about ending up in the open ocean had scared Aidan. She was paddling as hard as I'd ever seen her.

When our canoe hit bottom, Aidan jumped out and seized the bowline. I got out, and together we pulled it onto the island. We stood there in the sand, stunned by what Arey represented: our trip was over. Above us, glaucous gulls squawked in the cold, damp air.

We walked toward the center of the island and saw exactly what Arey is: a low, bleak, narrow bench of earth scattered with driftwood. Fourteen hundred miles to the north lay the northernmost point on earth, and nothing separated us from it but open water. We were at land's end.

Aidan turned in the other direction. "Look, Dad," she said. I could hear the pride in her voice. There, in the distance, were the white-topped mountains of the Brooks Range leaning against a blue sky.

If anyone had earned the right to gaze upon that scene, it was Aidan. The Arctic is secluded, but it's more than that. It is aloof. It is hard and unforgiving. Its beauty and solitude have to be earned; they do not come easily. Like the Eskimo girls who accompanied their fathers on hunting trips, Aidan had been bold, dependable, and tough even under difficult circumstances. She had risen to every challenge. My contribution was merely to bring her here.

If Alaska had shown me anything, it was that Aidan, like Dave, Chris, and me—like all of us, perhaps—craved what she could touch, feel, breathe, and see. She craved the primary experience of meeting the world directly. That world may have been frightening and dangerous, and often far less comfortable than the living room couch, but, in the end, it was Thoreau's "contact" that had the power to stir her soul.

We walked farther and saw that Dave and Chris had found the trunk of a large tree to hide behind, and we took shelter there, too. After a few halfhearted high fives, we dug into the sand as deep as we could to avoid the brutal wind. We boiled water and ate a freeze-dried meal, then pitched our tents in a shallow hollow on the leeward side of another large log. On the beach to the south, Cort and the others were lugging their rafts across the sand. They set up camp a hundred yards away. To hell with the bear fence, we said. Besides, what bear in its right mind would wander into a camp of eleven people?

The wind beat against the tent all night long. Although we tied the guy lines to heavy pieces of driftwood, I slept fitfully, worrying about whether the nylon might tear or a pole might snap. By morning, the wind hadn't let up a bit. Robert Thompson had said that August is a time of heavy seas, and he was right. Large waves broke onto the beach, and the sky threatened squalls and snow.

When I called Thompson on the satellite phone later that morning, the first thing he asked me was whether we'd seen a polar bear. I told him no, but he still warned me to be careful. He then told me that the weather report called for fog and high winds for the foreseeable future, and that he wouldn't be able to get us until the weather improved. When I broke the news to Dave and Chris, we confronted a problem none of us had seriously considered: not a shortage of food but a lack of drinking water. All we had left were our individual bottles and one more gallon in our hydration bladder. We talked briefly about taking our canoes back to the Okpilak and replenishing our supply with muddy river water, but decided to ration instead.

We spent much of the afternoon in our tent. We were dozing when we heard a commotion outside. Cort had been in touch with another captain from Kaktovik. Word was that he had a larger boat and was going to try to pick all of us up on the lagoon side. After a day of barely moving, we suddenly packed up at high speed. We were soon trudging through the loose sand, lugging our gear across the island. At the shore we waited and watched the open water to the west, looking for a boat.

By early evening, our hope was gone. We wrestled our gear onto our backs and toted it back to our campsite, where we set up our tents again and rerigged our guy lines. Cort invited us for a stew supper, but as good as the food was, there was little of the conviviality of our first meal together on the Okpilak. Everyone was tired, wind-beaten, and ready for bed.

AIDAN AND I woke early the next morning, our fourteenth day since leaving Grasser's and our twenty-eighth day since arriving in Alaska. We walked down to the beach and sat in the sand and stones and watched the water.

"I can't believe that's the Arctic Ocean," she said. "We're actually here." She stood for a moment and tried to skip a stone, but it hit a wave and sunk.

"Are you happy to finally be here?" I asked her.

"I've been waiting for this moment, when we'd be here on the island, getting ready to leave. But now I don't want to go. I want more."

"I know you do," I said.

"I'm not sure." She continued, "It'll be good to hear Mom's voice, and to see Rachel and Willa and everybody, but going will be hard, even harder than before."

I was tempted to say something, but I checked myself. I put my arm around her. She laid her head on my shoulder as she had when she was younger. She mustered up a halfhearted laugh and then cleared her throat. "I don't know if I can put it into words. Right now, it's mostly a feeling. I missed a lot not being home. Seeing my friends and going out. But sometimes I think about all the things I've seen that the rest of the world has missed."

She got up again. "I'll miss the beauty. You know on a clear day the sky has that quality, like it's not real, and how sound carries so far, how you can hear it up and down the river valley? And how sometimes on really cold days in winter the air seems to be filled with little sparkling diamonds? I'll even miss the roar of the river and the never-ending wind."

"That's pretty," I told her.

She scoffed. "I'm not trying to be pretty or poetic. I'm just trying to tell you something."

"I'm listening."

"I know you feel it, too, Dad," she continued. "I saw it in summer and in winter after we'd been home for a while. I know how much you love your family and I know you were happy to be back, but I could tell you were . . . you were . . ." She paused, searching for the proper words. "You were missing something. The wildness."

Then she sat back down. "Can we do this again, Dad?" she asked me, as she had that evening on Esetuk Creek.

More than anything I wanted to tell her that we could go on doing this forever. If I were given to prayer, I would have asked God that nothing ever change, that Aidan remain my sixteen-year-old daughter, and that I stay strong enough always to accompany her on wilderness trips. But the fact that I was wishing so fervently that time would stop was an admission that it moves on, gathering speed with every year. That scared me. I was a middle-aged man, achy with arthritis, on a too-fast downhill, closer, as they say, to the end than to the beginning. But I still had my dreams. Rachel and Willa were counting on father-daughter adventures, and Elizabeth and I had our own plans to explore the world—by bike, train, and kayak.

But I also still had home.

By urging Aidan to embrace Lodi, I realized that I hadn't embraced it myself. Even after living there for almost a decade and a half, I hadn't made an emotional commitment to it. But Alaska had taught me that I belonged to a place, as much as Heimo and Edna did. And knowing this would take the edge off my own *fernweh*. My restlessness, I knew, would come and go. But my home was in Lodi, with a wife and family that I loved, living a life that Elizabeth and I had worked hard to carve out, on a small piece of land that still had the power to surprise me with its beauty.

"Yes," I answered Aidan. "I hope we have the chance to do something like this again."

Aidan sat with me for a while longer. When she got cold, she returned to the tent to get into her sleeping bag. When she did, I stayed by the water, thinking about how quickly our moment together had already become a memory.

IT WAS EARLY afternoon, and Aidan and I were lying in the tent, trying to escape the coarse and frigid wind, when we heard someone yell out.

"What's that?" I asked Aidan.

"I think he said 'bear,'" she said.

I grabbed my shotgun and stood outside the tent. There was no doubt about it; he was yelling "bear."

Aidan and I hustled over to Cort's camp, and then we saw it—a polar bear. He was walking toward us.

"Oh, my God," Aidan said.

We gathered in front of the tents with some of the others, watching him. He didn't show a bit of fear or skittishness. He kept coming, in a curious kind of skip that is unique to polar bears. I could feel my heart beating, and I heard Aidan taking short, shallow breaths.

"Breathe," I said to her. "Breathe."

In a few minutes all of us were assembled with enough firepower to bring the bear down should he decide to become aggressive, but still he moved nonchalantly, thoroughly unimpressed with us or our weapons. Unlike the early European whalers and explorers, who shot polar bears indiscriminately out of fear and a kind of hatred, none of us had any desire to shoot him.

For a moment the bear sat on his haunches, as if posing for us, and then he moved on. John Muir, who visited Arctic Alaska in 1899, said that polar bears act "as if the country had belonged to them always." Muir nailed it. This bear, the only polar bear I'd ever encountered, went where he wanted to go. He investigated the windbreak where we had made our morning breakfast and a spot behind a log where Aidan had peed. Then he walked to the beach on the island's north side, waded into the water, and floated like Baloo, Kipling's easygoing *Jungle Book* bear. When he returned to land, he shook for a while and then resumed his wanderings. Aidan had not taken her eyes off him.

Comparing a grizzly to a polar bear is like comparing a Rottweiler to a Doberman pinscher. The grizzly has a broad head and chest, while the polar bear is taller, has a narrower build, a slender nose and head, and is slighter through the shoulders, without the grizzly's unmistakable hump. Despite lacking the girth of grizzlies, however, polar bears can weigh twice as much as their distant cousins.

The bear headed for our camp again. All eleven of us stood close together in a north-south line. Then we started moving toward him, talking as we approached. John, one of Cort's rafters who had some experience with polar bears, guessed he was an adolescent male because of his rangy build.

"Move on," we said.

He appeared to disregard us, and then, at some point, he turned and walked in the opposite direction, unhurriedly, like a brazen student sent to the principal's office. We followed him down the island, and then—when it looked as if he'd gotten the hint—we returned to camp.

Aidan noticed his tracks in the sand. They were enormous, almost as long as the blade of a canoe paddle, and nearly twice as wide. "I bet he'll be back," she said, looking over her shoulder. "He didn't move like he was scared."

"Lucky it isn't just the four of us," Chris said.

An hour later, we were lying behind a windbreak in our sleeping bags when I saw him again.

"Here he comes," I sounded the alarm.

In a split second, Aidan was on her feet with her pepper spray in her hand. The word circulated, and soon everyone was gathered near our tent.

This time the bear didn't keep a polite distance. It looked as if he intended to walk right through our camp. Again, we formed a line. But, this time, we talked more aggressively.

"Get out of here, Bear. Get lost."

Someone hurled a piece of driftwood in his direction, but he ignored it. We moved as a group toward him, shouting. John's dog was straining at its leash, and Cort had to pick up his feisty terrier to prevent it from attacking. As we approached the bear, he turned and walked in the opposite direction, again, very slowly.

We pushed him to the far western end of the island and watched as he waded back into the water. This time, we hoped, he was gone for good. As he paddled into the ocean's waves, Aidan kept a close watch on him, her can of pepper spray still in hand. Again I was struck by her confidence and how much she'd changed over the course of our three trips. After all her fear about grizzlies, now she was helping to chase off a belligerent polar bear.

THE WIND WAS blowing like a gale. Since we had no idea when we'd make it off the island, we spent the late afternoon lugging logs and constructing larger windbreaks. Then we gathered more wood for a bonfire. By suppertime, it was blazing, its flames five feet high. We ate quickly and made a plan for the night's bear watch: two people for every three-hour watch. The job was to be on the lookout for polar bears and to feed the fire. Another one of the rafters and I got the 2:00 to 5:00 a.m. graveyard shift.

When Chris came to the tent to tell me it was my turn, I was already awake. At the fire, the logs burned loudly and the wind wailed, so conversation was impossible. Mostly I just scanned the beach and daydreamed.

At 3:00 a.m., I saw the sun set. An hour or so later, when I noticed a thread of color along the horizon, I woke Aidan.

She heard my voice outside the tent and panicked. *"Bear?"*

"No," I said. "I just thought you might like to see the sun rise."

When I walked away, I had no idea if she'd decided to go back to sleep. But five minutes later, she came out, bundled up, carrying her notebook. She sat as close to the fire as she could and wrote. I went to collect more wood, and when I returned she pointed to the ocean. The rising sun was split in half by the horizon. It offered little warmth, but in this wind-hammered landscape, there was something about its light that lifted the spirits.

The sun had been up for a few hours when we sighted a boat from Kaktovik running up and down the shoreline, testing the wind and the waves. The captain signaled for us to bring our gear a quarter of a mile up the beach. Again, we broke camp in a hurry and lugged our gear to the appointed spot. I saved the eighty-five-pound canoe for last. We'd broken it down the day before and packed it, so I hoisted the bag onto my shoulder and stumbled through the deep sand. When I arrived, out of breath, I saw the boat heading back toward Kaktovik.

"Too rough?" I said to Chris.

He nodded. "What are you gonna do?"

We didn't have long to be disappointed. Later that morning, Cort discovered via the satellite phone that Wright Air Service out of Fairbanks had two pilots camped out near the mouth of the Hulahula. They would be picking us up shortly and flying us to Kaktovik.

"Is it for real this time?" Aidan asked from her sleeping bag.

"Yup," I said. "Just get everything packed, and fast."

Half an hour later, two planes touched down.

"Look," Aidan said, "it's the Helio Courier, the one we took to Heimo's last summer."

Just then, Daniel Hayden stepped out of the plane.

"Daniel," Aidan cried.

"Aidan, Jim," Daniel said, sounding as surprised as we were. "I see you guys made it."

"We did," Aidan said. "Barely."

While I helped Daniel load gear onto the plane, Aidan ran down to the water.

"Look," she said when she returned. She was holding some stones and the pretty white shell of a moon snail. She slipped them into her pocket and we climbed into the plane.

We were in the air in no time. Aidan tapped on my back and pointed out the window. To the south, the high peaks of the Brooks Range were set against a cloudless sky. She tapped again. When I reached back, she grabbed my hand and squeezed three times: *I—love—you.*

ACKNOWLEDGMENTS

FIRST ON MY LIST OF people to thank is my wife, Elizabeth, for her love, patience, and quiet strength, and for believing. Our time to travel the world together will come again. Thanks also to my adventurous and spirited daughters Rachel and Willa, who fill my life with laughter and joy and make me grateful to be a dad.

A wilderness of thanks to Heimo and Edna for opening their world to us and their cabin door, too; and to Edna, especially, for befriending Aidan, and for her watchful companionship and care.

To the best of buddies, writer, editor, fellow wanderer, and dreamer Burns Ellison, who first introduced me to Alaska and who read every page of my rough draft. Though he was not able to join us on our adventures, he was with us always. In so many ways, this book would not have been possible without him.

Thanks to my agent, David McCormick, who encouraged me

to be bold and make this book a reality; and to my supportive, inspiring, and insightful editor, Amanda Cook, and her very capable editorial team (Domenica Alioto, Meghan Houser, and Jon Darga), who worked hard to shape *Braving It* into a successful story. Many thanks, too, to Crown and Penguin Random House and to Sarah Breivogel, Annsley Rosner, Roxanne Hiatt, and Rachel Rokicki for bringing this book "out into the world" with so much enthusiasm.

Thanks to Dave Musgrave and Chris Jones, our able travel companions. Our friendship was forged in adversity and sealed by beauty. Thanks also to Kathleen Belgard Jones and Sheri Musgrave for the post-trip hospitality.

I'd also like to express my gratitude to our dear and generous friends David Singer and Diana Kapp, who have enriched our summers with their invitations to Idaho and who made our unforgettable Salmon River adventure possible. And to the Idaho Rocky Mountain Ranch for years of hospitality, great food, adventure, and the best views in the whole West.

A big and hearty thanks to Stu Pechek and Marta McWhorter for the loan of gear and for a good meal, great conversation, and warm beds when we returned from the cold Arctic. And a slap on the back to my buddy Bert Gildart, who always sounds as if he's ready to laugh at a good joke or sip a little whiskey, for the loan of the maps and the advice.

I'm grateful also to writer-friend John Rember for the use of his lovely turn of phrase and to John Hildebrand, whose evocative writing led me to the Inupiat concept of *uniari*.

Thanks also to my council of writer-friends (Steve Coss, David Gessner, Dean King, Charlie Slack, and Logan Ward) for their insights and commiseration and to long-time pal Danny

Brennan for plying me with pints and listening intently to my Alaska stories.

Thanks to Lodi friend Dale Fanney for the paddling instruction; to buddy Gary N-ski for the gear and the moral and tech support; to our neighbors Paul, Janeen, Shannon, and MacKenzie Grover for watching over the place; and to Big Joe Klinzing for the use of his GoPro.

To pilots Daniel Hayden and Kirk Sweetsir for delivering us safely; to Jennifer Reed at the Fish and Wildlife Service in Fairbanks for her counsel; to David Payer of the Fairbanks Paddlers club; to Alv Elstead at Pakboats, Rick Henegar at Gardline Communications, and Nick Chiodo at Clam Outdoors for their generosity; to Wisconsin's Bear Paw Resort; to Idaho River Adventures and Dustin Aherin and his band of merry rafting guides (and, especially, to Mara, who showed my three girls just how accomplished a woman can be); to Bill Schneider; Rick and Cheryl Schikora, and Cort and Connie Zachel; to the kind folks at the Golden North Motel in Fairbanks; and to corporate sponsors Garmin, Filson, Cabela's, St. Croix Rods, Coleman, and Bass Pro.

Thanks to Waldo Arms Hotel in Kaktovik for their generosity, good food, and convivial atmosphere. And to Robert Thompson for his counsel.

To the Madison Country Day School for being the kind of place to recognize Aidan's winter trip for what it was: an opportunity for her to grow, outside the normal classroom setting. Thanks, too, to her teachers for the extra work they put in to make her month away possible.

Thanks to father-in-law Daggett Harvey and to Yvonne Yamashita, who opened their hearts, and summer house, to my family while I was in Alaska and who pretended never to tire of our

Alaska stories when we returned. And to the Les Cheneaux Club for being the kind of place where two weary travelers can enjoy their recuperation.

A world of thanks to my wonderful mother, who has spent much of her life worrying about me, for her love, support, and prayers, and to my family and extended family for being a big part of the reason we decided to settle, and stay, in Wisconsin.